Lincoln Archaeological Trust
The Archaeology of Lincoln, Volume XIV-1

Early Medieval Finds from Flaxengate

J E Mann

Introduction

In 1972–76 excavations by the Lincoln Archaeological Trust at Flaxengate revealed a complex sequence of timber buildings dating from the late 9th to the late 12th centuries. This provided the first real opportunity to examine the character and development of urban life in Lincoln in that period.

The evidence of domestic life and crafts so recovered is unfortunately both unbalanced and imperfect. No organic materials (apart from the charred remains of timber, straw, etc) survived owing to the dryness of the soil. There are thus no textiles, leather, or wooden objects. The latter would most certainly have formed a major proportion of the domestic utensils, but their existence can only be inferred from the survival of bone and metal fittings, and by analogy with other better endowed sites of the same period.

Only part of the evidence which has survived is presented in this report, which is concerned with objects of antler, bone, and stone, and with the smaller quantities of clay or ceramic, jet, amber, horn, and ivory artefacts. The glass and metalwork, with a discussion of the evidence for industrial activity, will form a separate publication (AL **14**/2 forthcoming) while further reports will deal with the pottery (AL**17**/2) and the coins (**6**/2).

It would be misleading to draw general conclusions from the incomplete evidence of one site constituting a small part of the town, but it is hoped that the glimpse it provides of urban life in Lincoln in early medieval times will be augmented by future excavation, so that a more comprehensive assessment may then be made.

The site

The site lies within the eastern part of the lower Roman walled town, in the angle formed by Flaxengate to the east and Grantham Street to the south (Fig 1); both roads were previously thought to be of Roman origin. Roman occupation here, indicated by traces of a 2nd century timber building, and a substantial building of the late 3rd or early 4th century, is discussed elsewhere, in Vol III of this series; for an interim report see Colyer & Jones 1979, 52–5. The site was apparently uninhabited for some centuries following the Roman withdrawal, although finds from other excavations indicate a degree of continuity of occupation elsewhere in the town.[1] Flaxengate was surfaced in the late 9th century although the earliest evidence of a road along the line of Grantham Street dated to the late 10th century. Intensive post-Roman occupation of the site commenced in the late 9th century and continued with a sequence of 13 periods of timber structures, spanning the following three centuries (Fig 2). The structural and stratigraphical evidence is discussed in Perring 1981. In the late 12th or early 13th century a break in building traditions is marked by the construction of the earliest in a series of medieval stone buildings (Jones 1980).

The timber buildings, whose limits were defined by postholes and floor surfaces of sand, silt, or clay, were rectangular, and generally approximately 5 m wide by up to 16 m long. Walls may have been of horizontal planking secured by dowels (or in the later buildings by nails) to upright posts. Hearths were commonly placed centrally; and together with the insubstantial nature of the vertical posts of the walls, this suggests that the buildings were single storeyed.

The essential similarity of the buildings (apart from structure 9, which had stone footings and was perhaps used for storage of perishable materials such as grain) meant that any specialized functions could only be inferred from internal features and concentrations of finds (Perring 1981, 41). Thus the finds of glass objects and crucibles containing glass waste in and around structures 13 and 16 suggest glass-working, while the large numbers of copper crucibles and waste imply that both these and structures 17 and 20 were used for copperworking.

The majority of the unfinished copper-alloy tags came from structure 20 (many from feature F36; see Perring 1981, 17) and associated pits, suggesting their manufacture within this building. A difference in the floor surfacing of structure 17 could indicate a division into two rooms, and a domestic-type hearth was found in the room to the rear, suggesting a combination of working and living accommodation under the same roof. The absence of 'industrial' finds from the building on the corner of Flaxengate and Grantham Street suggests that it was primarily residential, although there was no difference between its structural remains and those of the workshops.

The establishment of an internal chronology for the site relies to a great extent on tracing the loam horizons which sealed each phase of buildings, presumably representing levelling prior to reconstruction. A chronology was established of an average of 25 years' duration for each of the 13 periods, and the dates adjusted according to the coins and the pottery, especially the Stamford ware (Perring 1981, 36). The destruction and rebuilding at each

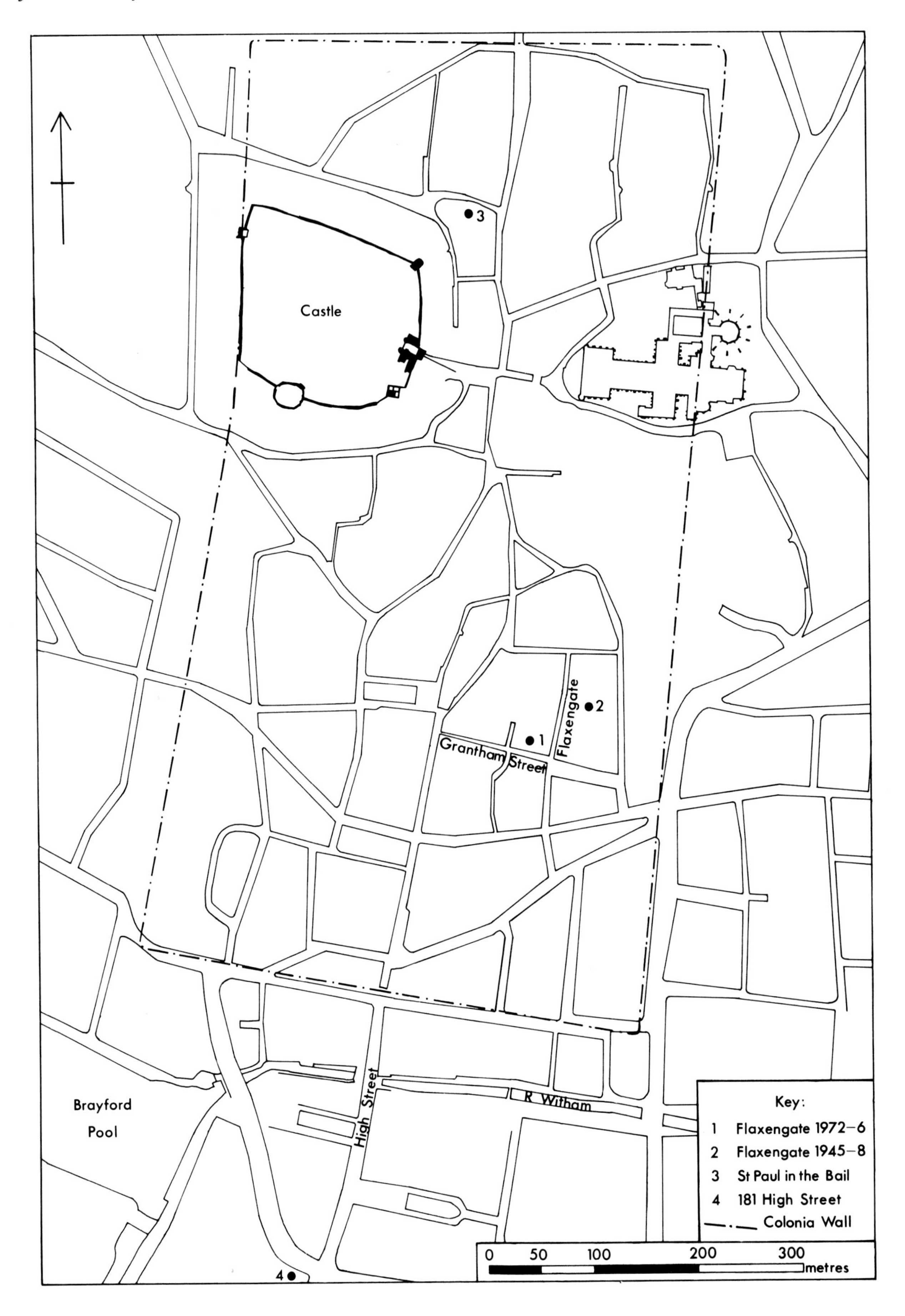

Fig 1 Location of sites referred to in text

Fig 2 The structural development of the site from the end of the Roman period to c 1200

period appear to have been conducted as a single operation across the site, the location and alignment of structures being frequently altered (see Fig 2). This may indicate that the area was under single ownership and that the establishment of the property itself may have been a direct result of the Danish conquest (Perring 1981, 43–4). Because the forms of the buildings do not betray any specifically Danish elements, it is to the pottery[2] and other finds that we must look for evidence of Danish settlers, and their possible impact on the development of this area.

An analysis of this material encounters certain major difficulties, the first of which is consequent upon the nature of the site. In common with most other urban excavations, a high proportion of the undiagnostic finds could well be residual—and Roman in date. Many such objects occurred in deposits related to the disturbance by pits and robbing of the late Roman building, or in the levelling horizons which contained high proportions of residual Roman pottery. While the ratio of residual to contemporary pottery may be indicative of the probable residuality of other finds, it can by no means be taken as proof. Objects regarding which there is an element of doubt are therefore included here, whereas those which can be identified as certainly Roman are omitted.

The second major problem concerns the dating of the early medieval finds. Most of the types of object discussed in this report cannot be assigned precise dates, and little of the Flaxengate material was found in securely stratified contexts such as floor surfaces. On the contrary, many objects came from the levelling between structural periods, or from pits, particularly at the western end of the site where no structures prior to the mid 11th century were found. The pits probably relate to the earlier buildings to the east but their sequence could not be associated directly with individual structural periods; they can thus only be assigned to a date range of up to two centuries.

A third major difficulty in interpreting the finds arises from the lack of information regarding the relationships between the finds and the structures, and between the finds themselves. During most of the excavation the exact location of each find was not recorded,[3] and thus their inter-relationships and distribution relative to each structure (of crucial importance as regards the industrial evidence) can only be imprecisely defined and imperfectly understood. The excavation of the site in 1975 by means of spits (for the method see Perring 1981, 4) gives some assistance in that finds are located to within an exact 2 m square, but vertical relationships were lost to some extent as each spit was excavated to an arbitrary depth of 0·10 m. Furthermore, although some surfaces and intrusive features were identified and recorded individually, this was not possible for areas external to the structures where the spits were excavated without regard to the stratigraphy. Many of the spits, and the associated finds, can only therefore be assigned a broad date range, overlapping several structural periods, and could relate to any of a number of buildings.

Notes

1 Recent excavations at St Paul-in-the-Bail revealed traces of a 10th or 11th century sunken-floored building, and the remains of a church (Gilmour 1979), which was previously thought to date to the 7th century, but may in fact be considerably earlier.
2 Report forthcoming, AL17/2, *Pottery from early medieval occupation at Flaxengate*, by Lauren Adams and Jane Young.
3 Three-dimensional recording was undertaken for the 1974 season only.

The finds

For ease of reference all numbers of the finds correspond with the Catalogue numbers and are printed in italic.

Combs

The comb fragments are, with one exception (*29*), of the single-sided composite type[1] commonly found on late Anglo-Saxon and Scandinavian Viking-age sites. A number of apparently unfinished pieces (*13–18, 26–7*), together with fragments of partially worked or waste antler (see below, p 37), may indicate manufacture on or near the site.

No *1* (Fig 3) is ornamented simply with paired horizontal lines running parallel to the edges of the connecting plates, perhaps to accentuate the angled back of the comb. A similar use of such ornament is seen on fragments of 9th century date from Hedeby (Tempel 1970, Abb 3, 5–8). The earliest examples of these combs bear ring-and-dot ornament in the form of a recumbent S, and are closely related to a late Carolingian Frisian type. They also occur at Dorestad (Roes 1963, pl 19, 3), Århus (Andersen *et al* 1971, 144–5), and Birka (Arbman 1943, Taf 160, 9) in 9th century contexts. A later development of the type is ornamented with a central panel of parallel lines (Tempel 1970, Abb 4, 8–10). The comparative dating of the Flaxengate piece to the 9th century is supported by the date of the context in which it was found (late 9th C).

The perforation through the end tooth segment suggests that it was originally provided with a case, both for protection and for ease in carrying. A small peg would be inserted through this, with a corresponding hole in the case to secure it; the case in its turn would be further perforated for suspension. Such an arrangement may be seen on an antler comb and case from Anglo-Scandinavian levels at Coppergate, York (MacGregor 1978a, fig 29, 11).

No *2* (Fig 3) is also from a late 9th century context. The end tooth segment projects beyond the connecting plates which are ornamented with a single vertical band of zig-zag. This style of decoration appears on combs of the late 7th or 8th centuries from Gotland and Grobin (Nerman 1958, 122–4; text figs 180–2; figs 67, 137, 163), and on other objects of later date from Scandinavian Viking-age sites, such as an antler handle from Birka (Arbman 1943, Taf 154, 1) and another from Lund (Nilsson in Mårtensson (ed) 1976, fig 197; dated *c* 1020–50). Two double-sided combs from York (one from Clifford Street,[2] the other unprovenanced) and one handled comb (also unprovenanced) bear similar vertical panels as part of their ornament (Waterman 1959, fig 17, 1 & 3; pl 18, 11). It also appears on a late Anglo-Saxon comb from Southampton (Addyman & Hill 1969, pl VIIa).

The end tooth segment of *3* (Fig 3) projecting beyond the connecting plates presents a gently flaring profile. Many late Anglo-Saxon and Viking-age combs have flared terminals, but most commonly the tooth segments have curved edges, producing an upturned end (Oakley & Harman in Williams, J H 1979, fig 137, 34; Waterman 1959, fig 16, 5). Its connecting plates bear a sketchily executed panel of lattice ornament; the terminals are decorated with converging obliques. Such simple linear ornament appears on Anglo-Saxon and Viking-age combs of all dates, as at Shakenoak (Brodribb *et al* 1972, figs 57, 58), Southampton

(Addyman & Hill 1969, pl VII), Birka (Arbman 1943, Taf 161–6), Trelleborg (Nørlund 1948, Tav XXX), and York (Waterman 1959, fig 16 & pl 18). The Flaxengate fragment came from a 10th century pit.

The end tooth segment of *4* (Fig 3) projects above and beyond the connecting plates; its back and edges are scalloped and ornamented with single ring-and-dot. The form of this terminal is such as to suggest an inturned animal head, its snout being emphasized by two small horizontal nicks, and by a saw-cut separating it from the upper edge of the connecting plate. A ring-and-dot 'eye' is placed just below the central, brow-like projection. The connecting plate bears a vertical band of zig-zag ornament below the animal snout, and a vertical step-pattern at its terminal. The upper edge of this plate is angled, suggesting that the back of the comb was steeply curved, or of triangular profile.

The projection of the end tooth segment above the connecting plates, and its shaping as an inturned animal head, are features reminiscent of 5th century barred zoomorphic combs from Spong Hill (Hills 1977, figs 129–32; Hills 1981, 100–1), examples of which are also known from the Frisian terps (Roes 1963, pls XII, XIII). They also appear on early types of Frisian winged combs, which are dated by Roes to the late 7th and 8th centuries (*ibid*, pl XXII, 1 & 2). The projecting terminals of these are almost triangular, but on both the eye is suggested by ring-and-dot, and the snout separated from the connecting plate by a saw-cut. The backs of these winged combs are strongly curved or sharply angled to form a triangular profile. Similar rudimentary heads, sometimes little more than projections above the back of the comb, are found on some Frisian crested combs, but one such has an animal head inturned, raised some distance above the connecting plates. The eye again is represented by a single ring-and-dot, while a line of such motifs ornaments the side of this terminal tooth segment (*ibid*, pl XXV, 5).

A comb terminal from Cloak Lane, London, dated to the 9th or 10th century, bears some resemblance to the Flaxengate piece in that the terminal is also shaped as an inturned animal head, but in comparison this is somewhat rudimentary (CGM 1908, pl 54, 15). While the end has a vertical profile, the back is scalloped, and the eye, placed below a central 'brow', is represented by a single ring-and-dot. The snout is emphasized by a horizontal nick, and a saw-cut separates it from the back of the comb. The connecting plates are sharply angled to form a triangular profile.

Combs with scalloped ends are occasionally found on Viking-age sites, as at Hedeby (Jankuhn 1943, Abb 75c), and perhaps represent an elaboration of the commoner flared ends, where the connecting plates are also upturned. A similar comb terminal appears among finds from Clifford Street, York (Waterman 1959, fig 16, 6); a second terminal (*ibid*, fig 16, 9) differs, although the end is scalloped, in that the tooth segment projects above the connecting plates, which are not upturned.

A further comb terminal (Fig 3, *5*) from a mid 12th century pit is obliquely cut, and projects above and beyond the connecting plate. The latter, of which only the terminal survives, is decorated with three groups of double vertical lines, a common feature on many late Anglo-Saxon and Viking-age combs of varying types, as at Southampton (Addyman & Hill 1969, pl 7a), York (MacGregor 1978a, fig 29, 6, 8, & 11), and Lund (Blomqvist 1942, Bild 1–8).

No *6* (Fig 3) bears a longitudinal panel of ornament, composed of a series of double interlocking step-patterns, unevenly executed and broadening as the connecting plate widens and curves gently upward. The plate is fractured almost directly along an incised vertical line which represents the border of a central panel of decoration interrupting the longitudinal ornament. The step-pattern motif is of little use in determining date, although it appears on Scandinavian Viking-age objects of the 9th and 10th centuries, as on several casket fittings from Birka (Arbman 1943, Taf 166, 5). A number of finds from Clifford Street, York, bear similar ornament: a wooden spoon (Waterman 1959, fig 15, 1) and three pins, one of bone (*ibid*, fig 12, 1), the others of bronze (*ibid*, fig 11, 13, 14). The latter belong to the category of plain-ringed, polyhedral-headed pins, originally dated by Fanning to the 9th and 10th centuries (1969, fig 1, 3–5), but which appear from recent finds in Dublin at High Street and Winetavern Street to continue into the 11th and possibly the 12th century.[3] A single vertical panel of the same pattern also appears on the terminal of 5, discussed above.

The arrangement of the ornament, however, may assist in dating this piece. The use of a single horizontal band of decoration, interrupted by a central vertical panel, thus dividing the connecting plate into two zones, is a feature of some late 9th and 10th century combs as found at Hedeby (Jankuhn 1943, Abb 75k) and Birka (Arbman 1943, Taf 159), many of which bear the characteristically early, horn-like protuberances of the terminals, representing stylized animal heads. Thus, although 6 was found in a deposit representing levelling activity which can only be loosely dated some time from the 10th to the second half of the 11th century, the way the ornament is laid out suggests that the comb itself dates to the 10th century, and perhaps before.

The ornament of many Viking-age combs is confined to the central portion of the connecting plates, either with or without a small band of decoration at the terminals, as on 5; many of the York combs show this arrangement (Waterman 1959, fig 16; pl 18). Two of the Flaxengate comb fragments (Fig 3, 7 & *10*) are clearly of this type; both are from 11th century contexts. The central panel of 7 is formed by a double row of incised zig-zag, separated by a double horizontal line. The borders of the panel are formed by a band of vertical lines. Only a small portion of the comb could be reconstructed, as it was badly fragmented when found. Its decoration is carelessly executed; the zig-zags are of uneven length, and no attempt has been made to match them on either side of the central dividing line. Similar ornament appears commonly on Anglo-Saxon and Viking-age combs as at Shakenoak (Brodribb *et al*, 1972, fig 57, 45), Hedeby (Jankuhn 1943, Abb 76b), Jarlshof (Hamilton 1956, pl 32, 1), and Clifford Street, York (Waterman 1959, fig 16, 3 & 7).

No *10* (Fig 3), a fragmentary connecting plate, bears part of a central panel of ornament formed in this instance by paired oblique lines, bordered by three pairs of vertical lines. A second fragment of connecting plate (Fig 3, *11*) bears similar ornament, but the piece is too small to indicate whether this also represents part of a central panel of decoration. This simple decorative technique, like that of 7, is of common occurrence on combs; there are numerous continental examples of Viking-age date. Pairs of oblique lines run

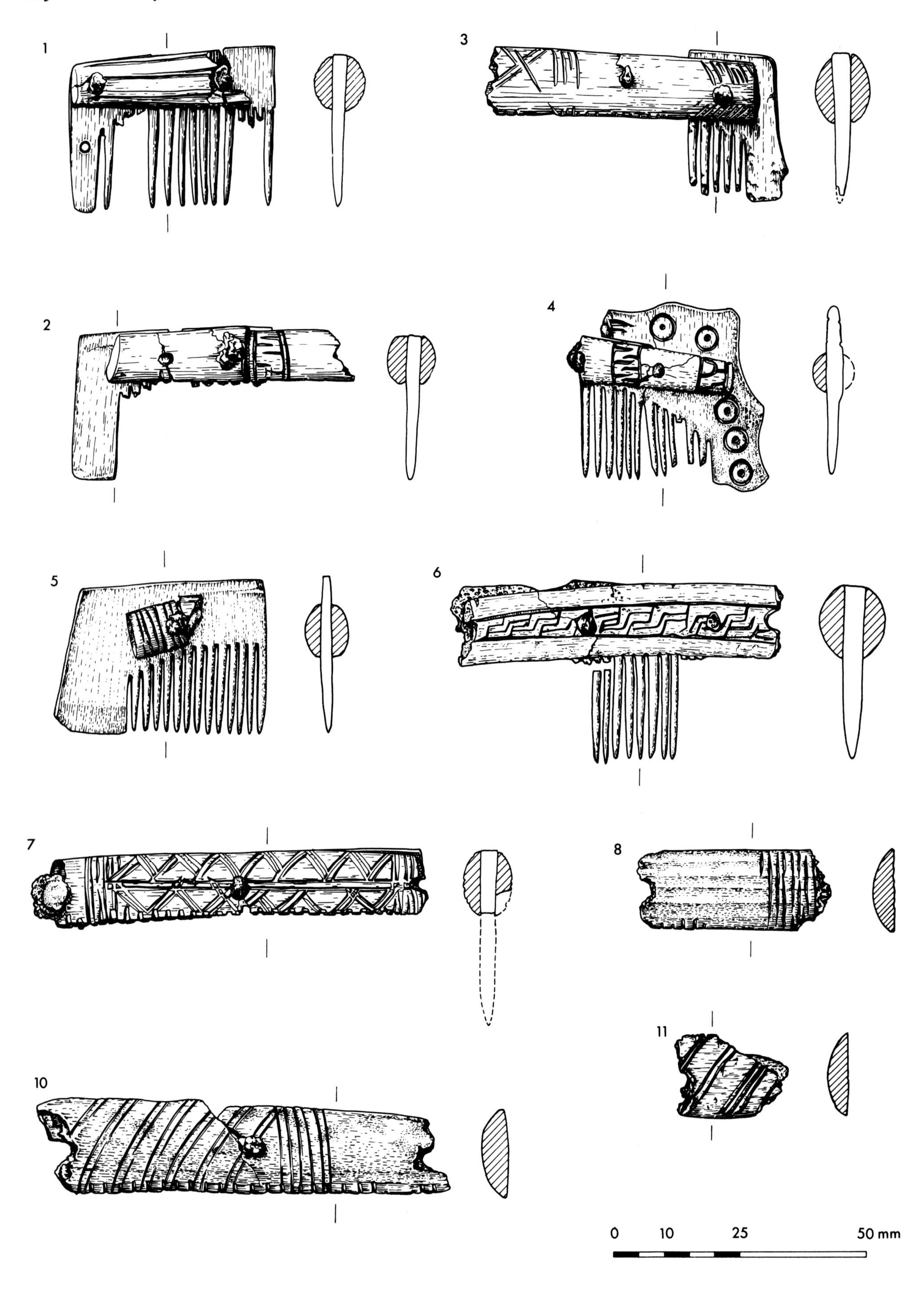

Fig 3 Bone and antler combs

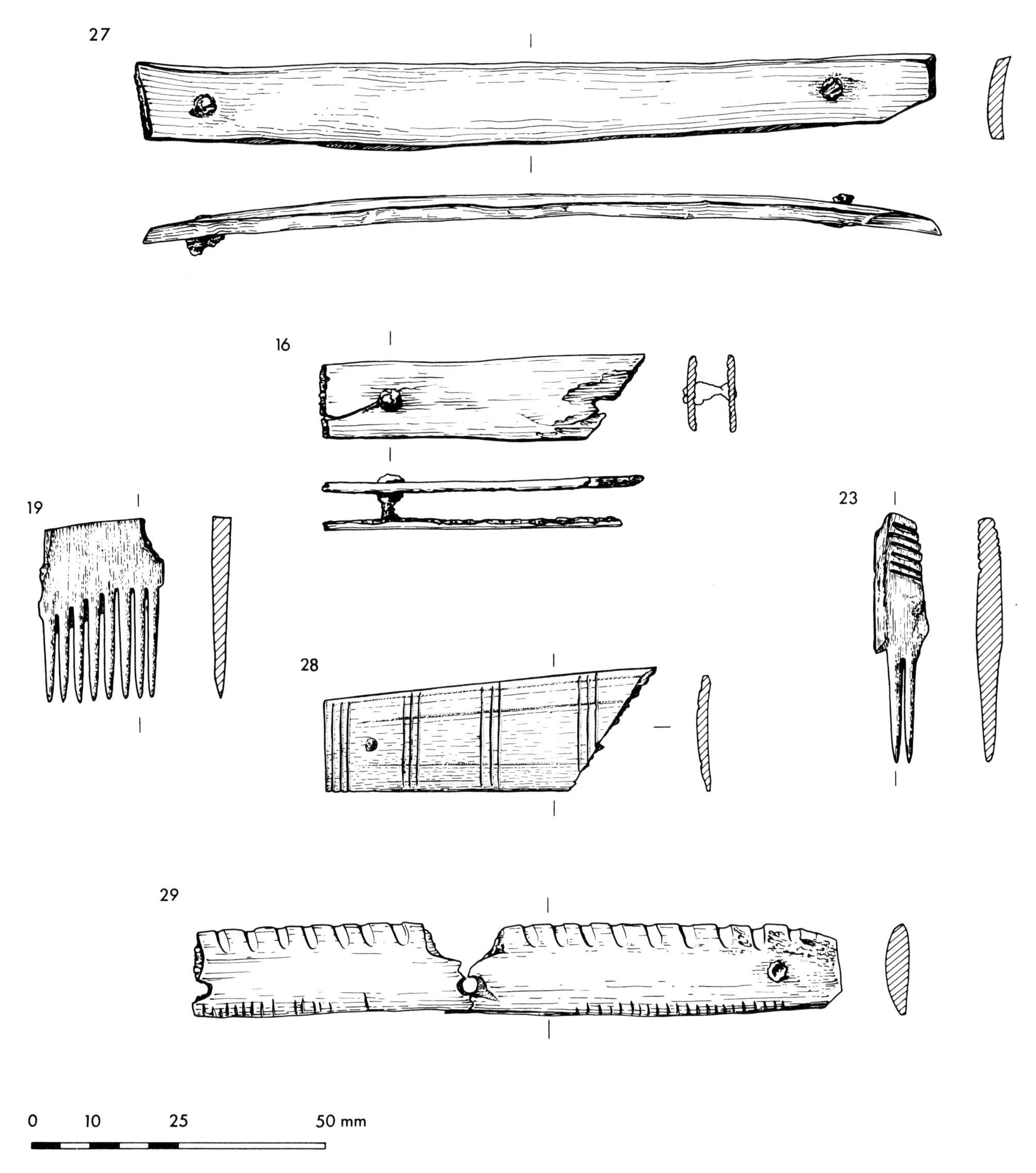

Fig 4 Bone and antler combs; 27, 28 are comb cases

the whole length of a Frisian winged comb (Roes 1963, pl 21, 1), while sets of four obliques ornament a late 9th or early 10th century piece from Hedeby (Jankuhn 1943, Abb 75b). A comb from Århus shows a similar arrangement to the Flaxengate fragment (*10*), with a central panel of paired obliques bordered by groups of verticals (Andersen *et al,* 1971, 148–9 ADV).

Two fragmentary connecting plates (*9* and Fig 3, *8*) bear crudely executed decoration in the form of a band of vertical lines. These may represent either a decorative feature repeated at intervals along the plate, or a single central panel, as on an 11th century comb from Lund (Persson in Mårtensson (ed) 1976; fig 288, 2A). Groups of two or more vertical lines placed at intervals along the connecting plate are a common feature of late Anglo-Saxon and Viking-age combs, eg at Southampton (Addyman & Hill 1969, pl VIIa), Hedeby (Jankuhn 1943, Abb 76f), and York (MacGregor 1978a, fig 29, 9).

The connecting plates of almost all the combs discussed above are of antler, while the tooth segments are of bone, a choice dictated perhaps by the need for greater strength in the plates. No *2* is the sole example of a comb constructed entirely of bone. In addition to the normal antler connecting plates, a number of thin bone strips of rectangular or plano-convex section (*13–18, 26–8*) were found in 10th and 11th century contexts. These are made from split rib bone, generally of cattle, but occasionally of a smaller animal such as sheep (*14*). The terminals of *26*, and *16* and *27* (Fig 4) show that the bone was partially sawn, then snapped off at the required length. The sides and ends of these plates are mostly rough and uneven, indicating that they may have been manufactured on the site, but not completed. No *16* (Fig 4), the terminal of a pair of plates, shows that they were originally secured together (with iron rivets) at some distance apart. Several other plates have iron rivets remaining, or perforations for rivets, either at each end of the plate (Fig 4, *27*), or with an additional rivet, or rivets, in the centre (Fig 4, *16*). All are undecorated; one piece (*26*) is stained green, but this seems to have been caused accidentally by contact with corroding copper in the surrounding soil.

These bone strips were probably intended for use as connecting plates on combs or comb cases, despite their weakness as compared to antler. Undecorated split rib connecting plates occur on a comb from Clifford Street, York (MacGregor 1978a, fig 29, 10), while ornamented strips from Leadmill Lane, York (*ibid*, fig 29, 12, 13) appear to be fragments from comb cases. By comparison with the York pieces, the Flaxengate fragments may thus be connecting plates; those with rivet holes only at the terminals (*26, 27*) for comb cases, those with interspersed rivets (*13–18*) for combs. One further fragment of split rib, ornamented with transverse groups of triple lines (Fig 4, *28*), may also be a fragment from a comb case.

Similar thin bone plates were found during the excavation of late Anglo-Saxon levels at Thetford (Knocker & Hughes 1950, 45). It was argued that these could not be comb cases because of the shortness of the plates ('only four inches or so long') and the occasional presence of a central rivet. Short combs are, however, not uncommon on both Anglo-Saxon and Anglo-Scandinavian sites of this period; the connecting plates of a comb case from St Peter's Street Northampton (Oakley & Harman in Williams, J H 1979, fig 136, 33) are approximately 130 mm (5 in) long, and those of a case from Coppergate, York (MacGregor 1978a, fig 29, 11) are approximately 115 mm (4½ in) long. Whereas the presence of a central rivet would indeed prevent the plates from having been used for comb cases, they could certainly have been used for combs, as on the York piece discussed above. An objection to the latter use (Knocker & Hughes 1950, 45) was that those plates still riveted together are too far apart ('¼ in') for the normal width of tooth segments. The distance between the two plates of the Flaxengate piece *16* is almost as great (*c* 5 mm); a possible explanation may be that the corrosion of the iron rivets has forced the plates apart to a greater distance than originally intended, so that the tooth segments have dropped out.[4] None of the Flaxengate examples was attached to tooth segments, but this may be due to the fact that they are probably unfinished. Split rib connecting plates are also known from such Viking-age settlements as Ribe (Ambrosiani 1981, 102), bone supplementing local supplies of antler (see p 45).

Adjoining fragments of an antler connecting plate (Fig 4, *29*) were recovered from mid 10th century contexts, and may represent the sole example of a handled double-sided composite comb from this site. A series of fine, closely spaced saw-cuts runs along one edge; along the other is a series of larger, more widely spaced notches. If both sets were made by the saw-cutting of the teeth, even the closely spaced nicks represent coarse teeth—approximately six per cm—and the teeth on the opposite side must have been extremely thick—approximately two per cm. These nicks may be purely decorative, but similar coarse teeth appear on late Anglo-Saxon double-sided combs from Southampton (Addyman & Hill 1969, pl VII, centre; Holdsworth 1976, fig 21, 2) averaging approximately three per cm.[5]

Single-piece and composite double-sided combs (without handles) are common on earlier Anglo-Saxon sites, such as Shakenoak (Brodribb *et al* 1972, figs 56–9, probably dating to the 7th century), but do not usually occur on Viking-age sites before the 11th or 12th century. None was found at Birka, Trelleborg, or Hedeby; at Jarlshof such combs first appeared in levels related to the 12th century (Hamilton 1956, pl 32, 5–9), and at Trondheim none occurred in levels earlier than the 13th century (Long 1975, 25).

Handled single-sided combs appear in England, Scandinavia, and the Rhineland (especially Dorestad) from the 8th or 9th century onwards (see Roes 1963, pl XXVIII), and a Frisian origin is suggested for the type (Waterman 1959, 89). It is possible that the double-sided handled comb, as seen at Southampton (Addyman & Hill 1969, pl VII), is of the same origin and owes its occurrence to trading contacts with Frisia. No *29* may well be a fragment of a comb similar to the Southampton piece. The antler connecting plate is slightly curved, rather than straight as would normally be the case with a handleless double-sided comb (*ibid*, pl VII, top; Waterman 1959, pl 18, 10 & 11; Persson in Mårtensson (ed) 1976, fig 290, 19D). The fractured end of the Flaxengate plate is broader and thicker than the remaining terminal, perhaps also indicating its projection into a handle. Its occurrence in an early context might also be suggestive of its Frisian affinities (see below, p 47).

A number of tooth segments (*19–25*) from single-sided composite combs were found in contexts of the early 10th to mid 12th centuries. These are all of bone, occasionally with a sloping upper edge from combs with a curved back. The upper portion of *23* (Fig 4) is ornamented with oblique lines, and would have projected above the connecting plates of the comb in the same manner as the terminal segment of *4* (Fig 3). Saw-marks are often visible on the teeth, which are occasionally beaded from wear.

Pins

Only one group of pins—those with expanded, perforated heads (*43–51*)—may with certainty be considered to be of late Anglo-Saxon or Viking-age date. The ball-headed (*30–40*) and nail-headed (*41, 42*) varieties are both types which occur on Roman sites, and the possibility that these and many of the fragments (*52–74*) are residual cannot be discounted, especially when they are from contexts associated with the demolition of the Roman building, or from levelling of the site prior to the construction of the earliest timber buildings (see above, p 4). These pins display no characteristically post-Roman features, such as a marked swelling or 'hipping' of the lower shank which occurs on many middle and late Anglo-Saxon bronze pins, as at Southampton (Addyman & Hill 1969, fig 26, 2–6, 9, 10) and York (Waterman 1959, fig 11, 5 & 9).

A number of the pins (Fig 5) are almost certainly Roman in date and are therefore omitted from the Catalogue. Three fragmentary polyhedral-headed pins, two of bone and the third of jet, came from late 9th century contexts. This type of pin head is common on Roman sites in both materials, as at Portchester (Webster in Cunliffe 1975, fig 116, 88–90) and York (RCHMY 1, pl 69, 11 & 16), but it reappears on Anglo-Saxon bronze pins. The lower surface of the head is generally more sharply angled than on Roman pins, and the facets are often ornamented with ring-and-dot, as at Whitby (Peers & Radford 1943, fig 14) and Southampton (Addyman & Hill 1969, fig 26, 6–8).[6] A plain polyhedral-headed bone pin from Clifford Street, York (Waterman 1959, fig 14, 30) and another of wood from Hedeby (Jankuhn 1943, Abb 72) suggest that the type may have survived in non-metallic pins. All three of the Flaxengate pins are however from late 9th century contexts, representing levelling prior to the construction of the first timber buildings, which contained a high proportion of residual Roman pottery. They are therefore most probably of Roman, rather than of later date.

Two pins (Fig 5) have a more complex 'turned' head: the first type, with one broad between two narrow mouldings, occurs on Roman sites such as York (RCHMY 1, pl 71) and Portchester (Webster in Cunliffe 1975, fig 116, 95, 96). The second has five narrow transverse mouldings surmounted by a squat cone. Although a pin of this type appears among finds from the Frisian terps (Roes 1963, pl 53, 5), this too could be of Roman date.

The head of the last pin (Fig 5) is carved to represent a seated bird; this was found in the early 10th century levelling over the Roman building. Finely carved bird-headed Roman pins are known from York (RCHMY 1, pl 71) and Lydney (Wheeler & Wheeler 1932, pl 32, 179); a much cruder pin, closer in appearance to the pin discussed here, was found in a Roman context during an earlier excavation near Flaxengate (Coppack 1973, fig 12, 13).[7] A further indication that this pin is of Roman rather than of later date, is the method of carving the head. The bird is presented sitting across the shank and is carved flat, ie, two-dimensionally. By contrast, the creatures depicted on Scandinavian Viking-age pins (more often animals than birds) are generally carved as a continuation of the shank and are treated in the round—ie three-dimensionally, as on pins from Hedeby, Birka, York (Schwarz-Mackensen 1976, Abb 4, 6 & 7), and Dublin (VMD 1973, 29–33).

Three fragmentary jet pins were also found; two from early 10th century levelling, the third from a late 11th century pit. Personal ornaments of jet are found on both British and Scandinavian Viking-age sites; these however are mostly pendants, rings, beads, and armlets. Bone and metal were apparently preferred for making pins. Although there is evidence for small-scale jet-working at Flaxengate mainly in the 11th century (see below, p 45), there is nothing to suggest that pins were included in the products. These fragments are most likely of Roman origin.

The most common type of the remaining pins is the ball-headed variety *(30–40)*, the head of which may be small and neatly fashioned (Fig 6, *32*), or large and occasionally mis-shapen (Fig 6, *35*). Slight faceting is often visible on both head and shank, and the upper part of the latter is often cut into to aid the shaping of the head. This is a long-lived type, occurring on Roman sites such as Fishbourne (Cunliffe 1971, fig 68, 22–4) and on Anglo-Saxon sites as at Whitby, where they are of both bone and bronze (Peers & Radford 1943, fig 14). Although such pins appear among finds from the Frisian terps (Roes 1963, pl 53), some with

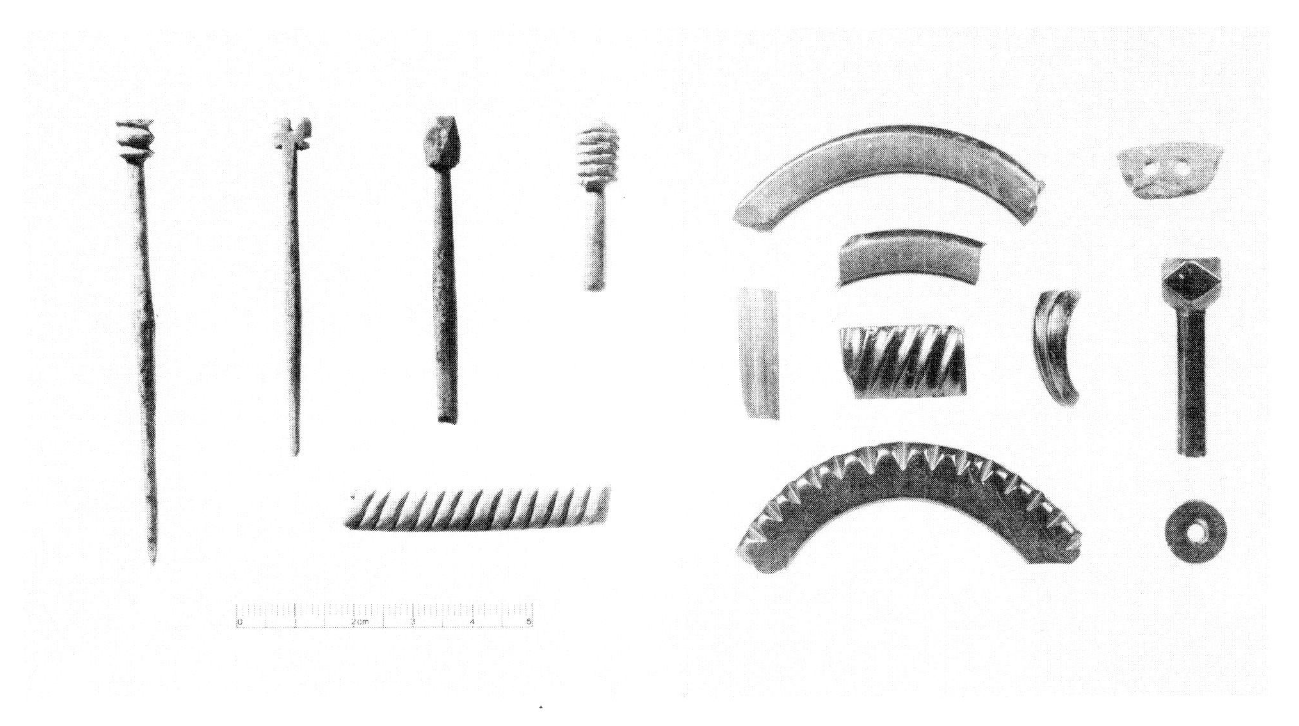

Fig 5 Roman jet and bone pins, bracelets, and beads from early medieval contexts

the characteristic post-Roman hipping of the lower shank, they do not seem to occur on Scandinavian Viking-age sites.

All the ball-headed pins from early medieval levels at Flaxengate are included here in the Catalogue, although some may be of Roman date. It is perhaps no coincidence that three of the four pins with large, sometimes mis-shapen heads *(34, 35, 40)* were more securely stratified in late 9th or 11th century deposits than many of those with smaller, more neatly executed heads which came from the 9th century levelling, pre-dating the first timber buildings, over the area of the Roman stone building.

Two nail-headed pins *(41, 42)* were found in late 9th to 11th century contexts associated with pits or robbing at the western end of the site (the area of the Roman stone building). No *42* has a small, centrally placed stump on the upper surface of the head, as though it is unfinished, or further ornament has been broken off. If the latter, this pin may belong to the series of Roman pins with complex ornamented heads. In appearance, however, it bears more resemblance to the slender form of *41* (Fig 6). The type is Roman in origin, examples occurring at Portchester (Webster in Cunliffe 1975, fig 116, 92), Shakenoak (Brodribb *et al*, 1971, fig 37, 11) and York (MacGregor 1978b, fig 19, 161). The nail-headed pins found in 10th and 11th century contexts in York, at Hungate (Richardson 1959, fig 19, 18)[8] and Clifford Street (Waterman 1959, fig 14, 32), suggest that the type may have survived into late Anglo-Saxon times.

There is little doubt regarding the date of the pins with expanded perforated heads *(43, 44, 46–8,* and Fig 6, *45, 49, 50)* as they are of common occurrence on Anglo-Saxon sites of all dates, as at Shakenoak (Brodribb *et al* 1972, fig 64, 105, 106) and Southampton (Addyman & Hill 1969, pl VIb), and on Viking-age settlement sites such as Freswick (Curle 1938–9, pl 48, 2), Jarlshof (Hamilton 1956, fig 59), and York (MacGregor 1978a, fig 30, 2; Waterman 1959, fig 14, 18–21, 23–5). They also occur among finds from Dorestad and the Frisian terps (Roes 1963, pl 52, 2 & 3), but are particularly numerous on Scandinavian Viking-age and medieval sites, as at Hedeby (Schwarz-Mackensen 1976, Abb 16, 1–6), Trelleborg (Nørlund 1948, Tav XLVIII, 17–24), Århus (Andersen *et al* 1971, 11) and Lund (Lindström in Mårtensson (ed) 1976, fig 240). These pins are all made from pig fibulae, whose natural shape lends itself particularly well to the purpose; they were probably made by the inhabitants of Flaxengate when required, as evidenced by an unfinished pin (Fig 6, *50*). A partially trimmed pig fibula (Fig 35, *306,* see below, p 33) may also have been intended for use as a pin. It is often suggested that these pins with expanded, perforated heads were used as needles (Brodribb *et al* 1972, 129); if this were the case the width of the head would certainly have restricted their use to coarse work such as netting or rush basket-work. They may possibly have been used in tapestry work, or for passing the weft in tablet and tabby-woven braids.[9] The function of such pins could have been twofold. They could have served as dress-fasteners, or perhaps have been worn in the hair. If used for the former, the garments must have been of coarsely woven cloth, as the shanks and points are generally quite thick. The perforation would then have served for the attachment of a cord to secure the pin to the garment (MacGregor 1972–4, 71).

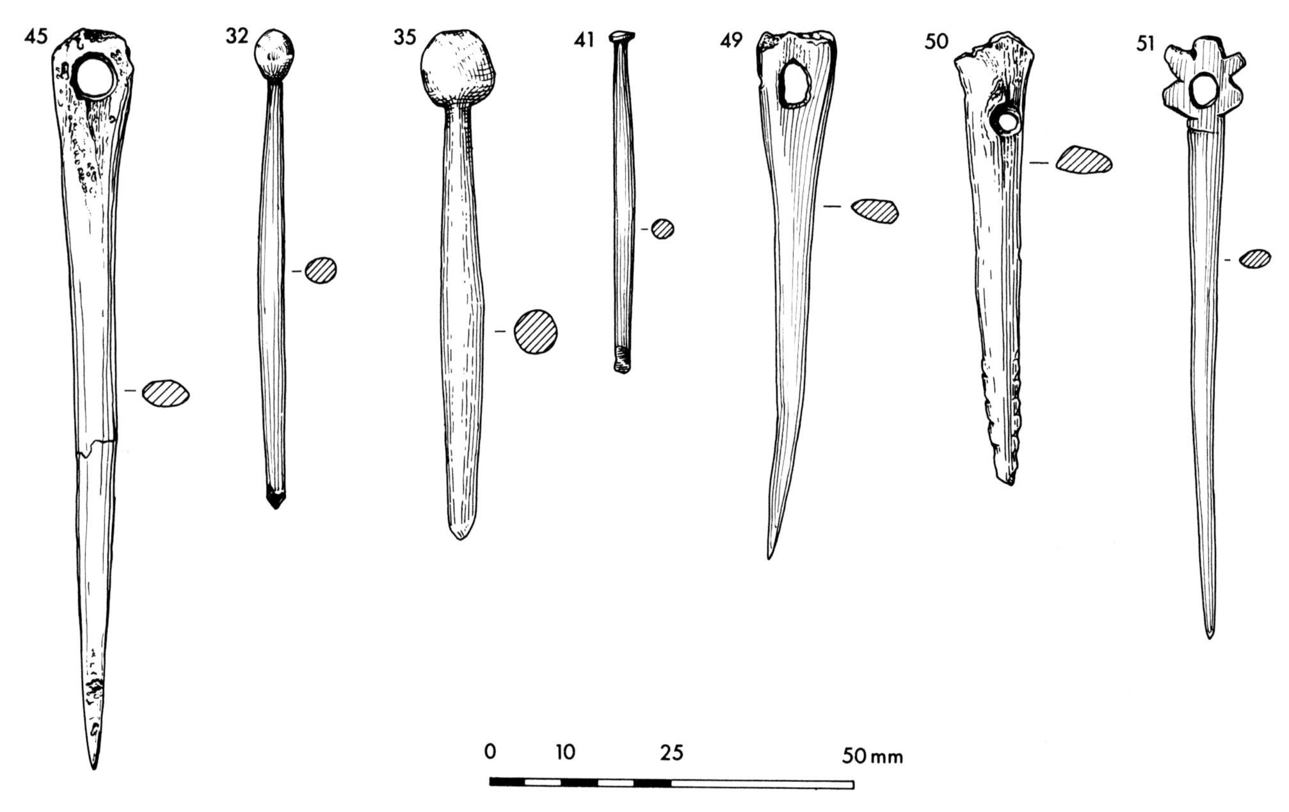

Fig 6 Bone pins

A variant of this type (Fig 6, *51*) has a perforated and decoratively scalloped head; this can be paralleled by pins from both British and Scandinavian Viking-age sites, as at York (Waterman 1959, fig 14, 10), Hedeby (Schwarz-Mackensen 1976, Abb 12, 6) and Århus (Andersen *et al* 1971, 110).

A number of headless pin fragments *(52–74)* were found, some in 9th century contexts associated with the levelling prior to the earliest timber buildings, or over the Roman building. These could therefore be of Roman date. The sharply pointed, slender-shanked fragments (eg *57, 58*) may be fragments of needles, rather than pins.

Finger-rings and bracelets

The five fragmentary jet finger-rings *(75–9)* are possibly all products of the 11th century jet-working at Flaxengate (see below, p 45). All are plain, and of D-shaped section; *75* (Fig 7) and *76* are very smooth and highly polished; the remaining three are unfinished. No 77 (Fig 7) has received only rudimentary shaping, and is probably a waste piece, broken during manufacture. The external surfaces of *78* and *79* (Fig 7) show traces of faceting and filing; final smoothing and polishing has not been applied. A sixth jet ring fragment (Fig 5), from a context associated with the late 9th to late 11th century pits at the western end of the site, appears to be of Roman origin, for it resembles Roman jet and shale bracelets in the ornament of its exterior with a median groove; the Silchester Roman bracelets commonly have two or more grooves (Lawson 1975, fig 5).

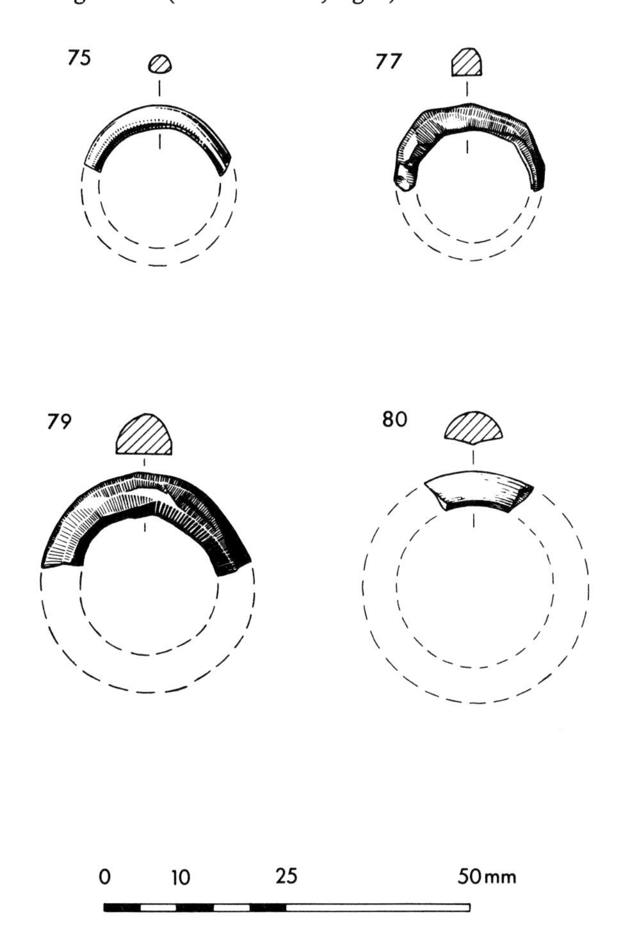

Fig 7 Jet and amber finger-rings

The small fragment of an amber finger-ring (Fig 7, *80*) was found in a 10th century context. This is a plain band of D-shaped section, with a median ridge on the internal surface which may result from the method used to cut out the ring from a core. Recent finds at Wood Quay, Dublin show that amber finger-rings were among the products of the craftsmen working there in the Hiberno-Norse period[10]; there is evidence for the manufacture of jet finger-rings at Coppergate, York at the same period.[11]

A number of jet and shale bracelet fragments were recovered, but are not included in this Catalogue. Jet armlets are known from Norse contexts in the Orkneys and the Isle of Man (Shetelig 1940, II, 86; IV, 74) but the Flaxengate pieces (Fig 5) are most likely of Roman origin, since the majority came from the early levelling, pre-dating the first timber buildings, or from levelling over the area of the Roman building. Furthermore, although most of the bracelets are plain, D-sectioned bands, a few bear ornament which may be paralleled by finds from Roman sites as at Silchester: 'chip' decoration, ridge-and-groove, and oblique grooving to produce a twisted cable effect (Lawson 1975, figs 4–6). There is also a fragment of a bone bracelet with incised oblique grooves similar to one recovered from a Roman context at Portchester (Webster in Cunliffe 1975, fig 117, 100).

Pendants and beads

An axe-shaped fragment of bone (Fig 8, *81*) probably served as a pendant; it is fractured across the socket (suspension loop). The wearing of pendants as protective amulets was a common practice from prehistoric and Roman times onwards; especially favoured by the Vikings were Thor's hammers and miniature weapons (Graham-Campbell 1980, 151–2).

The small piece of amber (Fig 8, *82*), fractured across its perforation, appears to be a fragment from a pendant. This may originally have been of sub-rectangular or triangular shape, as are a number of those from Hedeby (Graham-Campbell 1980, 133, no 461). Similar pendants found in York have been described as 'beads' (Waterman 1959, 95; fig 22, 1–7); others are known from Dublin.[12]

There are three stone pendants (Fig 8, *83–5*), one of which is unfinished. This *(83)* is a square-sectioned fragment of dark brown, siderite-bearing rock,[13] roughly worked to a rectangular shape with a tapered head. On the upper lip of the drilled hole is a small pit, as though two attempts at perforation were made. The piece is from an early 10th century context.

The remaining two pendants are from late 12th to mid 13th century levelling over the latest timber buildings (Jones 1980, 15). No *84,* of mottled red-brown Coal Measures Sandstone (?), is fractured across its small drilled perforation; it is of tapered rectangular form, square in cross-section, smooth and polished. No *85* is a triangular pendant of black limestone with rounded and perforated apex; this too is smooth and polished, although faint scratches are visible on both broad surfaces.[14]

A number of the perforated hones are so small and delicately fashioned that they might be classed as ornamental rather than functional pendants were it not for slight traces of wear on the surfaces (see below, p 29). These three pieces are treated here as purely

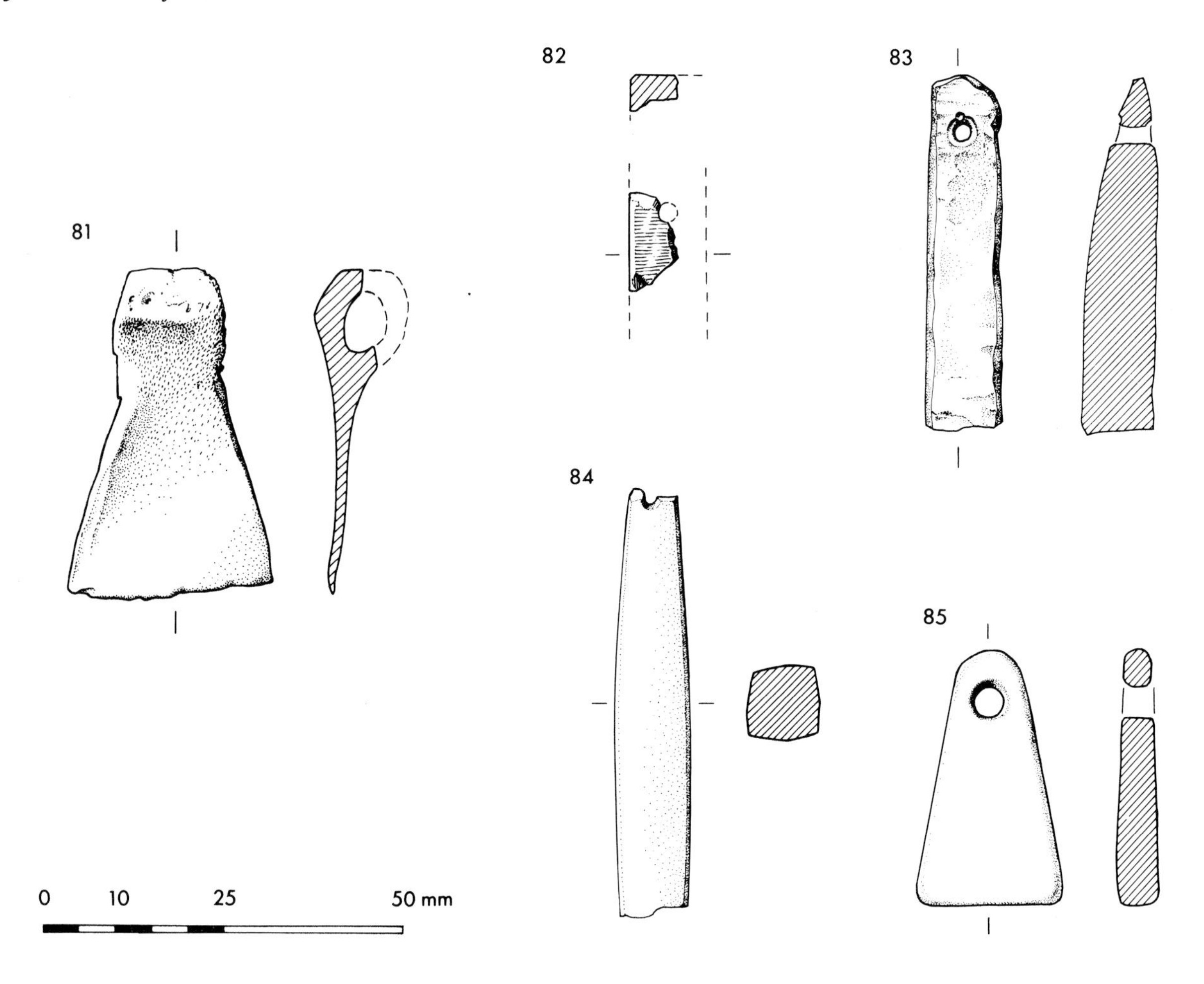

Fig 8 Pendants of bone, amber, and stone

decorative pendants on the basis of unsuitability of the rock types for honing, and the absence of any traces of such use. It is probable, however, that a number of the perforated hones from Birka served both functional and decorative purposes; these are of banded schist (Arbman 1943, Taf 188) and may have been chosen as much for their pleasing appearance as for their quality as hones.

The fact that *83* is unfinished suggests that it was made on site; two thin sub-rectangular fragments of jet may also be roughly worked pendants (see below, p 39 & Fig 44, *393, 394*). An antler object (Fig 38, *334*) may also have been used as a pendant but is not included here due to the uncertainty regarding its function (discussed below, pp 34, 36).

Several jet beads (Fig 5) were found, but these are probably of Roman origin; one of annular form came from the levelling pre-dating the earliest timber buildings. A semicircular bead with outer scalloped edge and double perforation is similar to those from a Roman context at York (RCHMY 1, pl 70), while a rectangular box bead with obliquely ribbed surface is paralleled by a Roman bead from Silchester (Lawson 1975, fig 2, 14). None of these beads, therefore, is included in this Catalogue.

Toggles

The eleven toggles *(86–96)* came from contexts dating from the early 10th to the late 11th century, and without exception are fashioned from the metapodials of young pigs as the distal ends are unfused. All but one (Fig 9, *88*) have a single perforation in mid-shaft, often penetrating it at a slight angle. The perforations were made either by drilling—leaving a neat hole as on *87* (Fig 9)—or by chipping out, leaving ragged edges as on *89* (Fig 9), which could have been neatened by bevelling, as on *96*, or perhaps worn smooth by use. The double perforation of *88* is unusual; this is fractured across one perforation and the lip between the two holes has also broken on one surface, perhaps from strain during use. Only one *(87)* shows further trimming along the shaft and across both ends. Most have some degree of polish on the perforated surfaces, as though from use, but there is generally little sign of wear around the lips of the perforations.

Bone toggles are found on late Anglo-Saxon, Viking-age and medieval sites in Britain, as at Northampton (Oakley & Harman in Williams, J H 1979, fig 139, 65–9), Freswick (Curle 1938–9, 97; pl 48, 11–14) and York (Waterman 1959, fig 19, 18), and on Continental sites of similar date, such as Hedeby (Jankuhn 1943, Abb 80) and Århus (Andersen *et al* 1971, 196). The pieces found at Århus were mostly in contexts dated by associated pottery to the 13th and 14th centuries; the distal ends of some of these are hollowed out (*ibid*, 196), but whether this relates to the function of the toggles is unclear. As with the Flaxengate examples, any wear is usually restricted to the shaft, where it is visible as a slight polish. Trimming of the ends, as on *87*, does not seem to have been a necessity as it so rarely appears, but the grooves at the distal ends of two of the Northampton toggles are artificially deepened by cutting (Oakley & Harman in Williams, J H 1979, 313).

Bone toggles are generally interpreted as dress fasteners, and occasionally as bobbins. Similar pieces occur on Iron Age sites such as Glastonbury Lake Village (Bulleid & Gray 1917, 421), Maiden Castle (Wheeler 1943, pl 35A, 11–13) and Cadbury (Alcock 1972, 153). These however are larger, being made from sheep metatarsals, and could have served as bobbins, as suggested by Wheeler (1943, 307). The smaller perforated bones from Flaxengate and other late Anglo-Saxon, Viking-age and medieval sites, are too small for such a purpose and would perhaps have been used for fastening garments. As toggles they would have provided an inexpensive and readily available substitute for metal brooches and pins.

Dice

Two bone dice came from early 12th century contexts. The smaller (Fig 10, *97*) is a rough cube with ring-and-dot markings only partially visible due to surface decay. The second (Fig 10, *98*) is a fragment of a larger, possibly rectangular die, with markings again of ring-and-dot, but too fragmentary to determine their arrangement (although it has a four on one side). Cubic dice with markings on opposite faces generally totalling seven were used in Britain from Roman times, but such larger rectangular dice are of typical Viking-age form (Rygh 1885, 475). The ends of these are often unmarked, or have only a single spot, with the remaining sides numbered 3, 4, 5, and 6. Both cubic and rectangular dice have been found at Lund, in contexts dating from the first half of the 10th to the first half of the 12th century; one rectangular piece has 4 on both ends, with 3, 4, 5, and 6 on the long sides (Persson in Mårtensson (ed) 1976, fig 329).[15]

Gaming pieces

The gaming pieces are all simple stone or ceramic discs, with the exception of one of ivory (Fig 11, *99*), and one unfinished antler piece (Fig 11, *100*). That of ivory is plano-convex in shape, with two concentric zones of ring-and-dot ornamenting the upper surface. Undecorated counters of similar form are commonly found on early Anglo-Saxon sites, as at Caistor-by-Norwich (Myres & Green 1973, fig 5, 98). Decorated pieces are also known from Sarre (Baldwin Brown 1915, pl XCVII; 413) and New Inns, Derbyshire (Howarth 1899, 192, no 117); many are lathe-turned. Although a number of similar pieces were found at Birka (Arbman 1943, Taf 150, 1; Grave 197), Viking-age playing pieces are generally more globular

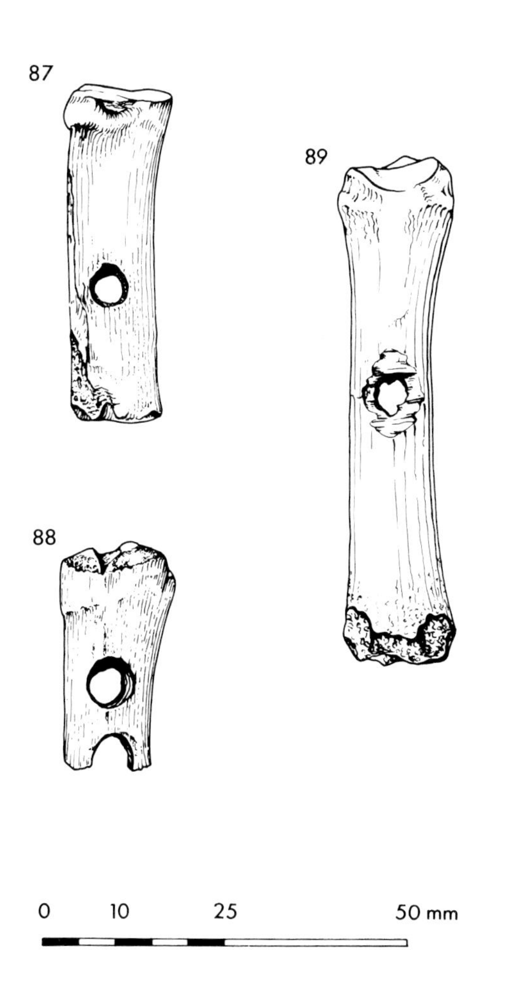

Fig 9 Bone toggles

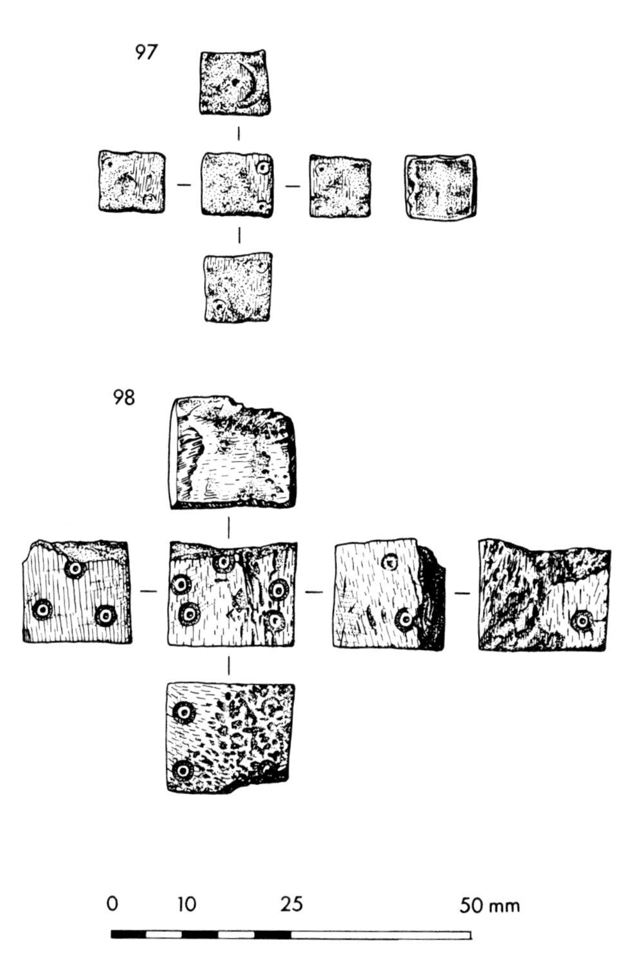

Fig 10 Bone dice

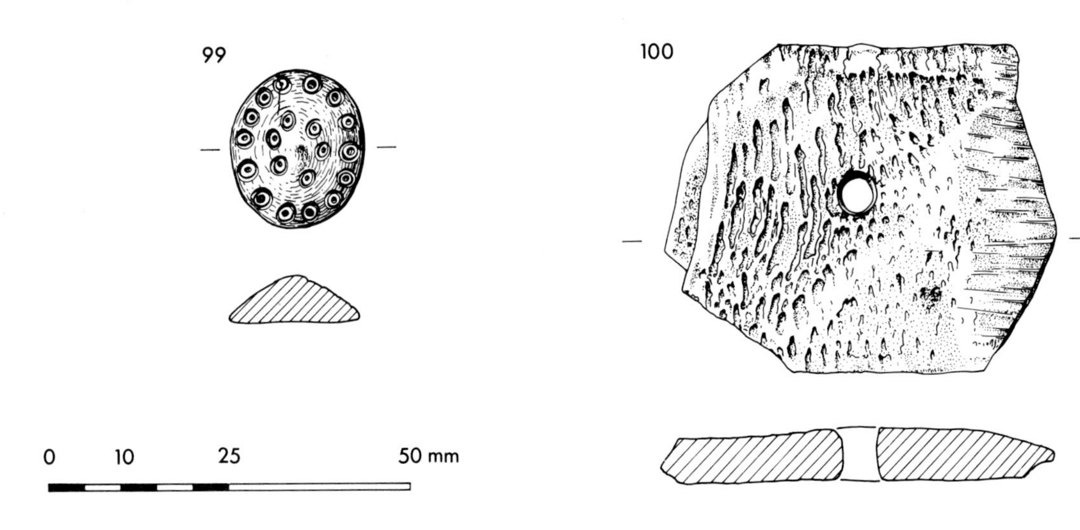

Fig 11 Ivory and antler gaming pieces

in form (Rygh 1885, 471–4; Arbman 1943, Taf 147–9). The Flaxengate counter came from a 12th century context.

The antler object *(100)* is likely to be an unfinished, disc-shaped gaming piece. The outer edges are sawn, and a small perforation has been made through the centre. Perforated antler gaming pieces are known from Hedeby (Jankuhn 1943, Abb 78; Ulbricht 1978, Taf 38), ornamented with incised lines or ring-and-dot. Similar pieces occur in 12th or 13th century contexts, as at Lund (Persson in Mårtensson (ed) 1976, fig 329), Århus (Andersen *et al* 1971, 212), and Oslo (Grieg 1933, figs 228–35). These are mostly of bone, either with or without the central perforation, and commonly ornamented with ring-and-dot, concentric circles, or a combination of both.

A similar series is found in Britain, again generally from 12th and 13th century contexts, although Wheeler suggested (1927, 48) that in technique they resemble many objects pre-dating the Norman Conquest. Such counters are known from Jarlshof (Hamilton 1956, fig 87, 5; associated with the medieval farmstead, built about the late 13th/early 14th century), King's Lynn (Clarke & Carter 1977, fig 143, 16; context dated *c* 1150–1200), Southampton (Platt & Coleman-Smith 1975, fig 247, 1930; from a pit dated *c* 1200–25), and Winchester (Cunliffe 1964, fig 52, 1–4; including one from a 13th century pit).[16]

The late appearance of this series of counters in Britain, and of those in later contexts in Scandinavia, may have been connected with the spread of a particular board game such as draughts. The game is thought to have been invented in the 12th century, perhaps in France (Murray 1952, 72). The unfinished antler piece from Flaxengate, however, came from a 10th or 11th century pit and may therefore have been intended for use in a game of more ancient origin, such as backgammon.

The ceramic discs are trimmed sherds of pottery *(101–4, 106–8, 111–17)* or tile *(105, 109, 110);* all but two of these *(115, 116)* are of Roman fabric. Most are roughly chipped to shape (Fig 12, *101, 109, 116),* but the edges of a few are wholly or partially ground smooth (Fig 12, *104*). They range in diameter from approximately 30 to 70 mm. The remaining discs, of limestone *(118)* and micaceous sandstone *(119–25),* are of similar size and commonly also have ground edges (Fig 12, *120, 121*).

Many of the discs came from late 9th century contexts relating to the destruction of and levelling over the Roman building, pre-dating the construction of the first timber buildings. Similar discs were also found in Roman levels, and it is probable that a number of those from the early medieval levels are residual. Such discs are frequently found on other Roman sites, as at York (MacGregor 1976b, 2; fig 2, 1, 16, & 28), but also occur in later contexts (Addyman & Priestley 1977, 139). A number of stone discs were found in Viking-age and earlier contexts at Jarlshof; the majority coming from 9th century levels (Hamilton 1956, fig 55, 8–11).These range in diameter from approximately 25 to 180 mm; it was suggested that the smaller may have been used as counters or plugs for skin floats, while the larger could have served as pot lids (*ibid,* 114). None of the Flaxengate pieces is large enough to have served the latter purpose. Another possible use for these discs is as stands (Addyman & Priestley 1977, 139). The stone discs from Scandinavian sites such as Lund (Persson in Mårtensson (ed) 1976, fig 333, from levels dated *c* 1150–1300) are generally termed gaming counters. They may have been used for such board games as backgammon or draughts.

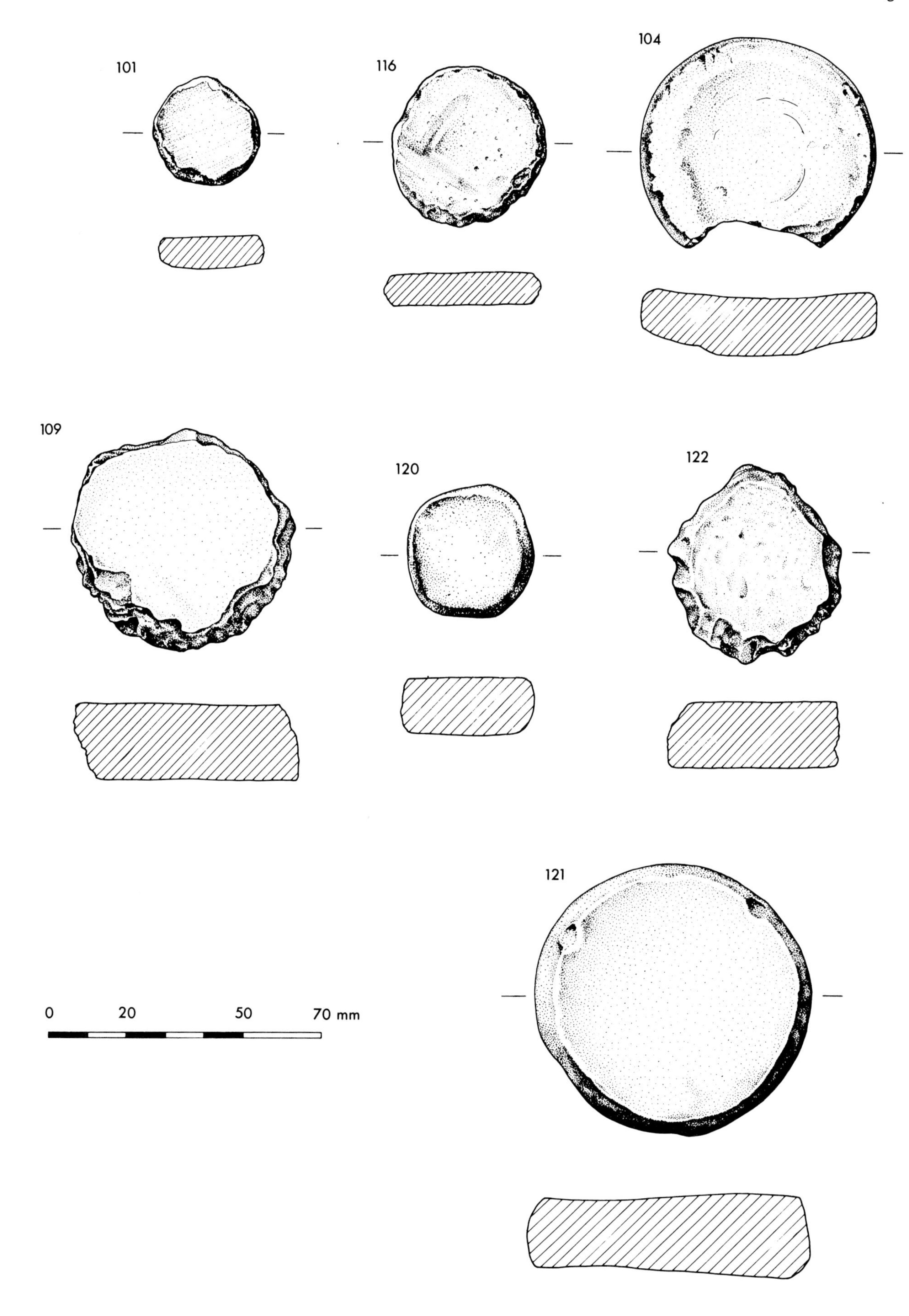

Fig 12 Ceramic and stone gaming pieces

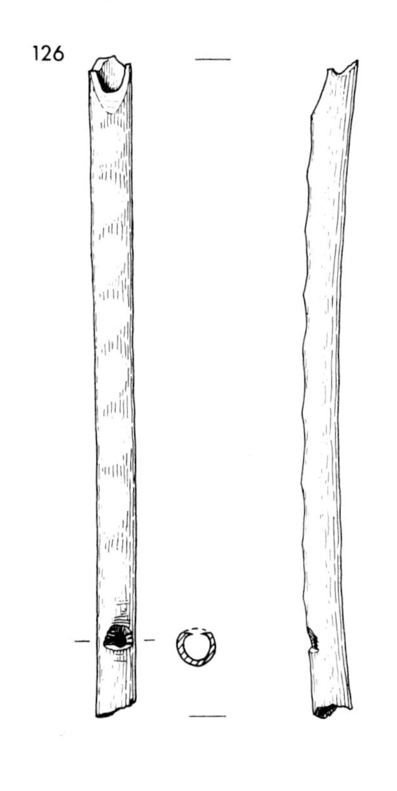

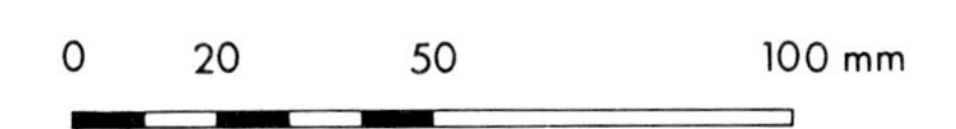

Fig 13 Bone flute

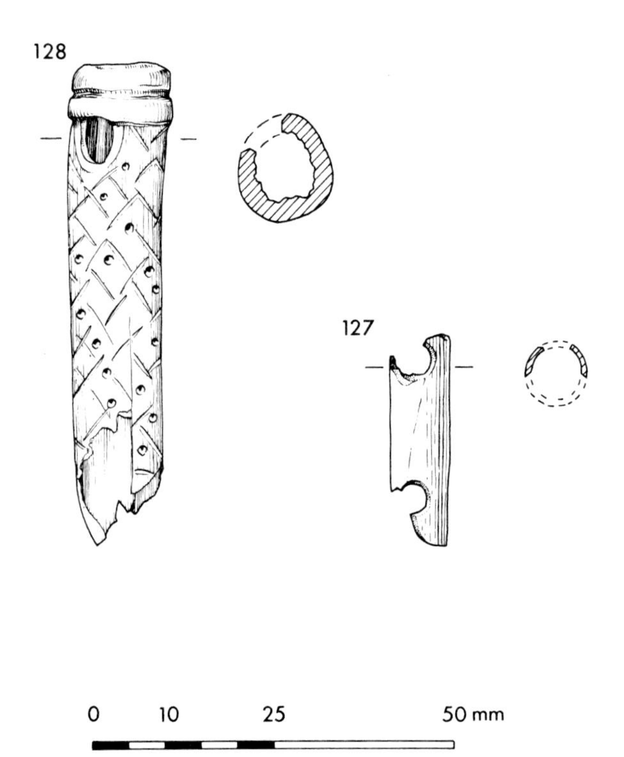

Fig 14 Bone flute and mouthpiece

Musical instruments

Of the three fragmentary instruments two are flutes *(126, 127)* and the third is the mouthpiece from a flute or pipe *(128)*. The better-preserved of the two flutes, *126* (Fig 13), is made from the ulna of a swan. The oval blow-hole and single remaining finger-hole are both made on the anterior surface of the bone, which has a series of shallow, natural undulations. The flute is fractured across the blow-hole and below the finger-hole; while the lip of the former is neatly bevelled, the edges of the latter are only roughly chipped out. The unfinished appearance of this hole suggests that the flute may have broken during manufacture. No *127* (Fig 14) is a splinter from a similar, but smaller flute, made from a goose bone; it is fractured across each of two finger-holes. The comparative neatness of the perforations and the smoothness and polished appearance of the shaft suggest that this piece was at least finished, if not played, before it broke.

Flutes of various types are commonly found on sites both in Britain and on the Continent from prehistoric times onwards (Megaw 1960; Crane 1972, 29–39); many are similarly fashioned from bird bone. Numerous examples are known from late Saxon, Viking-age and medieval contexts in Britain, including York (Waterman 1959, fig 19, 10, 11: late 10th/11th century), Norwich (Wilson & Hurst 1964, 267), King's Lynn (Clarke & Carter 1977, fig 143, 19, 20; contexts dated 1150–1200 and 14th century), and Southampton (Holdsworth 1976, fig 21, 7: late Saxon; Megaw in Platt & Coleman-Smith 1975—one of the best preserved examples, from a pit dated *c* 1300). Finds of similar date on the Continent are equally numerous, as from the Frisian terps (Roes 1963, pl LVIII, 1, 2), Hedeby (Jankuhn 1943, pl 79; Brade 1978, Abb 1, 1–3), and other Scandinavian sites (Crane 1972, 35). Many of these are broken in the same manner as the larger of the Flaxengate pieces, often leaving only one or two of the finger-holes.

No *128* (Fig 14), made from the tibia of a sheep, is ornamented with crudely incised and irregularly placed oblique lines and dots. A small blow-hole abuts the double-collared terminal; although the inner edge of this perforation is rough, the outer lip is neatly bevelled. It is fractured approximately 30 mm below the blow-hole, but may originally have had up to six finger-holes and was possibly of similar type to the end-blown flute from White Castle. This has five finger-holes and two thumb-holes, is ornamented with rows of impressed dots, and may date to the second half of the 13th century (Megaw 1961, pl XXIX). The Flaxengate piece is smooth and polished, as though from use.[17]

Bone skates

All three skates (Fig 15, *129–31)* are from 10th century contexts and are made from cattle metacarpals, with the anterior surface roughly cut or shaped; this face would have been in contact with the ice or light snow during use. The distal condyles of *131,* and to a lesser extent of *130,* are obliquely trimmed to form an upswept toe; those of *129* are broken off. The proximal anterior surfaces of *129* and *130* are slightly flattened, and the proximal end of the latter is trimmed to a sub-rectangular shape, with a shallow perforation in the articular facet. This hole appears unfinished; it is certainly too shallow to secure a wooden peg, around

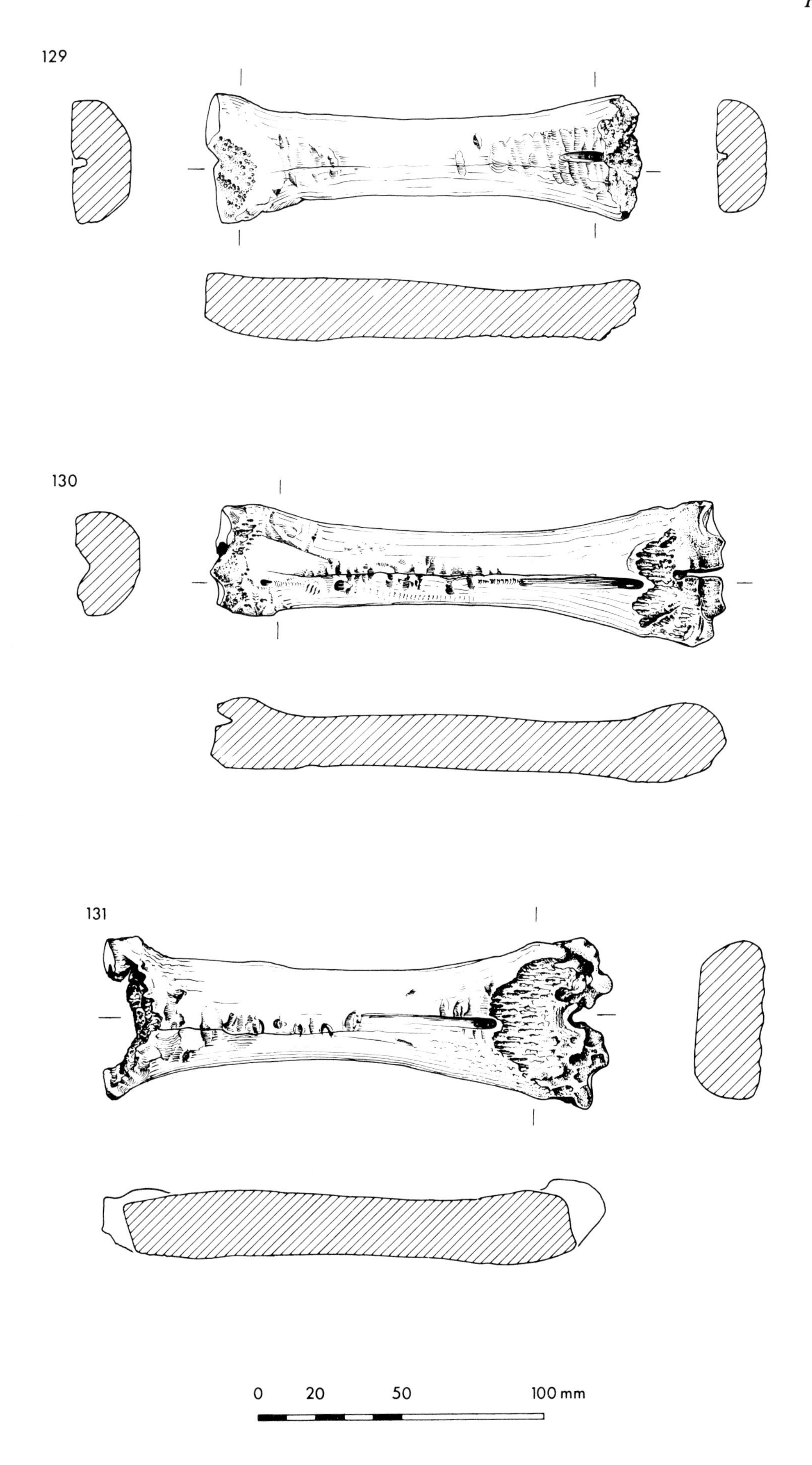

Fig 15 Bone skates

which a thong could be passed to secure the skate to the wearer's foot. Only one of the skates, *131*, appears to have been used; this is indicated by the faint striations and slight polish on the underside, although it has not been worn sufficiently to obliterate completely the preparatory tooling. The other two skates do not seem to have been used at all; the crude tooling and absence of final trimming suggest that these are unfinished. A small bone fragment, with one surface highly polished (Fig 33, *299;* p 33), may also be part of a skate.

Despite their crude appearance, there is little doubt that these objects were intended for use as skates; the arguments against such an interpretation are fully dealt with by MacGregor (1976a). Recent experiments have shown that such skates can be used successfully with very little preparatory trimming or smoothing of the underside, and that they rapidly become worn (MacGregor 1975). Little or no further shaping of *129* and *130* would thus have been necessary before use.

Comparison of skates from a number of British sites (MacGregor 1976a, table I) revealed a considerable variation in shaping and in the occurrence and placement of peg holes (or iron loops) for the attachment of thongs. Alternatively, thongs could have been passed through the natural cavity between the condyles of cattle metacarpals, but attachment to the feet was not really necessary in this form of skating, as the skates were always in contact with the ice, the skater propelling himself with one or two poles.

Bone skates were used in Europe from at least the Iron Age until the 19th century, although the earliest securely stratified examples from Britain are of early medieval date (MacGregor 1976a, 63–6). Three of late Anglo-Saxon or Saxo-Norman date were found during excavations at Holmes Grainwarehouse (181–2 High Street), Lincoln[18]; others are in the Trollope Collection.[19]

Skates are also commonly found on Scandinavian Viking-age and medieval sites, as at Hedeby, Birka (Arbman 1943, Taf 157, 6, 7), Trelleborg (Nørlund 1948, Tav 53, 1), Århus (Andersen *et al* 1971, 141, 142) and Lund (Cinthio in Mårtensson (ed) 1976).

Bone mounts

A number of thin bone strips (Fig 16, *132–7*) from 11th and 12th century contexts are fragmentary mounts, perhaps for small wooden chests or caskets. No *132* is made of scapula, the others of split animal rib; all are ornamented with ring-and-dot, and in one case *(134)* the central dots perforate the bone. Small circular rivet holes occasionally break the ornament, as on *132* and *134,* indicating that the decoration was applied prior to riveting. Although small bone pegs may have been used to secure the strips (see below), the absence of any metal staining in and around the perforations, together with a lack of surface polish, suggests that these may be unfinished pieces, perhaps offcuts or rejects. Only one *(133)* is apparently finished; one edge is smooth, rounded, and slightly polished.

No *138* (Fig 16) may also be part of a mount, although it is much thicker and different in style from the rest. It is lozenge-shaped, ornamented with a deep longitudinal groove and has snapped along a second, parallel groove. Both ends are sawn across, and faint oblique scratches on the upper surface indicate that it was smoothed by filing. There are no rivet holes for attachment. The possibility that this piece may be of Roman origin cannot be discounted since it was found in the fill of a late 9th century pit at the western end of the site (ie the area of the Roman building).

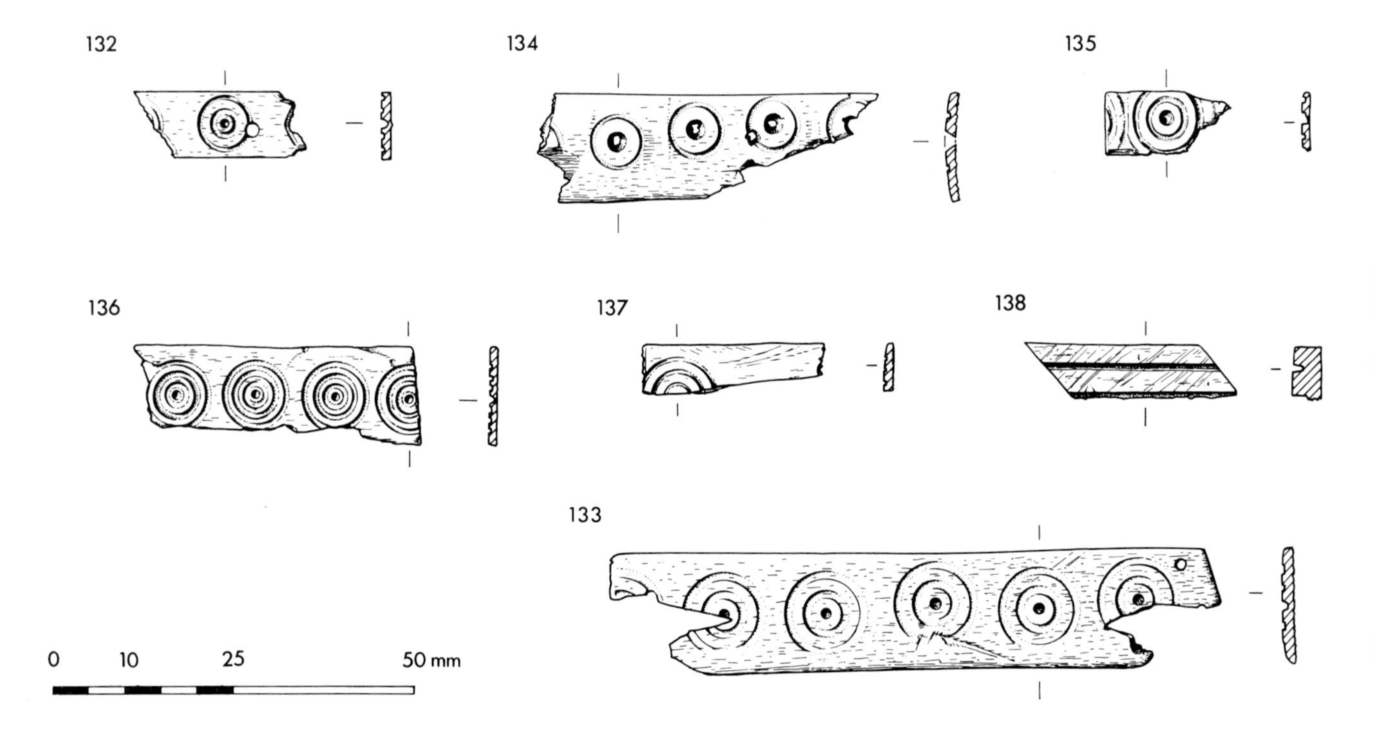

Fig 16 Bone mounts

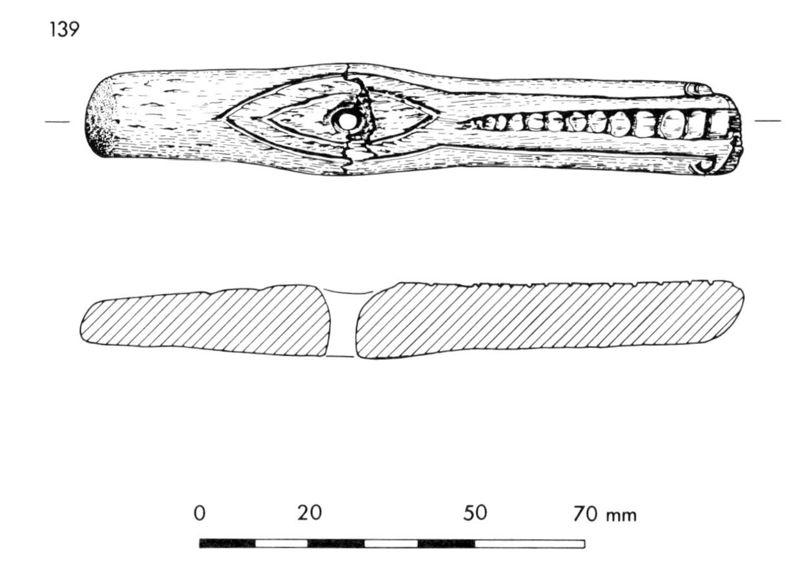

Fig 17 Bone sneck

Box fittings of bone with incised geometric and compass-drawn ornament are known from late Roman contexts, as at Richborough (Bushe-Fox 1949, pl LVII; Cunliffe 1968, pls LXI, LXII). Although many of these are perforated, and small bone pegs for securing them were found, a number have no rivet holes and must therefore have been inlaid or stuck on. One of these pieces is similar to *138,* in that it is lozenge-shaped and ornamented with two parallel, longitudinal grooves. In the same tradition as the late Roman mounts, and often using similar ornamental techniques, are the box fittings from early Anglo-Saxon contexts, as at Caistor-by-Norwich (Myres & Green 1973; fig 27 & pls XX, XXI; from Urn XII), Sutton Hoo (Bruce-Mitford 1975, figs 63 & 69; from Mound 3) and Spong Hill (Hills 1977, fig 138, 1351 & 1645). Two of the Spong Hill fragments are longitudinally, but shallowly grooved, and of similar form to *138.* Both these, however, and the Richborough fragment, are much thinner than the Flaxengate piece.

The remaining pieces *(132–7)* belong to the later Anglo-Saxon series of box mounts, dating from the 10th to the 12th centuries. Individual fragments are commonly found, such as the three pieces from Cadbury (Alcock 1972, pl 91; from an 11th century pit), while a number of pieces from Northampton, of probable late Anglo-Saxon date, appear to represent offcuts, trial pieces, and workshop waste (Oakley & Harman in Williams, J H 1979, 315, nos 83–91 & fig 141). More complete sets of mounts are known from Coppergate, York (Waterman 1959, pl XVII, 10th/11th century; MacGregor 1979, 11th century; both originally attached to oak lids), and Dublin.[20] The latest known example, from Ludgershall, is thought to date to the 12th century (Wilson & Hurst 1966, 192; pl XV).

Sneck

No *139* (Fig 17) is a thick bone strip of plano-convex section, markedly swollen around the off-centre perforation, across which it is fractured. Faint iron staining is visible around the edges of the hole, perhaps from a rivet. The piece may have broken in use and been discarded. The two adjoining fragments were found in different levels at some distance from one another, one from a late 10th and the other from a late 10th to late 11th century context. The longer of these pieces is stained green from contact with corroding copper in the surrounding soil. Incised ornament around the perforation and extending along the longest arm might possibly be intended to suggest a beast with staring eye and gaping jaws. Circular wear-marks are visible around the perforation on the underside, and both arms are angled slightly upwards.

In shape this resembles one side of the bone clamps used in the manufacture of combs and other articles (see below, p 30), but the pattern of wear indicates otherwise. The faint oblique ridges and circular grooves around the perforation show that the object swivelled about a rivet. If it had been used as a clamp, the driving of a wedge between the terminals at one end, to fix an object firmly between the jaws at the other, would most likely have left longitudinal marks; none such is visible on this piece. It may perhaps have served as a swivelling catch for a door or shutter; the slight angling of the underside of both arms was possibly intended to prevent excessive friction. Similar objects are known from Jarlshof (Hamilton 1956, 124) and Freswick (Curle 1938–9, pl XLIX, 1, 2).

Handles

The four bone handles (Fig 18, *140–3*) are all ornamented, although one *(140)* is probably unfinished. Three partially worked antler objects may also have been intended for similar use (Fig 39, *335–7;* p 36). Most of the knives and other small tools found on the site were probably provided with wooden handles, which have not survived owing to the dry soil conditions.[21]

Both ends of *140* are neatly finished, while the surface of the bone has been filed smooth, producing a rectangular-sectioned handle with sharply defined edges. Near the terminal on one surface is a small panel of incised ring-and-dot, with three separate motifs running obliquely away from the main group, thus presenting an unfinished appearance to the object.

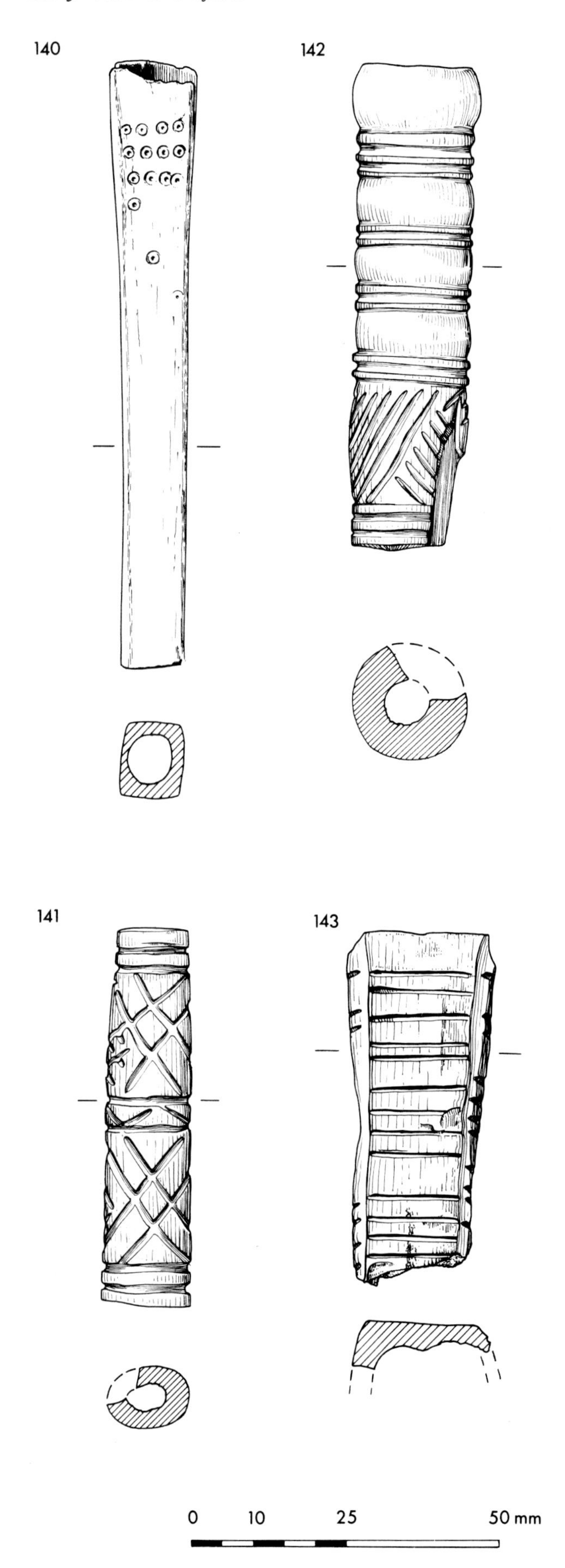

Fig 18 *Bone handles*

This and the shorter but thicker piece *142* are probably knife handles. The latter is made of cattle metatarsal, and ornamented with lathe-turned grooves and mouldings. A panel of incised, alternating oblique lines abuts the triple collar at the blade end, which shows traces of burning. One side of this handle is broken away, but it is otherwise smooth and polished. The ornamental technique of this piece resembles that of some late Roman handles from Lydney (Wheeler & Wheeler 1932, pl XXXIA, 152; XXXIB, 157), but a wooden knife handle from Lund, dated to the 12th century, is also ornamented with lathe-turned grooves and mouldings (Nilsson in Mårtensson (ed) 1976, fig 200).

A smaller handle, *141*, perhaps comes from an awl or bodkin. This bears deeply incised ornament and, although broken, is otherwise in good condition, being smooth and highly polished. No *143* is a small fragment of a rectangular-sectioned handle, ornamented with shallow transverse grooves.

Spatulae

The small bone spatula *145* (Fig 19) is made from a pig fibula; both the shaft and the natural ridges at the proximal end are trimmed, the latter to form a small, shallow bowl. No *144* (Fig 19) may also be a spatula, but although the end of the shaft is cut across in similar fashion to that of *145*, there are no further signs of modification to the shaft or to the ridges at the proximal end, where the bone is fractured. The cutting of the shaft might perhaps be the result of butchery rather than of deliberate working. The bowl of a similar spatula was found in an Anglo-Saxon context at Shakenoak (Brodribb *et al* 1972, fig 59, 71); another is known from Whitby.[22]

Late Anglo-Saxon and medieval spoons of bone, wood, or ivory generally have bowls of deeper, more rounded shape than the Flaxengate spatula(e), although a number of slender, shallow-bowled examples are known from London (LMMC 1940, pl XXV: bone), York (Waterman 1959, fig 15, 1, 2: wood) and Chichester (Waterman 1959, fig 15, 3: bone). The handles of the York spoons are ornamented, while the bowls of the London and Chichester examples are separated from the handles by animal-head mouldings.[23] A silver spoon-spatula and spoon-fork from Sevington, dated pre-850, are the nearest parallels in metal (Wilson 1964, nos 67, 68). A group of spoons or spatulae from Winchester has recently been published (Collis & Kjølbye-Biddle 1979); these are cut from large bones such as cattle rib or long bone shaft. While similar in shape to the shallow-bowled spoons discussed above, they are unusual in that most of them appear to be double-ended; moreover, the bowls and occasionally the handles are ornamented (*ibid*, figs 1–3). The Winchester spoon-spatulae are probably the products of a single craftsman working in the earlier 11th century. It is suggested that such bone or wooden implements were used for domestic purposes, and may have had Scandinavian connections (*ibid*, 389).

Soapstone vessels

The four small soapstone (steatite) vessel sherds (*146–9*)[24] are among the few finds which are to be considered as distinctively Viking in character (see below, p 42). No *146* is much abraded but appears to be part of a plain rim. The only other notable piece is *147*, consisting of two adjoining sherds of a vessel with

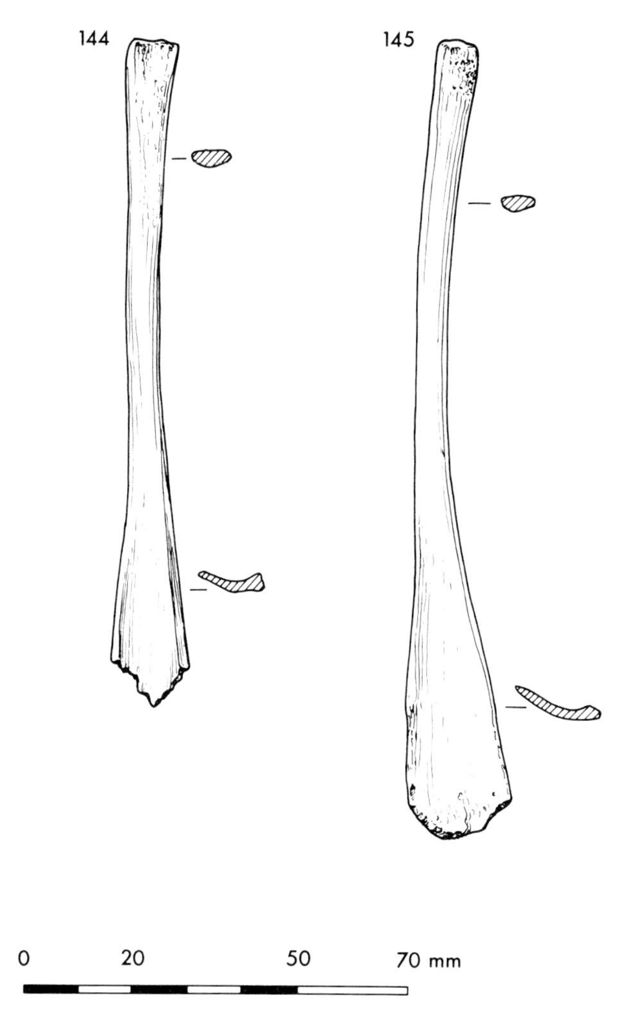

Fig 19 Bone spatulae

a decorative band formed by three shallow grooves, now only faintly visible. Similar ornament appears just below the rim of a bowl from Borge, Norway, (Petersen 1951, fig 191). Carbon deposits on the external surfaces of *147* and *149* suggest that they may have been used as cooking pots. All the sherds are too small for the forms of the vessels to be determined, but they are probably fragments of hemispherical bowls, the most common vessel-type in this material (Petersen 1951, figs 190–3; Graham-Campbell 1980, nos 40, 41). The only other known finds of soapstone in England are from York: two body sherds from Lloyds Bank (MacGregor 1978a, fig 21, 1, 2,) and a few fragments from recent excavations at Coppergate.[25]

The Viking exploitation of soapstone outcrops in south-west Norway for the manufacture of vessels, weights, spindle-whorls, and other objects was of major economic importance. Finds of rough-cut blocks and half-finished fragments at Kaupang (Blindheim 1969, 18) suggest the existence of a specialized industry catering for both local and international trade, the scope of which is in part demonstrated by finds of soapstone vessels at Birka and Hedeby. Outcrops of soapstone in the Shetlands were exploited by the Norse settlers; the Cunningsburgh quarries appear to have been the source of the material found at Jarlshof (Hamilton 1956, 206–10), although there are also other outcrops in the area. Thin-sectioning of the two fragments from Lloyds Bank, York (MacGregor 1978a, 37–9) showed them to be comparable with material from Cunningsburgh, but without samples for comparison from other sources, the possibility of their import from Norway could not be eliminated. For the same reason the source of the Flaxengate fragments cannot be determined.[26]

Querns

Three of the quern fragments *(150–2)* are made of Niedermendig (Mayen) lava from the Rhineland. No *150* (Fig 20), part of an upper stone, is fractured across the handle socket, which perforates the upper surface and side at an oblique angle. The shallow radial grooves of the lower surface, to facilitate grinding, commonly occur on Roman as well as later quernstones, and *150* may be of Roman date since it

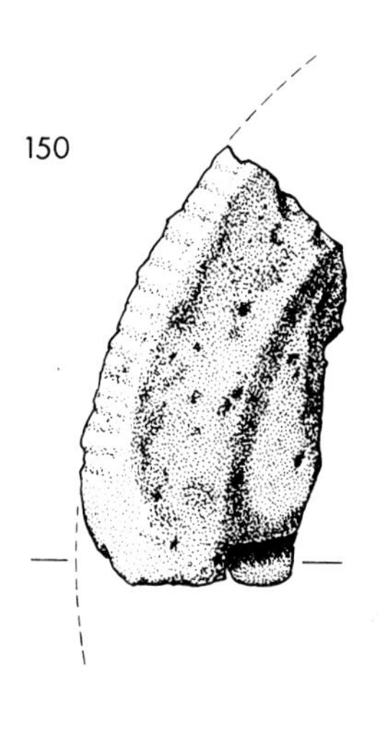

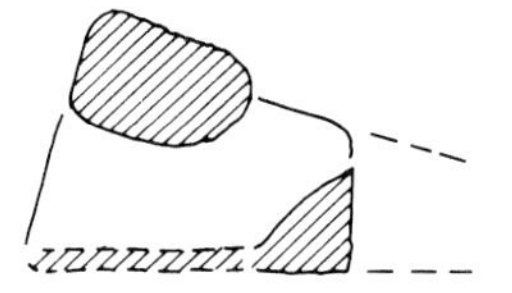

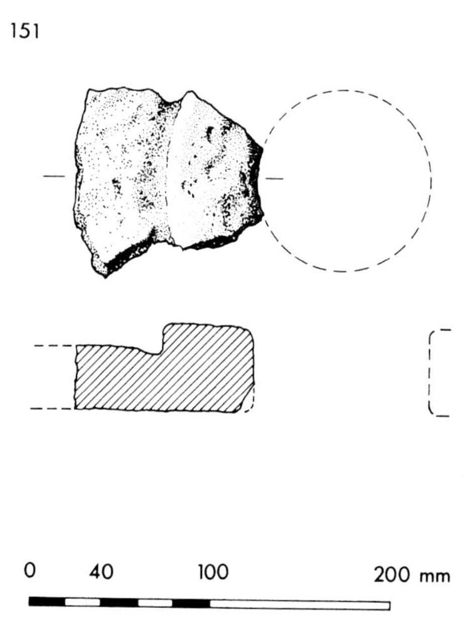

Fig 20 Mayen lava querns

was found in a context associated with the early 10th century levelling over the Roman building. No *151* (Fig 20), also a fragment of an upper stone, has a raised collar round the central perforation. No *152*, possibly from a lower stone, is grooved in similar fashion to *150;* its grinding surface is well worn. Nos *150* and *152* are too small to make an accurate estimate of diameter, but both appear to fall within the normal range of late Anglo-Saxon and Viking-age querns, comparing well with those from St Neots (Addyman 1973, 89) and Trelleborg (Nørlund 1948, Tav XX). The oblique perforation of *150* is paralleled by the handle sockets of two of the St Neots stones (Addyman 1973, fig 17, 1, 2); both the latter fragments also have a raised lip round the central hole, like the Flaxengate piece *151*. The same feature appears on a schist quern from the late Norse settlement at Jarlshof (Hamilton 1956, pl XXXV, 10).

Two of the remaining quern fragments *(153, 154)* are of Millstone Grit, probably from Yorkshire or Derbyshire. The grinding surface of *153* is radially grooved, as on the lava querns *150* and *152*. No *154* is more 'pecked' than grooved, with the markings concentrically placed. A quern fragment from a post-Conquest context at St Peter's Street, Northampton shows a similarly 'pecked' grinding surface (Oakley & Anderson in Williams, J H 1979, Q1). No *155* is of very coarse grit, probably from the Spilsby area.[27]

Spindle-whorls

Twenty of the fifty-two spindle-whorls are simply made from perforated cattle femur heads *(156–75)*. The only unfinished whorl (Fig 21, *161*) has a hole bored from the underside to within approximately 8 mm of the upper surface. A small pit on the latter suggests that perforation would have been completed from this direction, a method which might account for the angled perforation apparent on some of these whorls. The upper lip of the perforation is occasionally of triangular *(166)* or square outline *(165* and Fig 21, *160)*; the latter is also found on a bone whorl from St Peter's Street, Northampton (Oakley & Hall in Williams, J H 1979, 288, SW18: unstratified). Further shaping occurs rarely, and is limited to a slight bevelling of the lip *(163, 168)*. Bone whorls are commonly found on sites of prehistoric date onwards, due no doubt to the availability and easily worked nature of the raw material.

Six disc-shaped whorls *(176, 177* and *179–182)* are made from trimmed and perforated potsherds, two of Roman fabric *(176, 177);* a further whorl is made from Roman tile *(178)*. The edges of these three, and of a whorl in Saxon sandy fabric (Fig 21, *182*), are ground smooth—a feature also shown by some of the ceramic gaming counters (see above, p 14). The remaining three whorls are of fine shelly fabric, crudely trimmed *(179, 180* and Fig 21, *181*). Ceramic whorls of this type occur commonly on late Anglo-Saxon sites, as at St Peter's Street, Northampton (Oakley & Hall in Williams, J H 1979, 188, SW20–25: fabric of late Saxon/post-Conquest date) and St Neots (Addyman 1973, fig 18, 4: probably of Roman fabric). Two fragmentary whorls of fired clay were also found: one disc-shaped *(183)*, the other conical (Fig 21, *184*). The latter form is found frequently on Scandinavian Viking-age sites as at Trelleborg (Nørlund 1948, Tav LI) and on Norse settlement sites in Britain, as at Jarlshof (Hamilton 1956, fig 66, 5–8; of steatite).

With the exception of a fragmentary chalk disc (Fig 21, *185*), the remaining whorls are all of limestone *(186–207)*. These are of varying forms and many are ornamented, generally with simple incised designs and occasionally with paint. The disc appears in an unusually tall form, more as a cylinder, in *186* (Fig 21). No *187* (Fig 21), of the normal squat shape, has crudely faceted sides bearing random and irregularly incised ornament. A variant form, found in the four whorls *189–92*, is tapered, thus resembling a truncated cone (as Fig 22, *190, 192*). Only one of these *(192)* is ornamented, again with apparently random incisions. Whorls of similar form in a variety of materials are known from late Anglo-Saxon sites such as Whitby (Peers & Radford 1943, fig 23) and Southampton (Addyman & Hill, 1969, fig 29; Holdsworth 1976, fig 21, 12); these commonly bear neatly incised linear ornament or ring-and-dot. The irregular incised decoration of the Flaxengate pieces *187* and *192* is matched by that of a number of the whorls from Clifford Street, York (Waterman 1959, fig 20, 10, 11).

The earliest of the decorated whorls is from a mid 10th century context (Fig 21, *188*). This is of sub-conical form and its ornament, although carelessly executed, is the most elaborate of the designs. On both the flattened upper surface and the base is a mis-shapen, 8-pointed star; around the sides alternating panels of vertical, horizontal, or opposed oblique lines surmount an uneven zig-zag.

Three of the five hemispherical whorls also bear panels of incised ornament; alternating ladder-pattern and plain segments appear around the sides of *195* and *196*, and on the base of *194* (see Fig 22). The decorative panels around the sides of the latter are formed by carelessly executed, opposed obliques. Basal ornament also appears on *195*, but as simple radial lines rather than as panels. These three whorls are from 11th century contexts.

Two of the three globular whorls (Fig 22, *198–200*) have a flattened upper surface and base; both bear continuous incised ornament around the sides. On *198* this is an irregular chain-loop, on *199* a zig-zag formed by two more or less parallel lines. Around the sides of *200* are crudely incised crosses; faint traces of red paint are visible on this, and within the zig-zag of *199*.

Ornament on the remaining whorls is simpler; traces of red paint are again faintly visible on the otherwise plain bi-conical whorl *201*. The shallow concentric circles of the bi-conical whorls *202, 203* (Fig 22), and *206* are repeated on the single annular whorl *207* (Fig 22), while *205* (Fig 22) bears shallow radial lines. The concentric circles are very regular, evidently produced by lathe-turning; this feature appears on whorls from Scandinavian Viking-age sites such as Trelleborg (Nørlund 1948, Tav L), and on late Anglo-Saxon sites, as at St Peter's Street, Northampton (Oakley & Hall in Williams, J H 1979, fig 126, 5–8); the latter are from post-Conquest levels and thus correspond well with those from Flaxengate, which occurred in late 12th century contexts. In contrast, the whorls with continuous or panelled ornamental zones, or with painted decoration, are from late 10th and 11th century levels. The use of painted ornament may be paralleled on a pottery whorl from Clifford Street, York (Waterman 1959, fig 20, 5).

The weight of the whorls varies to a certain extent in accordance with the material. Those of bone weigh generally between 13 and 18 g while the stone whorls

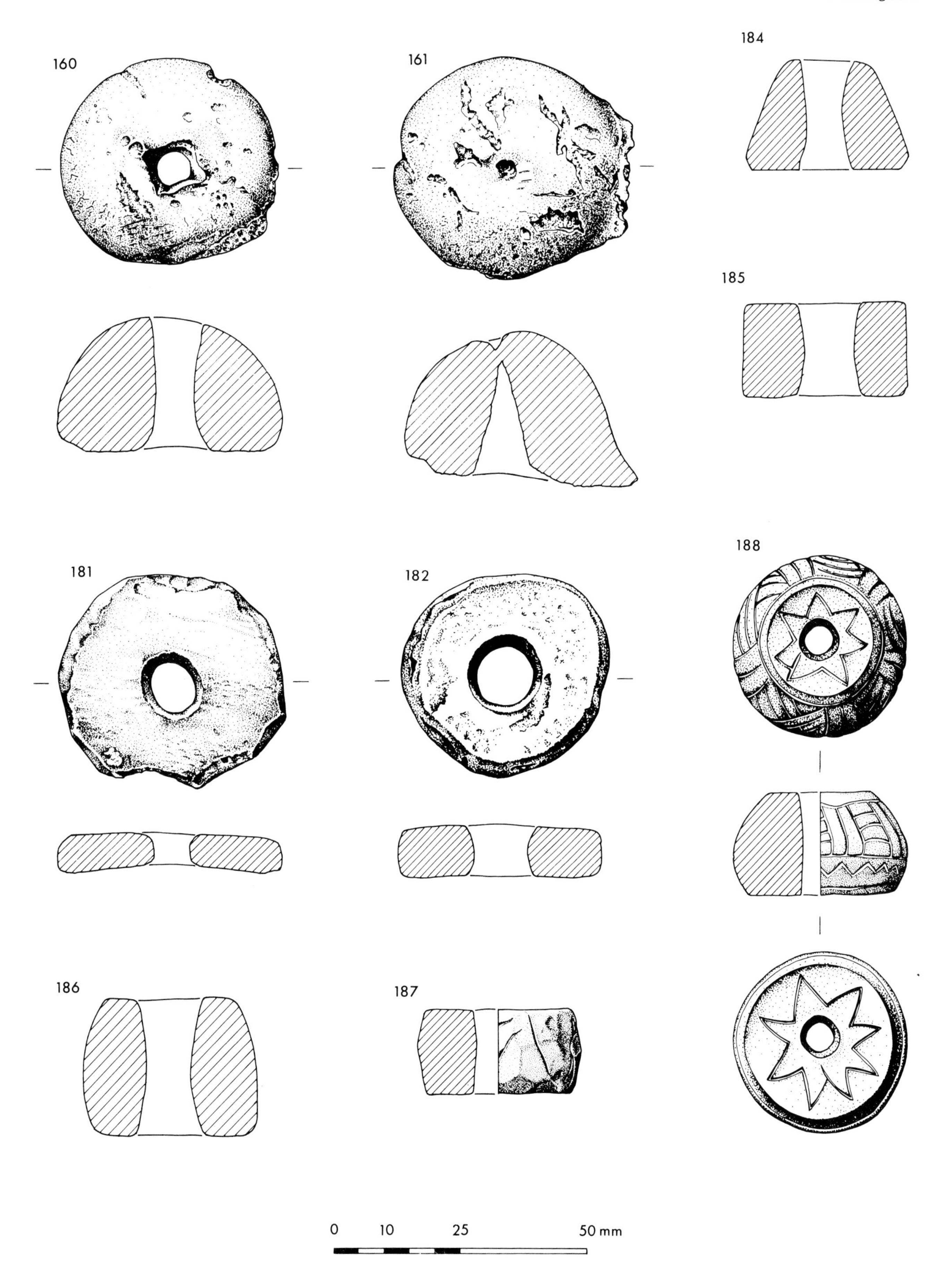

Fig 21 Spindle-whorls of bone, pottery, clay, and stone

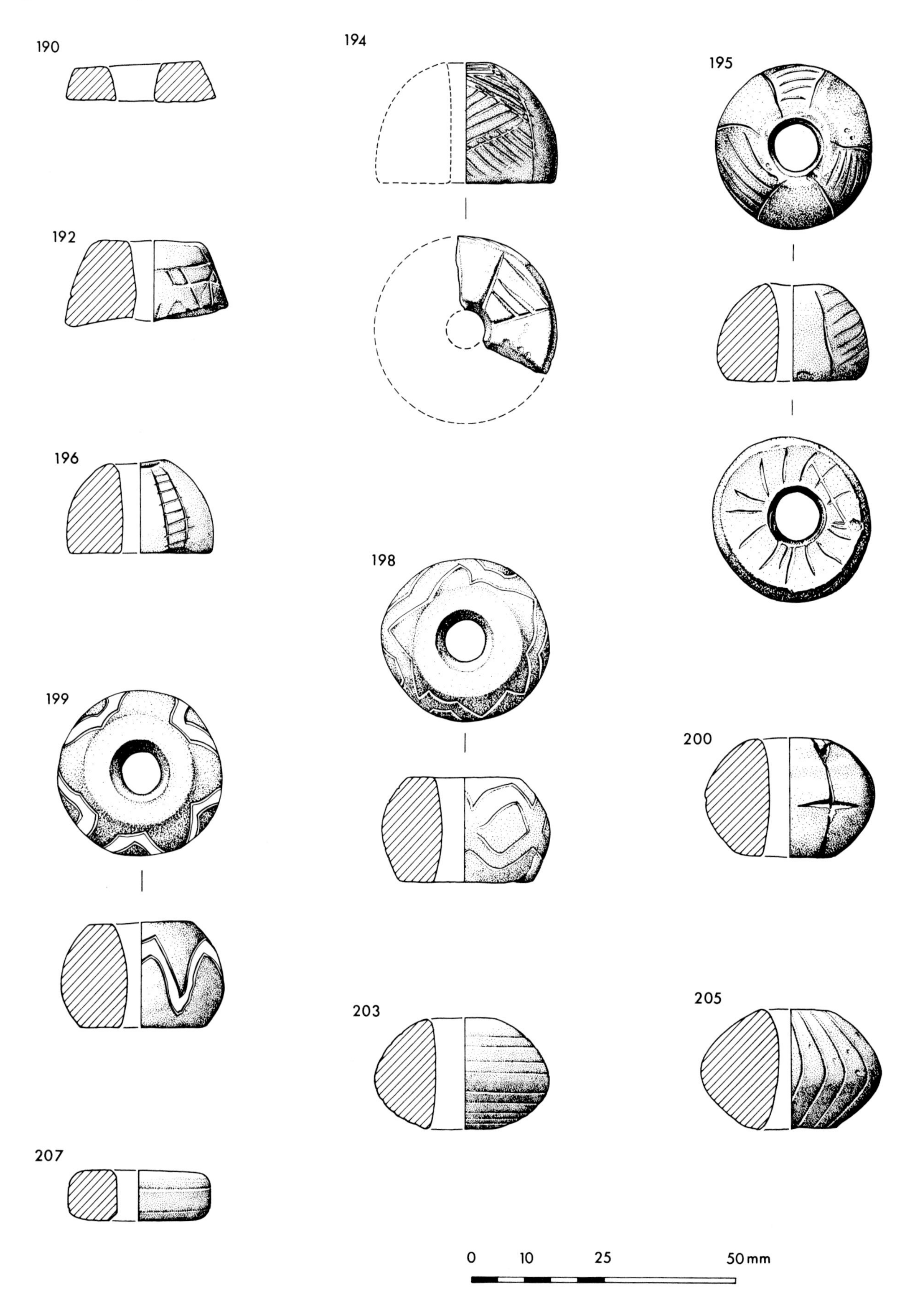

Fig 22 Stone spindle-whorls

are mostly between 20 and 27 g, with three at 30 g (the total weight is estimated for fragmentary specimens). Striking exceptions to this latter group consist of the unusually tall cylindrical form *186,* of 42·1 g, the smallest truncated conical whorls *(190, 191)* at 6 and approximately 9 g, and the single annular whorl *(207)* at 9 g. The clay whorls accord well with the heavier group, while the ceramic vary between the lighter (bone) group and the lower range of the stone whorls. While there is no sharp distinction between the two groups, the preferred weight was apparently between 13 and 27 g; the lightest whorls of 6 to 9 g were presumably used for producing finer threads and the unusually heavy specimen for spinning stronger yarns or plying threads together (see MacGregor 1972–4, 88–9; and below, p 43). A similar range is shown by the whorls from St Peter's Street, Northampton; these are mostly from post-Conquest levels, but fall into two distinct groups of 11–16 g and 20–34 g, with a preference for the lighter weight (Oakley & Hall in Williams, J H 1979, fig 125).

Loomweight

A single fragmentary loomweight of coarse felspathic grit (Fig 23, *208*) was found in an 11th century context. It is of irregular section with the sides worn at one point to a smooth tapered profile, presumably as a result of friction during suspension. Anglo-Saxon loomweights are commonly made of fired clay and are of two basic types: annular or bun-shaped, the first occurring in early Anglo-Saxon, the second in later

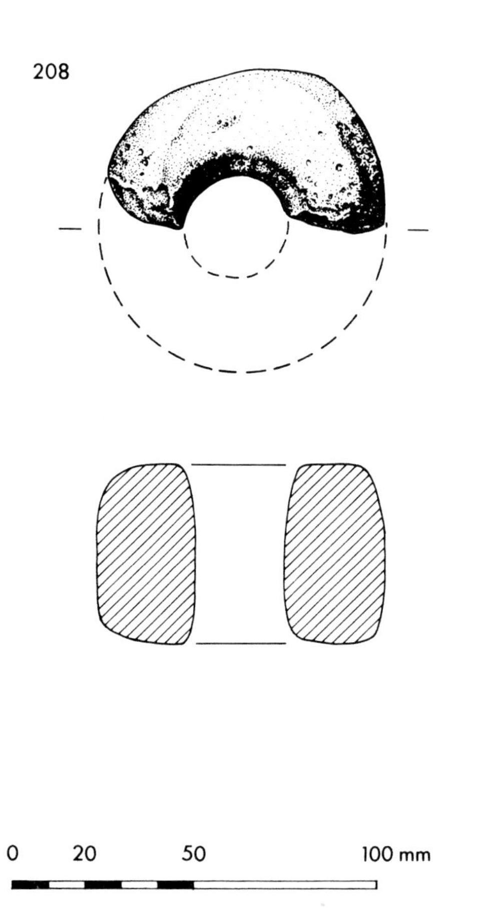

Fig 23 Stone loomweight

contexts (Hurst in Dunning *et al* 1959, 23–5). A third, intermediate form is known from middle Saxon contexts as at Whitby (Peers & Radford 1943, 83; described as 'bun-shaped'), Maxey, Northants (Addyman 1964, fig 12, 15), and from the excavation of late Anglo-Saxon settlements near St Neots (Addyman 1973, 90–1, & fig 18, 1, 2). The Flaxengate weight appears to belong to this intermediate type; the occurrence of this and the St Neots examples in late Anglo-Saxon levels suggests that the intermediate and bun-shaped forms may be chronologically indistinguishable.

Pinbeaters

Four small, single-pointed bone tools (Fig 24, *209–12*) were found in 10th and 11th century contexts; all four are smooth and polished. Such implements are generally known as pinbeaters (or 'thread-pickers') and are thought to have been used in weaving for adjusting stray threads, or perhaps for raising groups of threads in pattern-work. All four are of oval section, with facets flattened from wear on both broad surfaces. The upper end of *209* is extremely worn, tapering to an almost concave, spatulate terminal, suggesting that it might be of dual purpose, being perhaps used also as a smoother or burnisher. Small tools of this kind could have served a number of purposes, not necessarily connected solely with weaving.

The upper end of *210* appears to have been broken and trimmed for reuse; this and *212* are worn in a similar fashion to *209,* although to a lesser extent. Wear is also noticeable on the blunt points of *209–11,* being most pronounced on *209,* which has its point worn at a distinct angle to the shaft.

No *213* (Fig 24) may be a similar type of small weaving tool.[28] The rectangular-sectioned shaft with rounded edges is extremely smooth and polished, and wear is particularly noticeable around both the head and point—the latter (as *209*) worn at an angle to the shaft. A partially worked bone object (Fig 35, *307,* see below, p 33) may have been intended as a single-pointed pinbeater of more normal, oval section.

Double-pointed pinbeaters of oval or circular section are of common occurrence on Anglo-Saxon sites of all dates, as at Shakenoak (Brodribb *et al* 1972, fig 62), Maxey (Addyman 1964, fig 16, 21, 22) and Southampton (Addyman & Hill 1969, fig 29, A342.69, A343.69). They also appear in Carolingian levels at Dorestad and among finds from the Frisian terps (Roes 1963, pl XXXVI), and on Scandinavian Viking-age sites such as Birka (Graham-Campbell 1980, 21, no 79) and Hedeby (Schietzel 1970, Abb 8, 4; made of wood). The single-pointed pinbeater, however, is found only on late Anglo-Saxon and medieval English sites, as at Portchester (Hinton in Cunliffe 1976, fig 140, 65), Oxford (Radcliffe 1962–3, fig 15, 10), Seacourt (Biddle 1962–3, fig 32, 1, 3, & 8), and Northampton (Williams, F 1979, fig 21, 12, 13). The flattened, almost concave upper ends of the Flaxengate examples and the blunt points worn at an angle to the shaft are features matched by a number of the pinbeaters from St Peter's Street, Northampton (Oakley & Harman in Williams, J H 1979, 313, WB55, WB56, WB59).

Needles and bodkin

All three needles could be classed as pins but for the fact that they have slender, polished shanks with sharp points (where these remain). No *214* (Fig 25), with a sharply pointed head and small circular eye, is from an early 10th century context, although it might perhaps be of Roman date since needles of this type are found on sites such as Jewry Wall, Leicester (Kenyon 1948, fig 91, 1). However, they also occur on the Frisian terps (Roes 1963, pl LIV, 14, 16, 18) and on Viking-age settlements such as Hedeby (Schwarz-Mackensen 1976, Abb 16, 9) and York (Waterman 1959, fig 14, 35, 36).

No *215* (Fig 25) is a fragment of oval-sectioned needle with a flat-topped head and large circular eye. Pins with the same type of head are found commonly on both Anglo-Saxon and Viking-age settlements, as at Southampton (Addyman & Hill 1969, pl VI, b) and Hedeby (Schwarz-Mackensen 1976, Abb 9, 6); a similar object, described as a 'needle' is known from an Anglo-Danish context at Hungate, York (Richardson 1959, fig 19, 19). The more slender, sharply pointed flat-topped needle also occurs at Hedeby (Schwarz–Mackensen 1976, Abb 16, 9).

No *216* (Fig 25), made from pig fibula, is similar to the pins with expanded perforated heads (the possibility that the latter may also have served as needles for coarse work is discussed above, p 10). This is of a more streamlined form, however, and the shank tapers to a sharp point; it appears to be unfinished, as the shank has not been trimmed and smoothed to remove the rough shaping. This is the commonest type of needle found on late Anglo-Saxon and Viking-age sites, as at Southampton (Platt & Coleman-Smith 1975, fig 247, 1921) and Birka (Arbman 1943, Taf 1969, 10).

A large bodkin (Fig 25, *217*) was found on the floor of structure 40. This is made of cattle ulna, with a

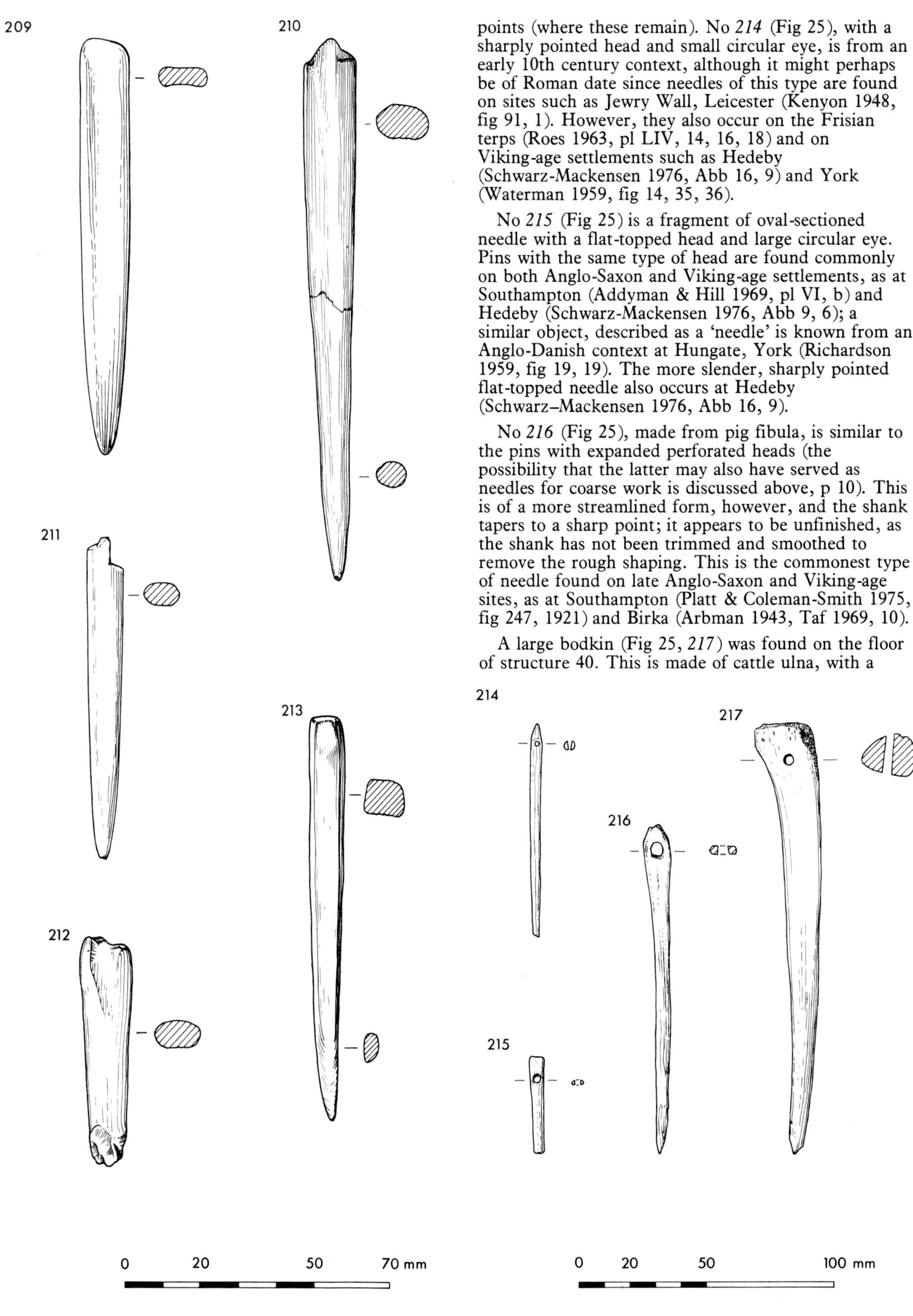

Fig 24 Bone pinbeaters

Fig 25 Bone needles and bodkin

small circular eye and rather blunt point. Similar objects are known from Clifford Street, York (Waterman 1959, pl 16, 1, 2).

Tallow-holders

Three shaped fragments of cattle metatarsal *(218–20)* were found in 10th and 11th century contexts. All three consist of the proximal end of the bone, chopped or sawn from the shaft at an oblique angle, and longitudinally perforated through to the natural cavity. The obliquely cut surface of *218* (Fig 26), and to a lesser extent that of *220,* is crudely trimmed. All three may be stood upright, although the slight trimming of the proximal end of *220* renders it more stable than the others. The largest and most complete *(218)* is 67 mm long.

A number of similarly shaped pieces of cattle bone occur among the Frisian terp finds; they are from 70 to 180 mm long, and unlike the Flaxengate pieces the smallest of them are carefully smoothed and finished (Roes 1963, pl XLII, 6–8). Roes suggested that they may have been used as tallow-holders, for use in waxing threads (*ibid*, 1963, 47), an idea supported by the carefully finished lips on the upper ends, and by the surrounding high polish. The only parallels known to Roes were similar objects from a late Anglo-Saxon context at Ipswich, which she suggested were imported from Frisia.

Three other fragments of obliquely cut, longitudinally perforated bone were found on Flaxengate (*290, 291* and Fig 32, *289;* see below, p 31), but these are more sharply pointed than the objects discussed here. They resemble certain socketed bone points found at York (Waterman 1959, pl XXII, 4–6) and elsewhere. A similar bone object from a late Anglo-Saxon context at St Peter's Street, Northampton is described as a possible tallow-holder (Oakley & Harman in Williams, J H 1979, fig 139, 72).

If these Flaxengate pieces are tallow-holders, they show little sign of use and are crude in comparison to those from Frisia. All three appear unfinished, suggesting that, far from being imports, they were made on site.

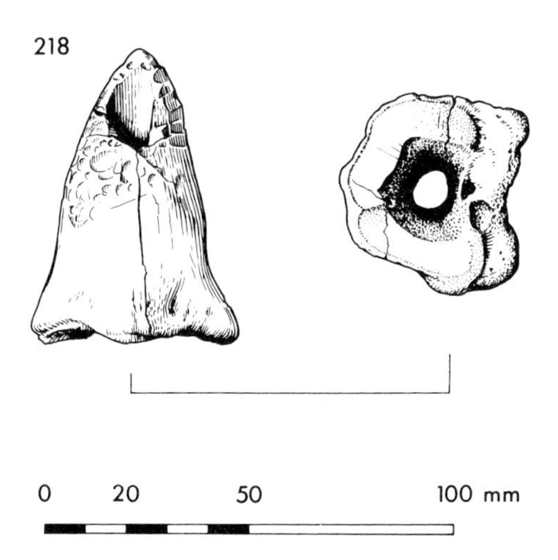

Fig 26 Bone tallow-holder

Hones

Over 60 hones were found in the early medieval levels; the majority of these have been thin-sectioned[29] and thereby assigned to four main petrological groups, classified after Moore (1978). Most numerous are the hones of Norwegian Rag or 'schist', followed by phyllite, comprising 47% and 27% respectively of the total number. Hones of Coal Measures Sandstone and Kentish Rag are fewer, representing 15% and 5%. The remainder are of varying rock types, each of single occurrence only.

The Norwegian Rag contains quartz, muscovite, calcite and chlorite, and iron ore, and is of characteristic texture; its source is near Eidsborg, Telemark, in Norway (Ellis 1969, 150; Moore 1978, 65). The material was probably cut from quarried blocks as rectangular-shaped rods, which were further shaped through wear. Most of the Flaxengate fragments *(221–51,* see Fig 27) are between 60 and 100 mm in length, the largest being approximately 150 mm.

The phyllite hones *(252–69,* see Fig 28) are of much finer grain (Ellis 1969, fig 4a) and generally smaller than the previous group, averaging between 40 and 70 mm in length (although one large piece measures approximately 150 mm). These features suggest that such hones were used for sharpening fine, delicate blades and small tools. Containing quartz and muscovite, the 'blue phyllite' could be a variant of Norwegian Rag, but its provenance is still unknown at the time of writing.[30]

The Coal Measures Sandstone hones *(270–9,* see Fig 30) are of a carbonaceous grit, containing quartz and muscovite, possibly from the Bristol or Forest of Dean coalfield. The hones, of rectangular section, are generally between 50 and 100 mm in length. Several large pieces appear to be fragments from slabs or blocks (see Fig 30, *270*); *275* is a lozenge-shaped slab of irregular hexagonal section (Fig 30). These are likely to be 'secondary hones', ie pieces of stone whose original function was otherwise, such as architectural, but which were subsequently used as hones (Moore 1978, 65).

Three hones of Kentish Rag were found *(280–2,* Fig 30); these are of quartz-microfossiliferous limestone from the Upper Greensand, Wealden area. One is shaped to an ovoid section, probably through wear (Fig 30, *282*). One of the remaining four hones is of quartz-bearing limestone *(283),* and another of quartz-muscovite-microfossiliferous limestone, possibly from the Purbeck Beds *(284).* There is a single example of micaceous siltstone *(286),* while a fragment of contact rock (quartz-carbonate rock streaked with quartz-biotite-calcite rock) is of similar form to the small, delicate phyllite hones (Fig 29, *285*).

The pattern of wear shown by the Flaxengate hones suggests that one or both broad faces were most commonly used, the latter often producing an irregular section (Fig 27, *225, 235, 242;* Fig 28, *253;* Fig 30, *272*); this is occasionally pronounced, resulting in a lozenge-shaped profile (Fig 27, *228, 229*). The narrow faces were also used, while wear on all faces occasionally produced a hone of lozenge-shaped section (Fig 27, *241;* Fig 28, *269*).

Shallow longitudinal grooves appear on two of the Coal Measures Sandstone hones (Fig 30, *270, 278*) and on one each of Kentish Rag (Fig 30, *281*) and Norwegian Rag (Fig 27, *244*). These were used for

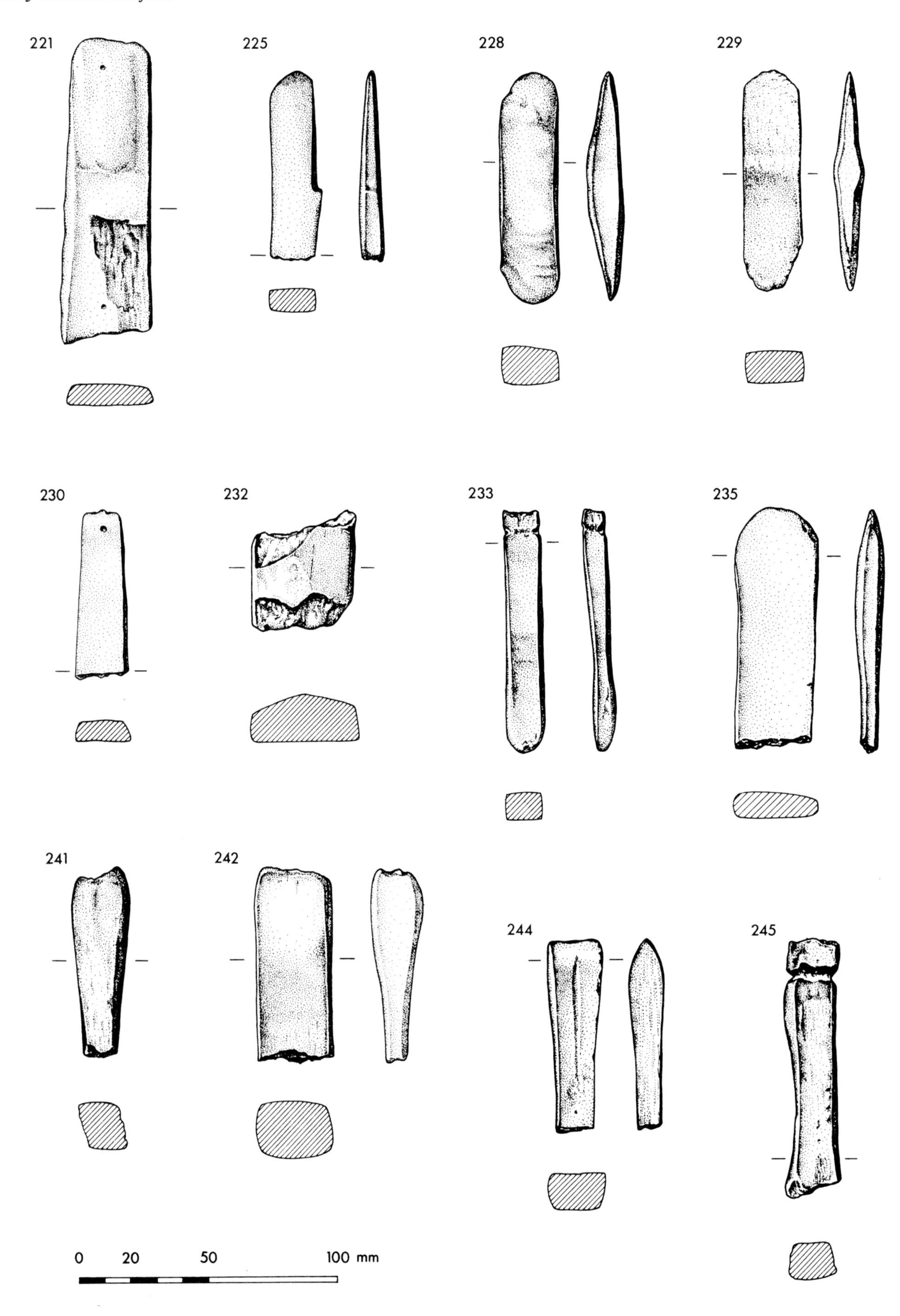

Fig 27 Norwegian Rag hones

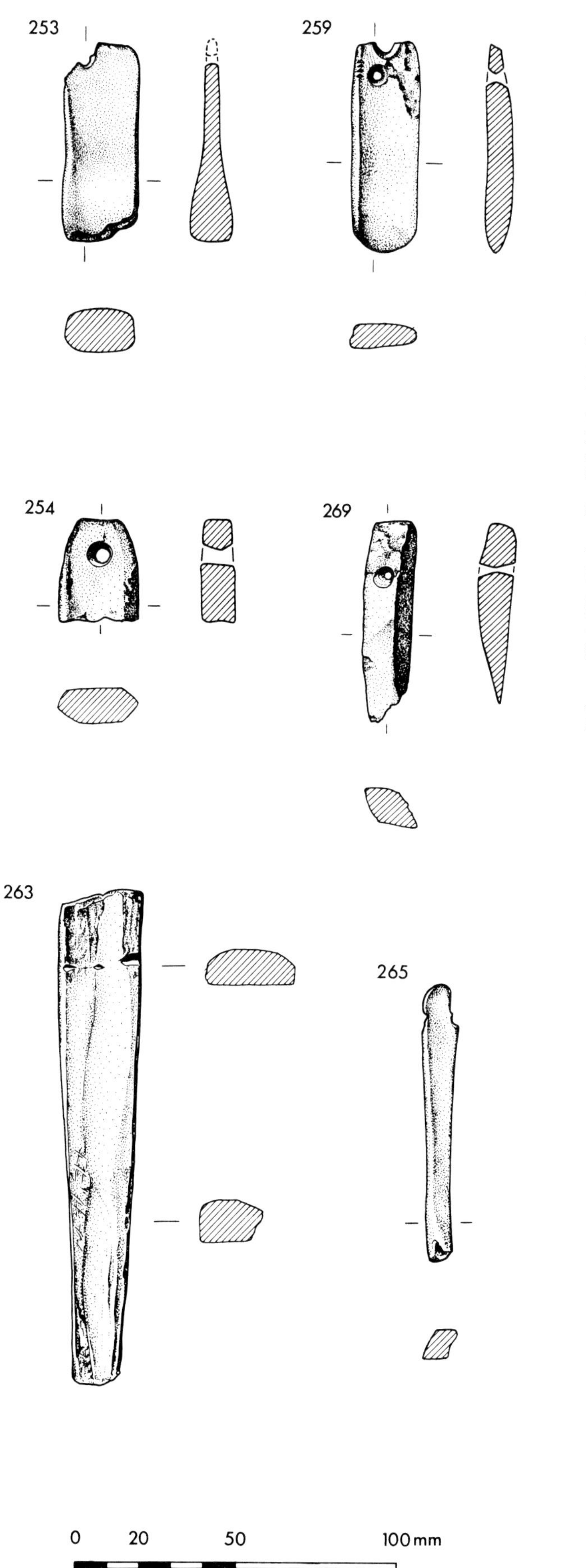

Fig 28 Phyllite hones

point- (or 'needle'-) sharpening, and appear on Anglo-Saxon hones of all dates (Evison 1975, fig 4e, f; Alcock 1963, 161 and fig 35, 1, 5, 9; Moore & Oakley in Williams, J H 1979, fig 123, 34). The infrequency of such grooves on the Flaxengate hones is perhaps explained by the relatively high proportion of fine-grained phyllite hones since these are admirably suited to such a purpose.

A number of the hones—mostly of phyllite—are perforated for suspension (Fig 28, *253, 254, 259, 269*). The smallest pieces are so fine and delicately fashioned that, were it not for the slight traces of wear, these might easily be described as purely ornamental, rather than functional pendants (Fig 29, *236, 264*). Several pieces are fractured across the perforation, but this type of damage did not always result in the discarding of the hone, as shown by *259* (Fig 28). This is fractured across its original central hole, with a second perforation drilled just below, and to one side of it. Two hones have small shallow pits drilled on one surface, possibly representing unfinished perforations (Fig 27, *221, 230*). This suggests that rough-cut blocks were imported and then worked to their final shape, being perforated on site. An alternative method of attachment for suspension is seen on two of the Norwegian Rag hones; these have horizontal nicks or grooves around one end (Fig 27, *233, 245*).

Perforated hones occur commonly on late Anglo-Saxon and medieval sites, as at Northampton (Moore & Oakley in Williams, J H 1979, fig 123), and

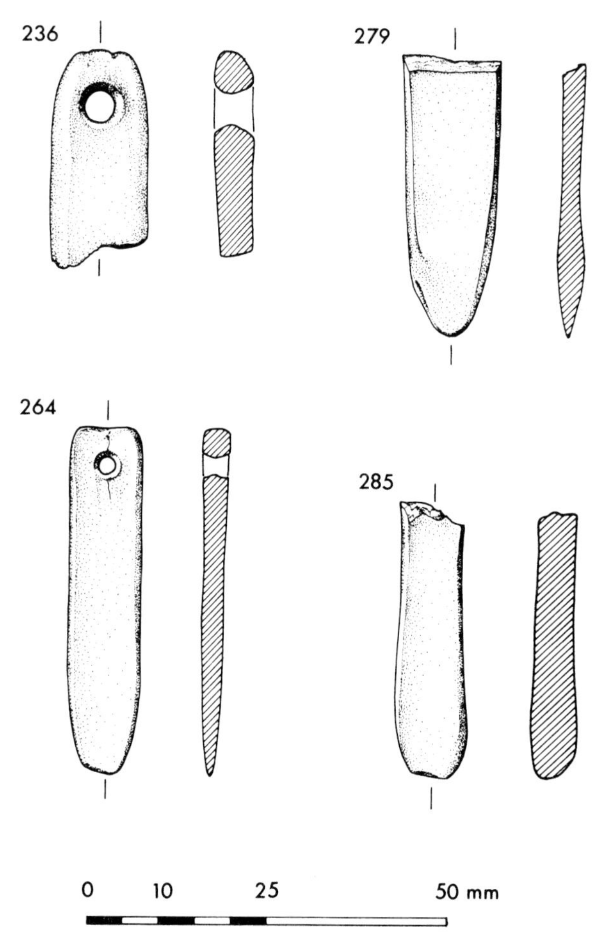

Fig 29 Pendant hones

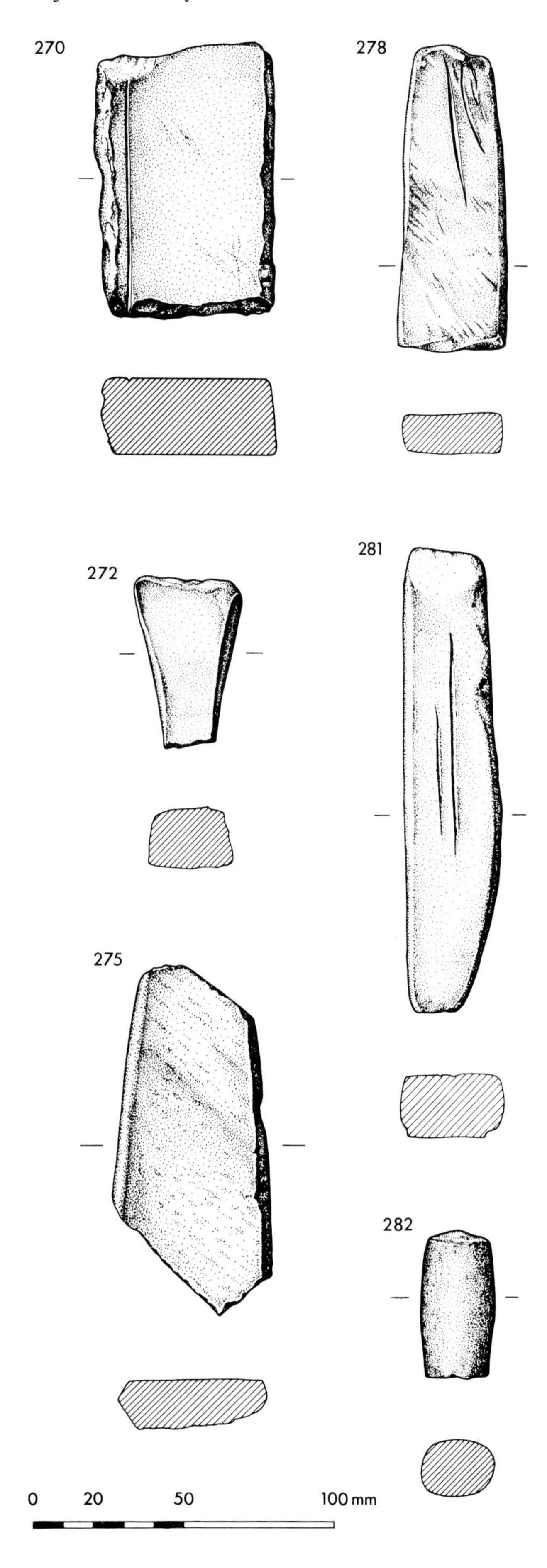

Fig 30 Hones of Coal Measures Sandstone and Kentish Rag

on Scandinavian Viking-age sites (Petersen 1951, fig 142), such as Hedeby (Jankuhn 1943, Abb 68) and Trelleborg (Nørlund 1948, Tav XXIX, 2–7, 9). A number of the hones from Birka have suspension-rings of iron, silver, or bronze, or traces of such rings, inserted through the perforations (Arbman 1940, Taf 186, 1, 2; Taf 188, 2, 7, 9, 10, 12, 16, 18), while one is broken with a secondary perforation drilled below (*ibid*, Taf 186, 4); others are furnished with horizontal nicks or grooves for suspension (*ibid*, Taf 187, 5–7, 11), as is one from Trelleborg (Nørlund 1948, Tav XXIX, 8).

Examination of hones from other sites in England has shown that a distinct change in the use of rock types occurred during the late Anglo-Saxon period. Both Kentish Rag and Coal Measures Sandstone hones were commonly used during Roman times, but the former are of infrequent occurrence thereafter. From the 10th century, native rock types were displaced, and greatly outnumbered, by imported hones of Norwegian Rag (Moore 1978, fig 3). The appearance of these hones, mainly in the north and east, largely reflects the pattern of Scandinavian invasion and settlement (Ellis 1969, 180–1), and although other types of rock remained in use after the 10th century, the continued import of Norwegian Rag ensured its predominance until at least the 13th century (Moore 1978, 72), as demonstrated by finds from a number of sites in King's Lynn (Clarke & Carter 1977, 317–20).

The hones from Flaxengate confirm this pattern (see Table 1)[31]; the earliest occurrence of Norwegian Rag is in a late 9th century context, and it was commoner than local stone throughout the early medieval period. A small proportion of the hones are of Coal Measures Sandstone and other rock types, with only three of Kentish Rag. The rare occurrence of the latter is emphasized by the probability that two out of the three pieces in this material, from levelling contexts pre-dating the construction of the earliest timber buildings, may be residual.

The large number of hones from the site and the high proportion of phyllite may be of some significance. The quantity found is more than one might expect from normal domestic activity, and may thus be connected with the various crafts engaged in by the inhabitants, whether at an individual level or on a larger scale.

Bone clamps

Two fragments of thick, plano-convex bone strip (Fig 31, *287*, *288*) came from 10th and early 11th century contexts. In both cases the remaining terminal is rounded; *287* is fractured across a single (?central) perforation, while *288* is split longitudinally. The upper convex surface of each is rough and the internal tissue of the bone exposed; the sides are smooth and faintly polished as if from use. Although these are of comparable size and shape to the 'sneck' discussed above (p 19; Fig 17, *139*), the distinctive circular wear-marks on the underside around the rivet hole are absent from *287*. This bears more resemblance to the two-piece bone and antler clamps found on a number of Scandinavian Viking-age sites, formed by pairs of matching plano-convex strips with the flat surfaces secured together by an iron rivet. A fine wedge driven between the slightly angled terminals at one end would force closed the opposing terminals, thus securing any small object placed between them.

Table 1 *Hones*

Material	late 9th C	10th C	Date 10/11th C	11th C	12th C	Post-timber & unstrat	Total
Norwegian Rag	1	4	3	11	9	3	31
Phyllite	–	6	6	5	1	–	18
Coal Measures Sandstone	2	2	2	–	4	–	10
Kentish Rag	2	–	–	1	–	–	3
Other	1	–	–	1	1	1	4

Such clamps have been found at Hedeby, made both of antler (Jankuhn 1943, Abb 74, a, b; Ulbricht 1978, Taf 40, 7–9) and iron (Müller-Wille 1973, Abb 2, 3, 4); Trelleborg (Nørlund 1948, Tav XXIX, 1) and Trondheim (Long 1975, Fig 11, g) have also produced examples of this type of tool, which is generally thought to be part of the comb-maker's equipment. Such restricted use is unlikely; clamps were presumably employed in a variety of crafts (Graham-Campbell 1980, 135, no 472). Several complete or fragmentary clamps were found during recent excavations in Dublin, on sites which also produced evidence for bone- and antler-working, and for metalworking.[32] These crafts were also practised at Flaxengate (see below, pp 44–5), and it may be significant that the most nearly complete of the two fragments *(287)* came from a level associated with structure 17, where copperworking took place.

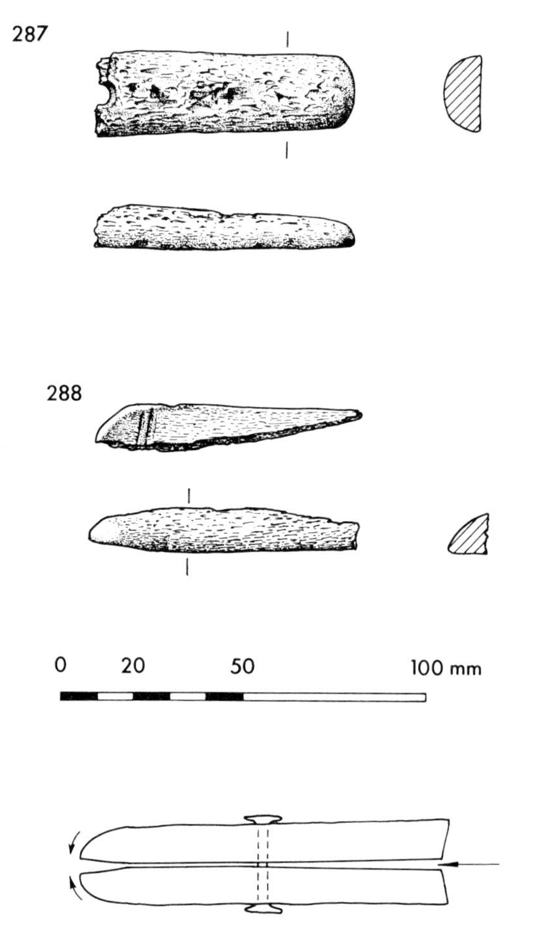

Fig 31 Bone clamps, with reconstruction below

Socketed bone points

The three socketed bone points *(289–91)* are of uncertain use. Nos *289* (Fig 32) and *290* are made from the proximal ends of cattle metatarsals, *291* from the distal end of a cattle tibia; a hole bored through the articular surface of each connects with the medullary cavity to form a socket. The shaft is obliquely cut and trimmed to a point, which on all three is smooth and polished. Similar objects are known from a number of sites in York (eg MacGregor 1978a, fig 31, 9, 10), often bearing incised ornament (Waterman 1959, pl XXII, 4–6).

These are unlikely to have functioned as tallow-holders (see above, p 27), since the latter have rounded, rather than pointed ends. Despite the suggestion that similar objects from London may be the tips from skating poles (CGM 1908, 154), it is doubtful whether a long, slender point such as that of the Flaxengate piece *289* could have withstood the strain of being thrust into ice. A more probable interpretation is that they are tools of some kind, perhaps gouges for leather-working.

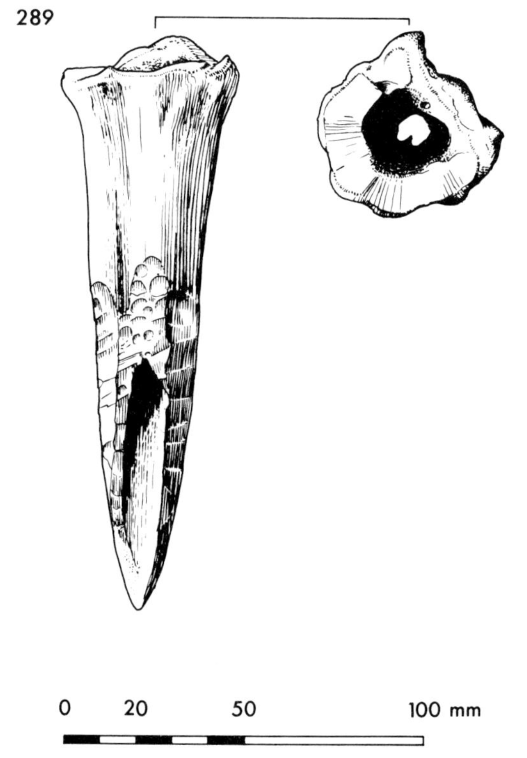

Fig 32 Socketed bone point

Miscellaneous objects, including waste material

Bone

Among the objects of uncertain function discussed in this section, two (Fig 33, *292*, *293*) resemble pegs, although they are dissimilar in form and apparently in function. No *292* is circular for two-thirds of its length, ornamented with transverse grooves and mouldings. The remainder of the shaft is square and tapered, with the terminal broken off. Two shallow longitudinal grooves, cut on adjacent sides of this squared portion and extending half-way along the remainder of the shaft, interrupt the ornament. The object appears to have been both functional and decorative; the lack of ornament on the tapered portion suggests that this would have been hidden from view while in use. The tapering suggests that the peg may have been inserted into a socket, but if this were the case, a peg of circular section throughout would surely have been more practical and more easily made.

The grooves were perhaps for securing the terminals of two strips at right angles to one another, and the peg may thus be the corner-post or foot from a small item of furniture such as a casket. The same arrangement of grooves on two adjacent sides is seen on a rectangular-sectioned bone object found in a Roman context during previous excavations to the north-east of the present site (see Fig 1; Coppack 1973, fig 12, 11). This has a conical head and is ornamented with transverse grooves and mouldings, while the lower shaft (along which the grooves seem to continue) is broken off; it has been identified as a 'bone mounting from the corner of a box or casket' (*ibid*, 83). The similarity between the two pieces suggests that, although *289* is from a level dated to the late 11th century, this too could well be of Roman origin.

The second peg, *293* (Fig 33), is rectangular in section for approximately half its length, with both broad faces tapered to produce a wedge-like profile; the remainder of the shaft is circular in section. Both ends are sawn across and smoothed, while further trimming of the shaft has produced slight facets and oblique striations. In shape this resembles a tuning peg from a stringed musical instrument, with the rectangular-sectioned terminal functioning as a hand-grip, in which case it must be unfinished for there is neither slot nor perforation for securing the string, and further trimming would be necessary to produce the slender profile normal on such pieces (Lawson 1980, fig 7). On the other hand, the degree of polish exhibited by the shaft suggests that the piece is

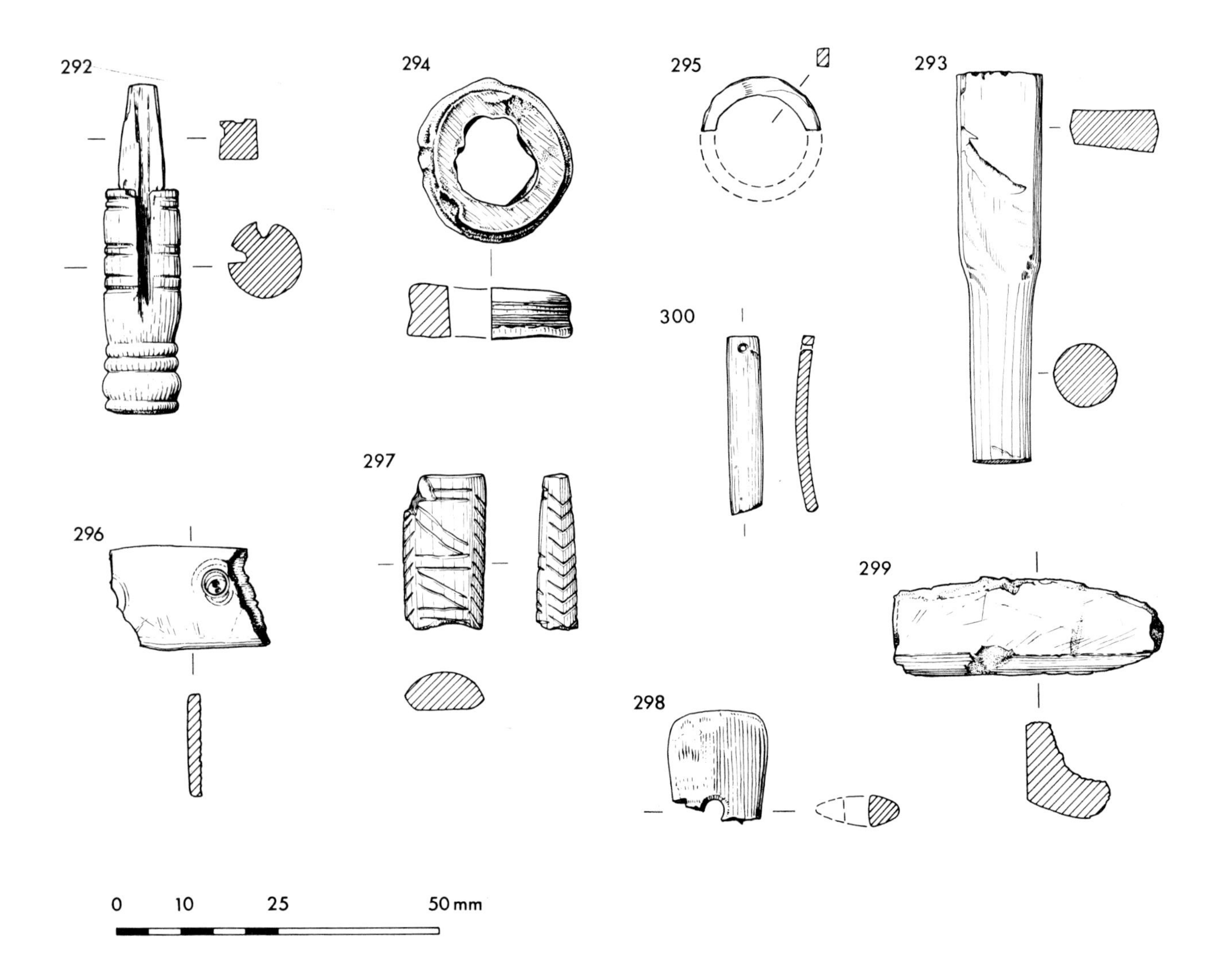

Fig 33 Worked bone

in fact finished and has been used.

The lathe-turned ring (Fig 33, *294*) is made from a sawn section of cattle metatarsal; the internal edges are untrimmed. This is too clumsy to be a finger-ring; similar objects from late Anglo-Saxon levels at Southampton, often ornamented with simple incised lattice, were used as spindle-whorls (Holdsworth 1976, fig 21, 12), but these are much larger than the Flaxengate piece. No *295* (Fig 33), a semicircular fragment cut from a scapula, also appears to be part of a ring but is so thin (approx 1 mm) that it is almost certainly a waste fragment.

A small fragment of polished strip, of split cattle rib, is fractured across a ring-and-dot motif at each end (Fig 33, *296*). One of these motifs is bungled, and the piece might therefore be a reject. Ornamented split rib plates were used in the manufacture of connecting plates for combs and comb cases (see above, p 8) and of inlay (see above, p 18).

The terminal of a thick, plano-convex tapering strip (Fig 33, *297*) bears incised ornament on all faces, which discounts its use as an applied mount or comb connecting plate. Both broad faces are flattened and taper towards the terminal in a manner reminiscent of the single-pointed pinbeaters (see above, p 25), of which ornamented examples are occasionally found, as at Northampton (Oakley & Harman in Williams, J H 1979, fig 138, 56, 58, 59). These, however, are generally of oval rather than plano-convex section.

A second terminal (Fig 33, *298*), of tapering oval section, is fractured across its perforation. This may be a fragment of an awl, or of a perforated pin of the type discussed above (p 10). A further terminal, *300* (Fig 33), is very thin and slightly curved, although the latter may be the result of warping. Despite its perforation this appears too fragile to be part of a pin or needle. Small, thin applied strips were occasionally used to ornament combs and comb cases (Arbman 1940, Taf 159, 11, 12; Taf 161, 12, 16), but these are of plano-convex section whereas *298* is oval.

The smoothness and high polish of one surface of *299* (Fig 33) suggest that this may be part of a well-worn skate, while *301* (Fig 34) is a fragment of a hollow cylinder. This is presumably complete in length, as both its ends are sawn across and ornamented with a series of transverse shallow grooves, but it appears to be too short for use as a handle, even for a small tool such as an awl or bodkin. Two other fragments could be from handles (Fig 34, *302, 303*); *302* is a fragment of cattle metacarpal with a single incised ring-and-dot but no other traces of working, while *303*, of cattle metatarsal, is incised with irregular cross-hatched ornament. One end of the latter is sawn across.

A number of the remaining fragments are partially worked objects. Two short lengths (*305* and Fig 35, *304*) are crudely knife-cut and were perhaps intended for use as pegs for securing bone mounts (see above, p 19). No *306* (Fig 35) is probably an unfinished pig-fibula pin, the point of which has broken; the lower shaft is knife-trimmed. A crudely worked length of bone cut to a point at one end (Fig 35, *307*) may be an unfinished awl, or perhaps a pinbeater, for the upper end is gouged out and oblique striations on one broad face suggest that final smoothing had commenced to produce a tapered, spatulate terminal.

A fragment of unsplit cattle rib is more difficult to interpret (Fig 35, *308*); the edges are crudely trimmed and cut to a point at one end. This is unlikely to represent a stage in the manufacture of connecting plates for a comb or comb case (see above, p 8) since the rib would almost certainly be split apart before shaping. A bone tool, similarly made of trimmed animal rib but with indented edges, came from a 10th century context at St Peter's Street, Northampton (Oakley & Harman in Williams, J H 1979, fig 139, 64). Fragments of cattle rib, generally shorter, but provided with toothed edges on one, two or all four sides, occur among finds from the Frisian terps (Roes 1963, pl XLIII, 1–5); Roes suggests that some of the larger pieces are scrapers, for scaling fish or cleaning pelts (*ibid*, pl XLIII, 3, 4; p 48).

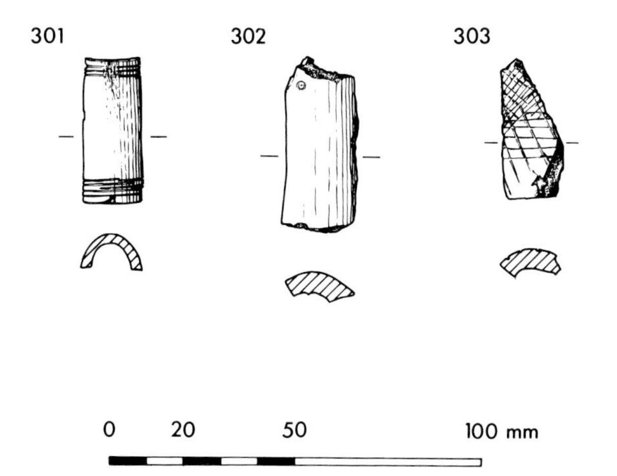

Fig 34 Worked bone

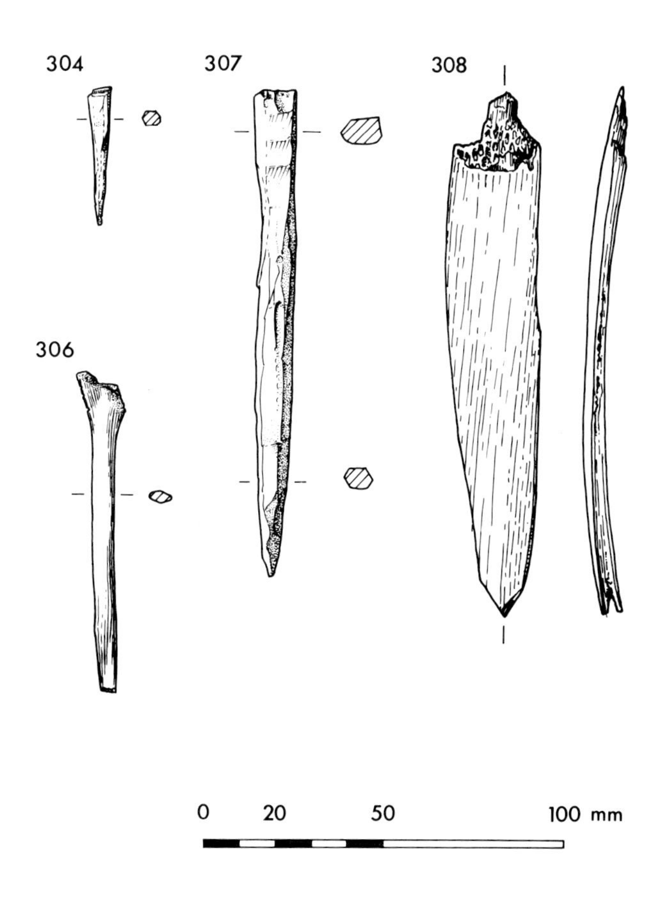

Fig 35 Worked bone

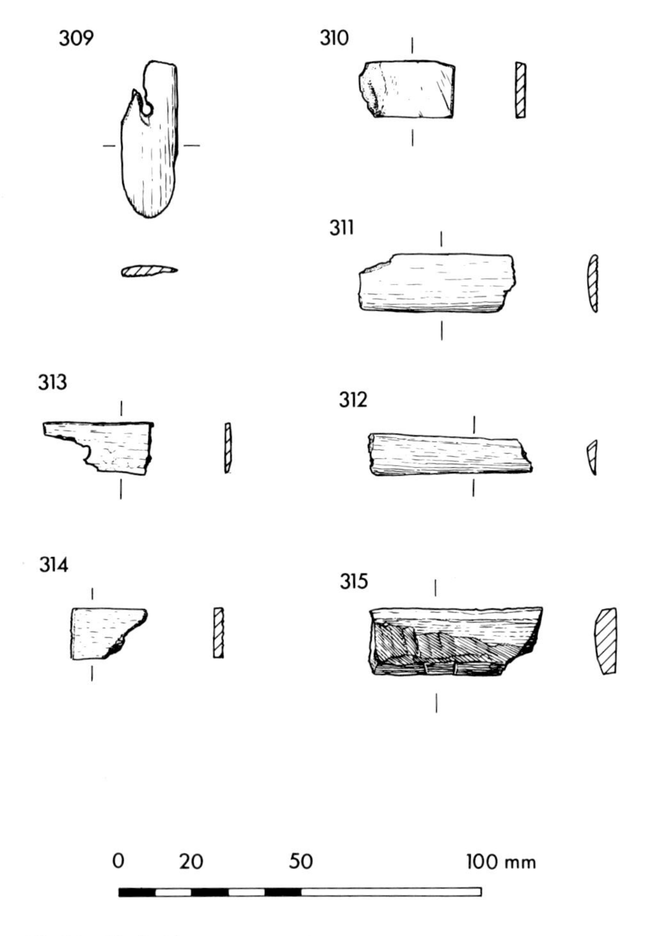

Fig 36 Worked bone

Nos *309–14* (Fig 36) are almost certainly waste fragments from comb manufacture; *310,* a fragment of solid rectangular plate, is possibly the broken blank for a tooth segment. Nos *309* and *311–14* are partially worked fragments of split rib, probably for connecting plates, although an alternative use was as mounts for ornamenting small chests (see above, p 18). No *315* (Fig 36), a somewhat broader and thicker piece of plano-convex strip, was possibly intended for a similar purpose; saw-marks and oblique striations are visible on all its surfaces.

Five shaft fragments are perforated longitudinally from the proximal articular surface through to the natural (medullary) cavity *(316* and Fig 37, *317–20).* The smaller pieces *316* and *320,* both of sheep metatarsal, and *317,* of sheep tibia, may have been intended for use as handles for bodkins, awls, or tools of similar size (cf Fig 18, *141*). None shows any signs of further working, and the shafts of *317* and *320* are simply snapped across, presumably at the required length. The shaft of *319,* a cattle metatarsal, is also snapped, although this end is crudely trimmed. This too may be an unfinished handle (cf Fig 18, *142*). A second fragment of cattle metatarsal, *318,* is obliquely cut across the shaft in a manner reminiscent of the socketed bone points (Fig 32), but the proximal end is trimmed flat. This surface was perhaps intended as a base, and the piece could be an unfinished tallow-holder (cf Fig 26, *218*).

Several fragments are perforated transversely (Fig 37, *321–3*), and may be waste. Nos *324* and *325* were more certainly discarded as waste, the former being the distal end of a cattle metatarsal which is sawn through and finally snapped (Fig 37). The shaft of this type of bone is suitable for producing handles (cf Fig 18, *142*), or rectangular plates might be cut from the surface for the tooth segments of combs (cf Fig 4, *19*). In Scandinavia cattle metatarsal shafts were also used for making short-handled, long-toothed weaving combs, and the sawn off distal ends found at Århus were apparently connected with this process (Andersen *et al* 1971, 122). No *325* (Fig 37) is the distal end of a pig metatarsal, also sawn from the shaft.

Little can be said of the remaining pieces *(329* and Fig 37, *326–8, 330–3),* except that they are partially worked but of unknown function. Perhaps these too represent discarded material.

Antler

The pieces discussed in this section are unfinished or waste products, with the single exception of *334* (Fig 38), an apparently finished and well-worn piece from a mid 10th to mid 11th century context. This is made from an antler tine, the natural shape of which has been used to produce a curved, tapering object. It is of irregular pentagonal section with a broad sub-circular collar, transversely perforated at the upper terminal. The outer edge of this collar and of the shaft immediately below is worn to expose the internal tissue, suggesting that the collar may have been circular in section, but was subsequently broken and worn to sub-circular shape. The corresponding area on the inner edge of the shaft formed by the junction of two adjacent, sharply angled sides is worn smooth. The lower shaft terminates in a squat, blunt point, surmounted by a narrow, double-collared moulding. The workmanship of the piece is not particularly competent, as the shaft is irregular and the point set at a slight angle. Faint transverse scratches across the shaft may be the result of finishing. Apart from the area where the internal tissue is exposed, the object is extremely smooth and highly polished, indicating that it was well used or burnished before use.

The tapered form and point of *334* suggest that it may be some kind of tool, with the perforation functioning as an 'eye' similar to that of a needle. Its angular section and projecting collars would however impede its passage through most materials (unless of very coarse mesh, such as net). It is unlikely to be a weaving implement because these must have a smooth, rounded or oval section, such as the pinbeaters discussed above (p 25). Its use as a piercer is equally improbable because the squat, blunt point would be ineffective; in any case it shows little sign of wear. A series of antler points, with zoomorphic heads perforated for suspension, is known from Scandinavian Viking-age sites such as Birka (Arbman 1940, Taf 154, 1), Hedeby (Ulbricht 1978, Taf 44, 6), and Tuna (Arne 1934, Pl I, 10; Pl XVIII, 3). These are of circular section, tapering continuously to the point, and are thus much more convincing as tools than the Flaxengate piece.

A closer parallel to *334* is provided by a bone object from a 10th century midden at Jarlshof (Hamilton 1956, 149; pl XXIX, 2). This also has a squat, blunt point surmounted by a narrow projecting collar of similar angular section to the shaft. In this case, however, the latter is square and provided with a raised central band. Both band and shaft are decorated, while the upper end terminates in a stylized animal

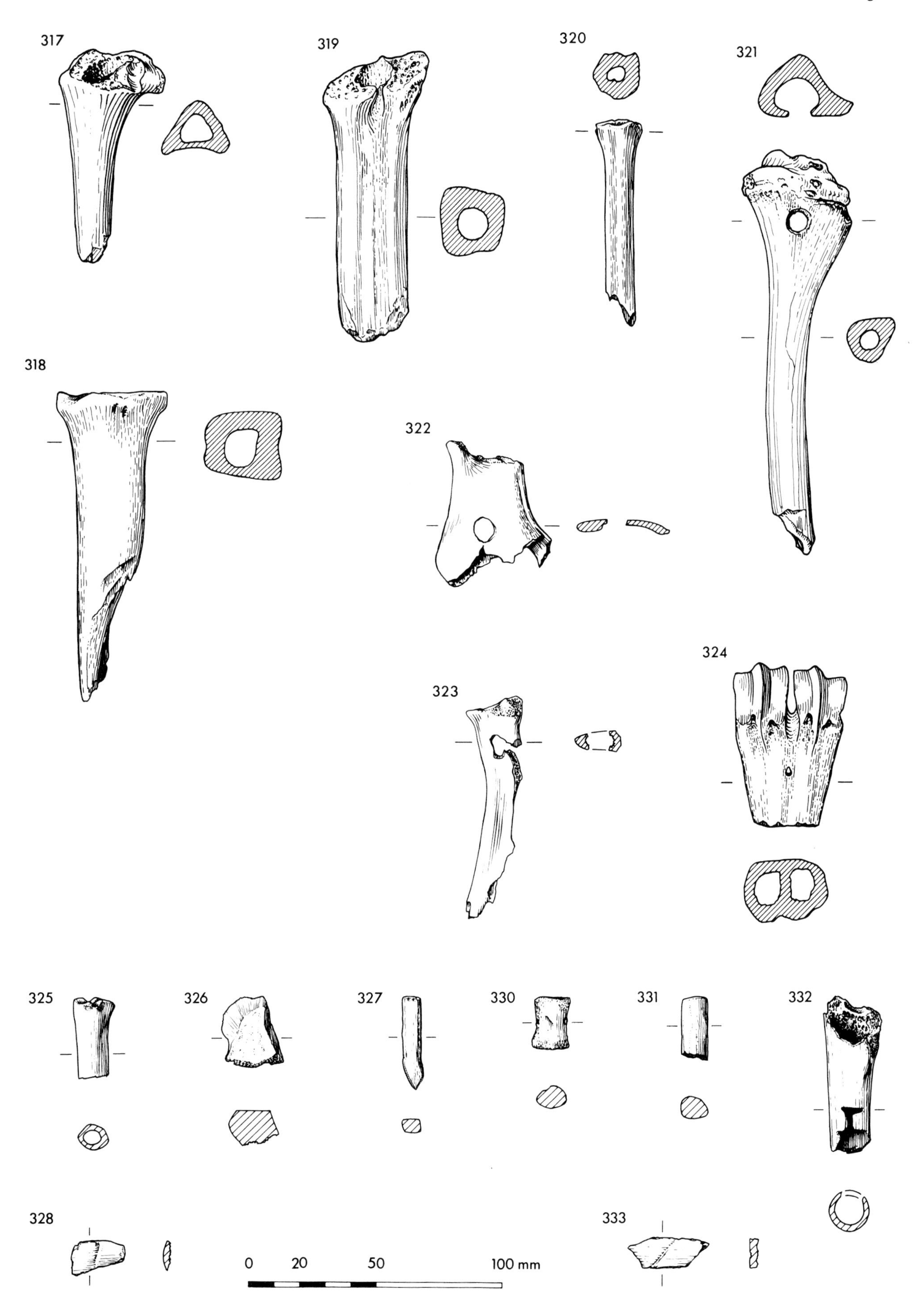

Fig 37 Worked bone and waste

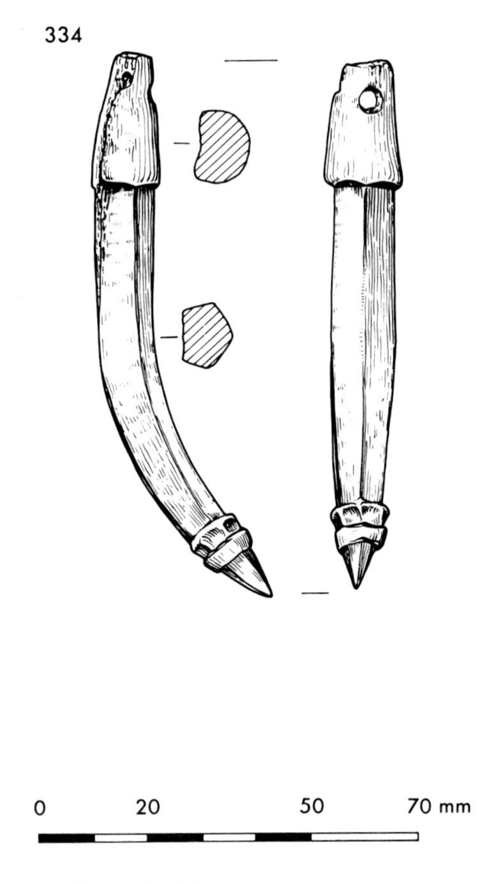

Fig 38 Antler object

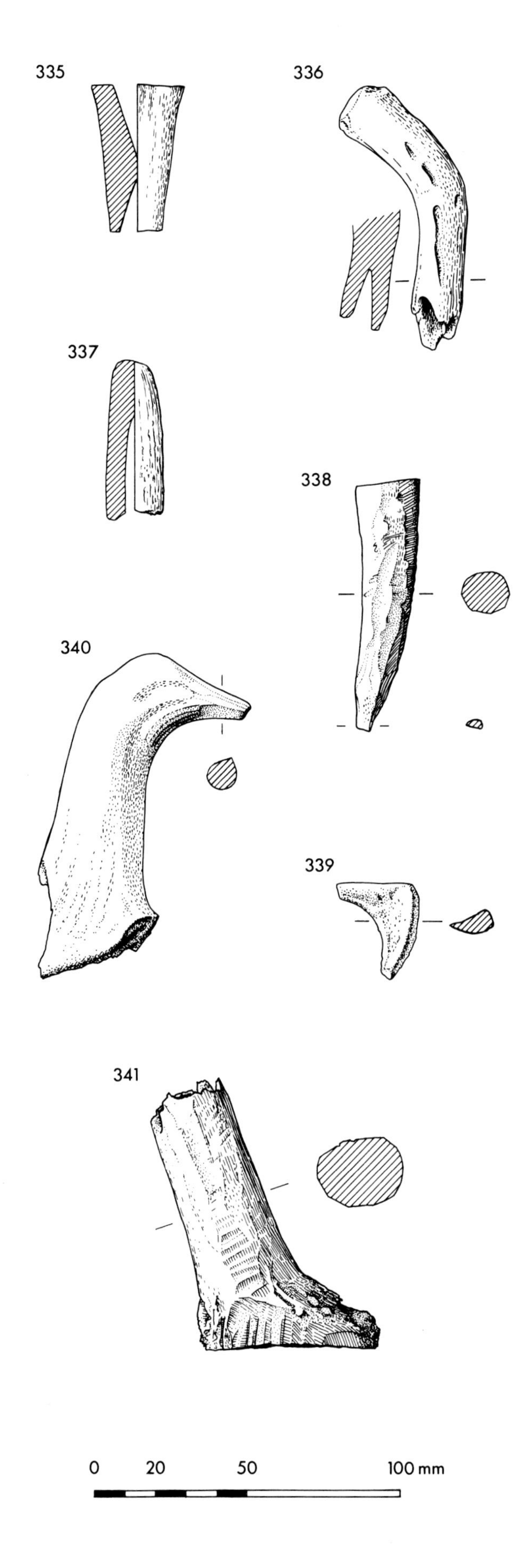

Fig 39 Worked antler

head with gaping jaws. A perforation through the ventral side opens into the throat of the animal. This in turn is apparently related to similar zoomorphic pieces from York (Allen 1904) and London (Wheeler 1927, fig 28, 7), both described as possible knife handles *(ibid,* 51).

Neither the antler tools from Scandinavia nor the 'knife handles' from York and London are directly comparable with the Flaxengate piece. Moreover, certain features of the latter suggest that, in common with the Jarlshof piece, it is not functional in purpose. Perhaps it is best interpreted as a pendant, of more pedestrian quality than the Jarlshof 'ornament'.

Nos *335–7* (Fig 39) are partially worked tines. No *335,* of red deer, is partially hollowed from both ends as if to produce a socket running the entire length of the piece. No *336,* a fragment of roe deer tine, is sawn across at the base. It has been partially hollowed and subsequently fractured, but apart from preparatory knife-trimming of the surface, there are no other signs of working. No *337* is also longitudinally hollowed for most of its length. All three are probably unfinished handles, *335* being for a small tool such as a bodkin.

No *338* (Fig 39) is a partially worked point of red deer tine, which is also damaged by rodent gnawing. One face of the shaft is pared away and faceted, to produce a wedge-shaped tip. Considerable numbers of worked antler points have been found in Anglo-Scandinavian levels at various sites in York, such as Clifford Street (Waterman 1959, pl XXI) and Coppergate (MacGregor 1978a, fig 31, 1–5). These could have served a variety of purposes, for example as

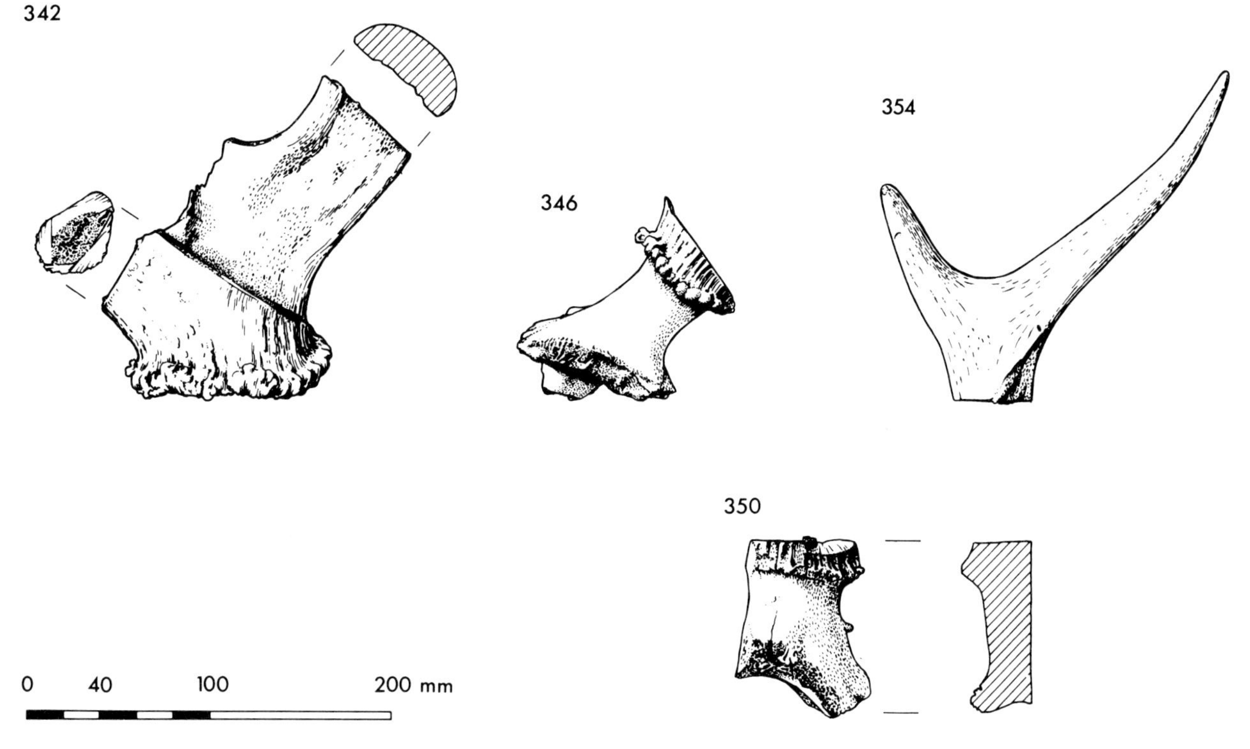

Fig 40 Antler waste

wedges, or possibly for separating the strands of rope for splicing (Waterman 1959, 93). In addition to working of the point, many of the York pieces are ornamented with simple linear incised decoration, or punched dots; some are also socketed or perforated. An alternative use for antler tine points is perhaps demonstrated by a number of the finds from excavations in Dublin at Christ Church Place, and, in particular, High Street. Examination of these antler tips in various stages of manufacture suggests that they may have been used as the handles of small draw-knives.[33]

A small lunate fragment taken from the base of a red deer tine (Fig 39, *339*) may be an off-cut, or perhaps an unfinished pendant. This is partially shaped by a saw-cut along the curved outer edge, while the tips of both arms are also sawn across. No *340* (Fig 39), a red deer tine, was removed from the beam by sawing and snapping; subsequently the lower end fractured. The only signs of modification are around the point, the extreme tip of which is broken, where knife-trimmed facets have produced a beak-shaped profile so that the object resembles the head and neck of a bird; it was perhaps intended as a terminal of some kind. A second fragment (Fig 39, *341*), a brow tine sawn from the beam and knife-trimmed, may also be an unfinished terminal, or perhaps a handle.

The remaining antler fragments *(342–87)*, comprising burrs, crowns, tines, and surface fragments of beam, probably are debris from comb making; these may have been discarded as waste, although they could have been used to make a variety of objects, as demonstrated by the Hedeby material. Here, solid, flat circular discs were cut from burrs to produce gaming counters, spindle-whorls (Ulbricht 1978, Taf 38), and even moulds (*ibid*, Taf 36 & 37, 3). Tines were fashioned into handles (*ibid*, Taf 41), awls (*ibid*, Taf 44) and a variety of tools (*ibid*, Taf 45–9).

The most useful part of an antler was the beam, for its solid surface could be cut into rectangular strips to form the connecting plates of combs (see Ulbricht 1978, Abb 3). The burr, lower tines, and crown were first removed by chopping, sawing, or snapping, as demonstrated by the Flaxengate waste pieces *(342–67)*. The burr was often removed with a single saw-cut (Fig 40, *346*), or two oblique cuts removed both this and the first tine (Fig 41, *351, 360*).

The first three tines on one fragment (Fig 40, *342*) are each sawn through from several different angles before being snapped off. The beam is longitudinally split from the point where the third tine was removed, down to an oblique saw-cut just above the burr, presumably to obtain a length of solid, workable material. Longitudinal splitting occurs on a second piece, but from below the burr down to the frontal bone of the skull (Fig 40, *350*).

The crowns were sawn off and occasionally discarded with the tines still attached (Fig 40, *354*), although the tines *(368–81)* were generally sawn off for further use (Fig 41, *362*). A number of sawn and snapped tine points (Fig 41, *373, 379*) suggest that their lower shafts may have been removed for the manufacture of such objects as knife handles (see Fig 39, *335–7*). The tips were discarded, or perhaps used for making small wedges (see above) or objects such as arrowheads (Ulbricht 1978, Taf 46, 1–17) and gaming counters (Andersen *et al* 1971, 212). Only one small fragment displays any traces of working other than saw-cutting; this (Fig 41, *378*) is the extreme tip of a tine, with transverse saw-cuts and faceting around the base.

Several small pieces from the surface of antler beams were found *(382–7)*; these are probably off-cuts from the preparation of rectangular strips, perhaps for combs, and are sawn across at one (Fig 41, *382*) or both ends (Fig 41, *385, 387*).

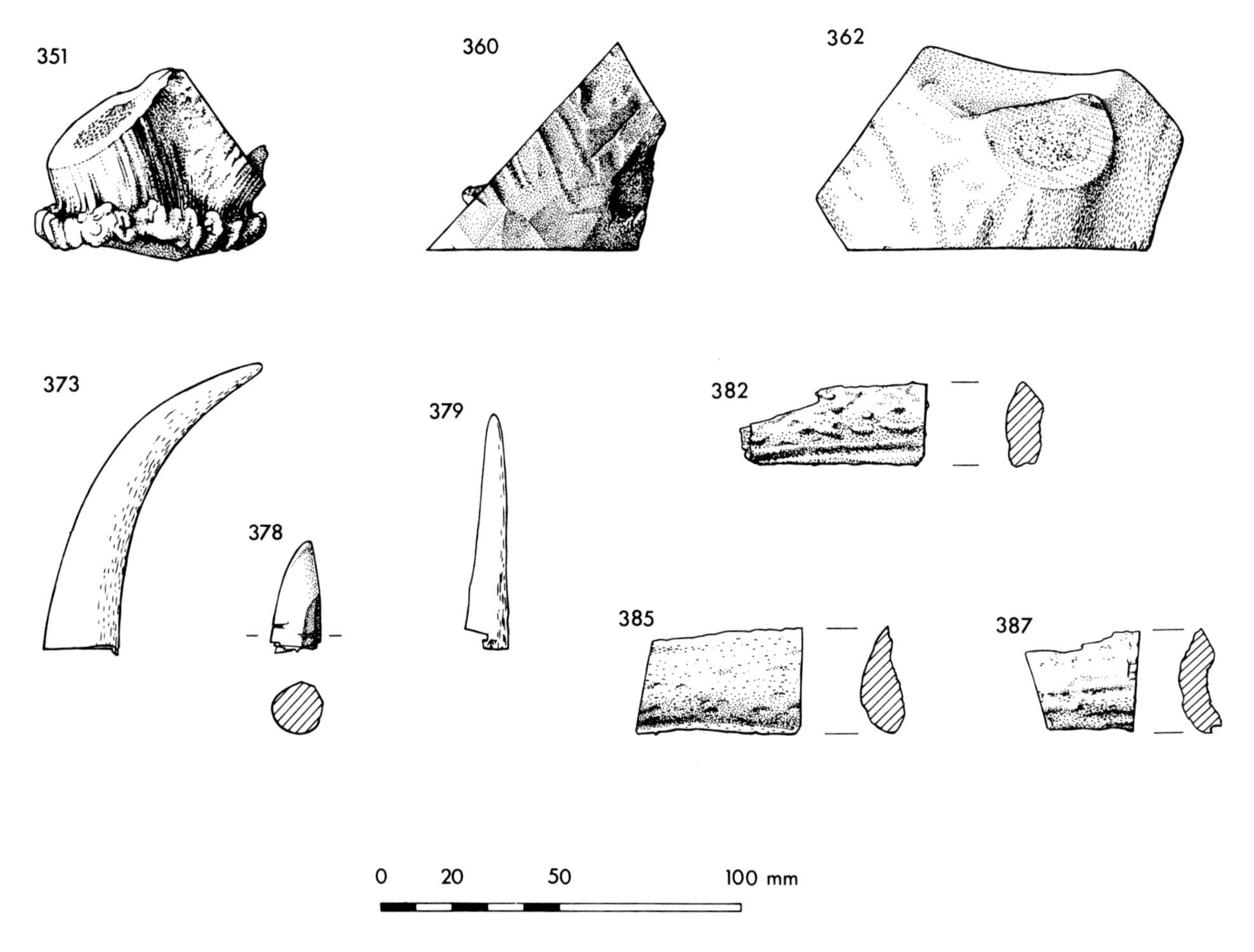

Fig 41 Antler waste

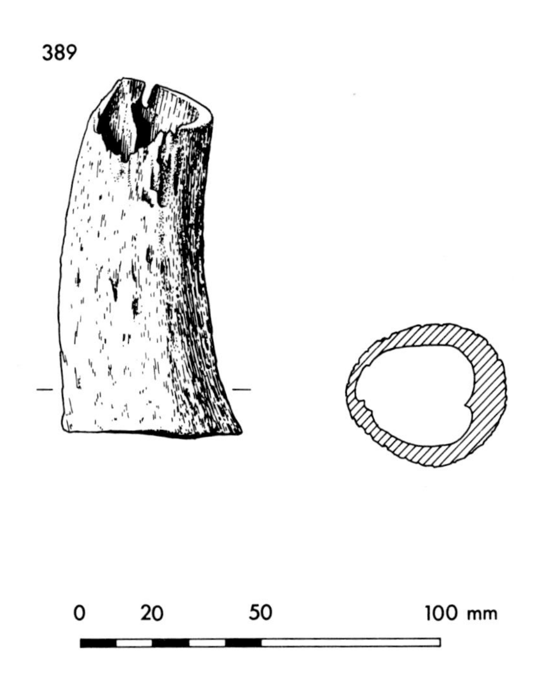

Fig 42 Horn waste

Horn and ivory

Three fragments of horn, two of cattle *(388* and Fig 42, *389)* and the third of sheep *(390)*, were recovered from 12th century contexts. Horn sheaths were used to produce thin, transparent sheets; the tip and base of the horn were sawn off and discarded, although the latter could also be fashioned into small objects such as candle holders. The Flaxengate fragments seem merely to be waste pieces because, apart from oblique saw-cuts just above the base or below the tip, there are no other signs of working.

No *391* (Fig 43) is the terminal of a thin, flat rectangular strip of ivory. Both broad faces are ornamented with a series of four irregularly incised longitudinal lines, each terminating in a shallow V-shaped notch at its junction with a single transverse line approximately 5 mm from, and parallel to, the terminal. On one broad face two small pits are visible in the intervening spaces, with a similar pit or notch at the point of fracture on both faces.

This is unlikely to be part of a strap-end or buckle plate because it seems too insubstantial for such a purpose and it has no perforation or other method of attachment. The irregularity and crudeness of the surface markings suggest that it may be an unfinished object, broken during manufacture; the lines and pits may have been intended as guides for the carving of a complex, possibly open-work motif, with the plate intended for use as a plaque or mount. The piece was found in the floor of structure 29, dated to the late 11th century.

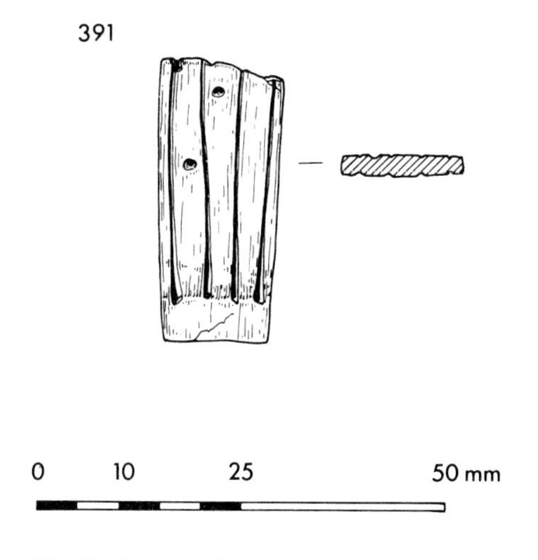

Fig 43 Ivory terminal

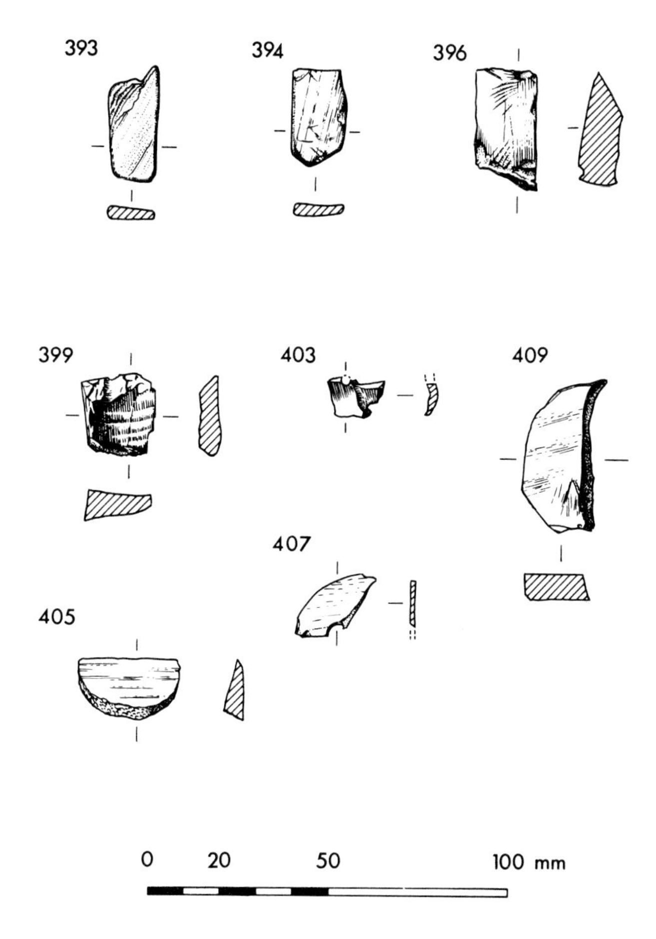

Fig 44 Worked jet and waste

Amber and jet

A small fragment of amber *(392)* with weathered surfaces was found in a 10th to early 11th century context; this appears to be unworked.

Two thin (*c* 2 mm), rectangular-sectioned fragments of jet from early 10th century contexts appear to be pieces of inlay. One, of sub-rectangular shape, has three straight, bevelled edges and a high surface polish. The second, a sub-triangular fragment, is ornamented with crudely incised running-loop ornament parallel to its single straight edge. A small piece of jet inlay from Skeldergate, York, is decorated in similar fashion with a running zig-zag; this is of Roman date, although found in a post-Roman context (MacGregor 1978b, fig 31, 275). Both Flaxengate fragments came from levels containing a high proportion of residual material; these too are probably of Roman origin and are therefore omitted from the Catalogue.

The remaining fragments of jet *(393–410)* are from mid to late 11th century contexts associated with the levelling over either structure 26 or the road (surfaces F748, F749), as are most of the unfinished finger-rings *(77–9;* see above, p 11); the only exception is an unworked fragment *(395),* from the eastern area of the site. The majority of these pieces are indeterminate waste flakes and small chips, over 50 of which *(401)* were found together within the levelling over the late 11th century road (surface F749).

Two thin sub-rectangular fragments (Fig 44, *393, 394*) are possibly unfinished pendants; *393* has smooth, polished edges and rounded corners, although this is probably due (at least in part) to weathering. No *394* is more crudely shaped, and cleanly fractured. A small sub-rectangular block (Fig 44, *396*) may also be the rough-out for a pendant. Two thin slivers are each fractured across a single perforation (Fig 44, *403, 407*); these may have splintered from rough-cut blocks during perforation.

Several of the partially worked flakes have split, producing a wedge-shaped section (Fig 44, *399*); others are semicircular in shape, with a 'pecked' outer (curved) edge (Fig 44, *405*). A larger semicircular piece, of rectangular section, has a partially faceted outer edge (Fig 44, *409*). There is no conclusive evidence to indicate that objects of jet other than finger-rings and (?) pendants were manufactured at Flaxengate. Although beads and bracelets may have been made, those found on the site in early medieval levels are most likely to be of Roman origin (see above, pp 11–12).

Chalk and stone

A number of chalk fragments *(411–24)* were found in late 11th and 12th century levels, and one (probably residual) piece in a late 13th or 14th century context. Two are fairly substantial blocks (Fig 45, *411, 412*), but the majority are small, between 20 and 60 mm in length, and of irregular rectangular, circular, ovoid or polygonal section (Fig 45, *415, 418, 419, 423*). The uneven faceting is apparently produced by wear, rather than deliberately cut. The ends of two pieces *(422, 424)* are worn at an oblique angle, suggesting that the fragments may have been used as 'rubbers', perhaps in some kind of finishing process.

Two pieces of igneous rock (Fig 46, *425, 426*) may be fragments of smoothers or polishers; both are very smooth, with rounded edges, and the remaining (fractured) end of *425* is tapered from wear. It has been suggested that similar stones from late Anglo-Saxon contexts at Southampton, some almost indistinguishable from natural pebbles and others carefully shaped, are finishing tools for textiles or for leather-working (Addyman & Hill 1969, 74; fig 30, 1–3).

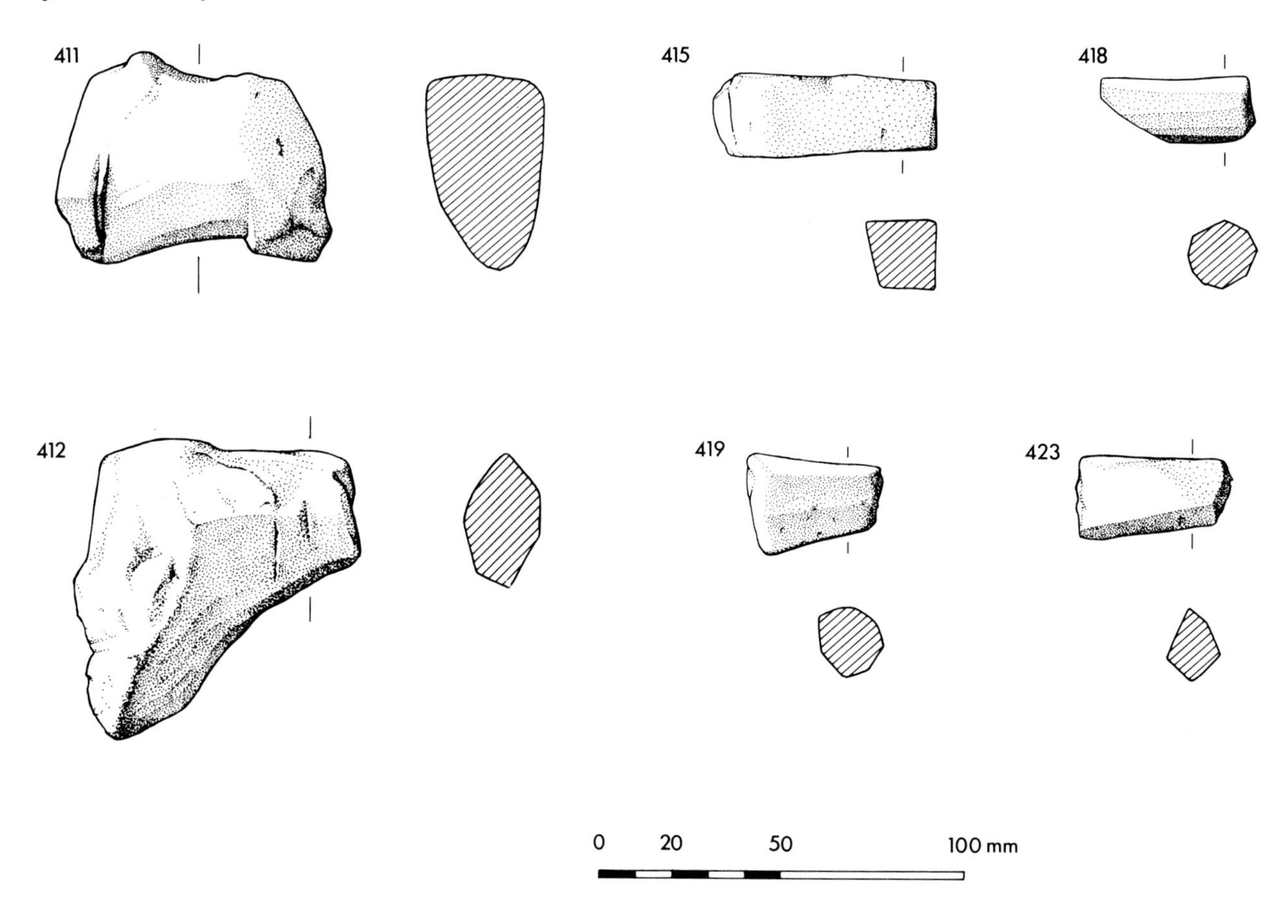

Fig 45 Chalk fragments

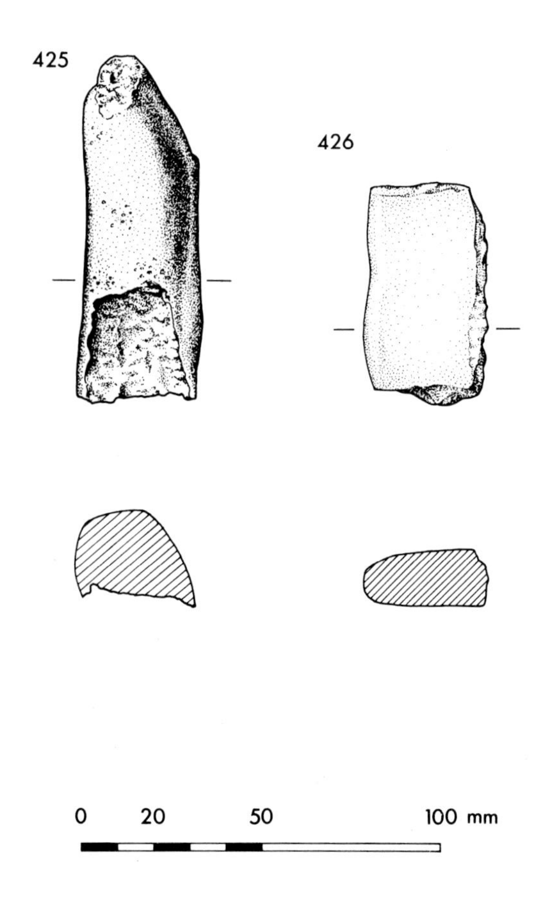

Fig 46 Stone ?smoothers/polishers

Ceramic

Several partially trimmed potsherds were found, two of which (Fig 47, *427*, *428*) may have been intended as gaming counters (see above, p 14). One *(427)* is fractured, as though it broke during manufacture; both are of late Saxon shelly ware. The base sherd of a Roman grey ware vessel (Fig 47, *429*), with part of the wall still attached, is fractured across a central perforation as though this too broke before being completed. It was possibly intended as a spindle-whorl (see above, p 22).

A fourth piece, *430* (Fig 47), has no parallel among the finished objects from the site, and its purpose is uncertain. This is a body sherd of Roman grey ware which has been trimmed to an irregular polygon; its edges are smooth and abraded as though from wear.[34]

Notes

1 The terminology used in describing the combs is that proposed by Galloway (1976).
2 The objects from Clifford Street are thought to represent debris from nearby workshops. They were found in association with a coin of William I, but the earlier date of some of the material suggests that the group as a whole may belong to the late 10th or 11th century (Waterman 1959, 68).
3 Personal communication, Mr T Fanning. A bronze pin of this type was found in the floor of structure 30 (Period 8: *c* 1080/90–1100); publication forthcoming, AL **14**/2. Inv no: F73 Ae290.
4 A pair of split rib plates found in a 10th/11th century context at Holmes Grainwarehouse, 181–2 High St, Lincoln, is secured by three iron rivets. One of the plates is fractured across the central rivet hole and has sprung out of alignment; the gap between the plates at this point is 10 mm. The length of the unbroken plate is 104 mm. Inv no: HG72 B20.
5 Others are unpublished (information from Mr J Graham-Campbell).

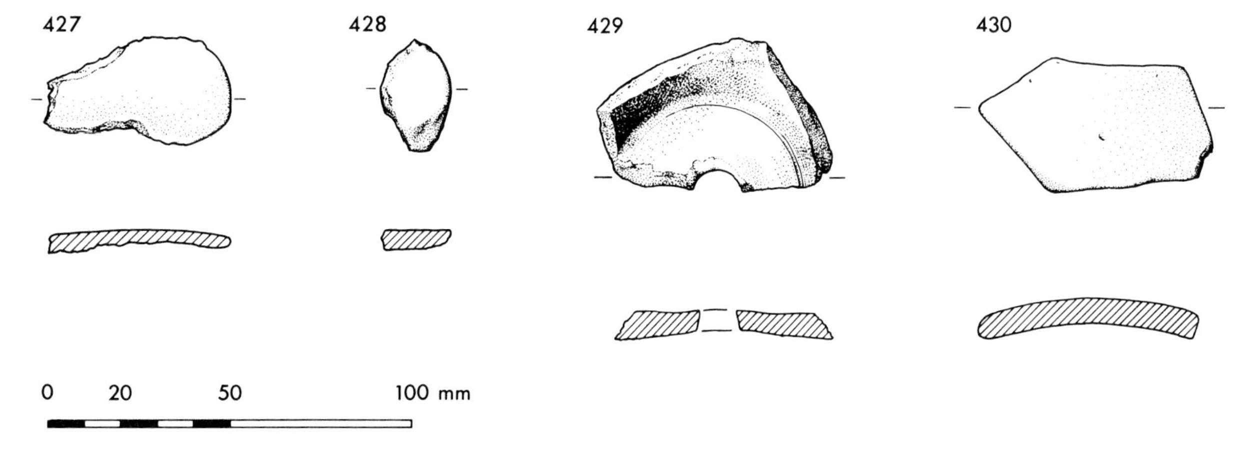

Fig 47 Trimmed potsherds

6 A bronze pin of this type was found in the levelling over structures 3 and 5 (Period 2: *c* 900-930/40); publication forthcoming, AL**14**/2. Inv no: F76 Ae64.
7 The area excavated lay some 36·6 m to the north-east of the site discussed here (see Fig 1).
8 The Hungate material, from within or immediately under the brushwood anchoring raft of the Anglo-Danish embankment, includes objects which can be paralleled on Scandinavian Viking-age sites such as Birka, Hedeby, and Trelleborg. The date thus suggested for the finds is between the later 9th and the end of the 10th century (Richardson 1959, 64–5).
9 Personal communication, Miss E M Crowfoot.
10 Information from Mr P Wallace (Assistant Keeper), National Museum of Ireland.
11 Information from Mr D Tweddle (Assistant Director), York Archaeological Trust.
12 These include a rectangular pendant and a fragment, fractured across the perforation, from Christ Church Place (National Museum of Ireland: E122.16919 and 16888).
13 The pendant was thin-sectioned and identified by Mr D T Moore, Department of Mineralogy, British Museum (Natural History).
14 This, and a number of the small perforated hones (see above, p 29) were examined by Dr A Oddy (Research Laboratory, British Museum), who concluded that none could be classed as touchstones.
15 A rectangular die in the Trollope Collection in the City and County Museum, Lincoln (88/23a 50), has 3, 4, 5 & 6 on its long sides; both ends probably number 5. The markings are of double ring-and-dot, but the central spot on one of the ends is represented only by a single dot without encircling rings.
16 Two bone counters of this later series were found in contexts associated with the medieval stone buildings; publication forthcoming, AL **15**/2. Inv nos: F73 B13 and B14.
17 Information and advice on the flutes and mouthpiece from Mr G Lawson and Professor J V S Megaw.
18 From 10th to 12th century contexts: inv nos: HG72 B30, B32, and B36.
19 City and County Museum, Lincoln: 88/36 50–88/40 50.
20 A wooden box-lid from Christ Church Place, Dublin, is ornamented with bone mounts, secured by iron rivets. Some of the plates are ornamented with ring-and-dot, others are plain and probably repairs (National Museum of Ireland: E122.16343). Numerous other bone mounts from this site are mostly ornamented with ring-and-dot.
21 Traces of wood were found on the tangs of some of the knife blades; publication forthcoming, AL **14**/2.
22 Mr A White, Keeper of the City and County Museum, Lincoln, kindly drew my attention to the Whitby spatula (publication of this, and of other finds from Whitby, forthcoming).
23 A bone spoon from Broadgate East, Lincoln, may be of the same type. This has a shallow, almost flat, oval bowl, separated from the handle by a rectangular projection. It was sealed between successive floors of a timber building in a context dated to the late 10th or 11th century; inv no: BE73 B22. Publication forthcoming.
24 Previously identified as 'griesen' (*recte* greisen) in Colyer & Jones 1979, 58 & 60. X-ray diffraction analysis of the sherds by Dr N G Berridge and Mr K S Siddiqui of the Institute of Geological Sciences, Leeds, has since identified the material as soapstone. Two vessel sherds were also found in 10th century contexts at Holmes Grainwarehouse, Lincoln; inv nos: HG72 M63 and M66.
25 Information from Mr D Tweddle (Assistant Director), York Archaeological Trust.
26 X-ray diffraction analysis (see above, n 24) showed a similarity in composition between sherds *143* and *145*, and between one piece of *144* (the adjoining sherds of which were examined separately) and *146*. This may indicate that the vessels could all have come from a single quarry of variable mineralogy.
27 The rock types used for the querns (and of many of the other stone artefacts) were identified by Dr F W Anderson.
28 Miss E M Crowfoot suggests that a rectangular-sectioned tool, even if it did not lie so well in the hand as a circular- or oval-sectioned pinbeater, might be useful if passing coarse-pattern threads needing a wider shed (personal communication).
29 Thin-sections undertaken by the Department of Mineralogy, British Museum (Natural History): these, and the other hones were identified by Mr D T Moore. Both Mr Moore, of the Department of Mineralogy and Mr M Fenton, then of the Lincoln Archaeological Trust, gave freely of their time and advice, without which this section could not have been written.
30 The precise source of the 'blue phyllite' hones remains in question, pending further analysis. Moore (1978, 68) suggested a German or central European provenance, based on the scarcity of this type of hone in Norway and its abundance at Hedeby; more recent work, however, has indicated that the blue phyllite may be a facies variation of the Norwegian Rag (Moore, personal communication). A hone from a late 19th century context at Flaxengate (inv no: F72 M4; publication forthcoming, AL **15**/2) was found to be an atypical Eidsborg schist (Norwegian Rag), which may have blue phyllite affinities.
31 Many of the finds can only be loosely dated to the 10th or 11th century (see above, p 4). These could be tabulated under the latest possible period but this would probably produce a biased distribution favouring later levels and under-representing earlier contexts. In Tables 1–3 such objects are therefore entered in a separate column headed '10th/11th C' in order to avoid too great a distortion.
32 Complete clamps have been found at Christ Church Place and Winetavern Street; the former appears to be broken and re-perforated (E122.9091; E81.2177). Single, perforated plano-convex strips, also probably from clamps, some of which are fractured across the perforation, came from Christ Church Place (E122.9604, 12678, 16555, and 17112), Winetavern Street (E81.2687) and High Street (E71.9927, 9938, and 15493—the last of wood). Unpublished; National Museum of Ireland. It is significant that evidence of comb making was found at both Christ Church Place and High Street, and of metalworking on the latter site.
33 Suggestion from Mrs C Morris. A group of worked antler tines from Christ Church Place, Dublin, shows the stages in manufacture. The tip of the tine was pared away on both sides (as for a wedge), and shallow notches cut on the inner curved face (finger-grips?). The base of the tine was perforated transversely in the same plane as the notches, and a slit then made in the sawn base to connect with this perforation. The thin flat tang of the draw-knife could then be inserted into the slit, and secured by a rivet through the perforation (E71.6972, 7046–7054, and 7279). Unpublished; National Museum of Ireland.
34 Mrs J Young suggests that the piece may have served as a pottery 'rib' for shaping vessel rims; such a use could well explain the abraded edges.

General discussion

The material discussed here forms only a small part of that recovered from the site so that any assessment of its significance must be regarded as tentative. More definitive conclusions about the Flaxengate area will only be possible when the analysis of its pottery, metalwork, and glass has been completed. At the same time, the site is not necessarily representative of the early medieval city as a whole. Nevertheless this material provides useful information about the origins of the inhabitants of the site, their daily lives, and by extension, the development of crafts and trade in Lincoln between the late 9th and the late 12th centuries.

The inhabitants and their possessions

The coincidence in date between the Danish conquest of Lincoln, as documented in the *Anglo-Saxon Chronicle* (Whitelock 1961, 48, *s a* 874), and the construction of the first timber buildings on this site (*c* 870/80)[1] suggests that the two events were directly linked. Both Flaxengate and Grantham Street may have been laid out as part of a reorganized street system. Perring (1981, 45) suggests that if the Danes organized and apportioned the land in this area of the town, the properties alongside both streets may initially have been held by them.

There appears to have been comprehensive reconstruction on the site on several occasions; this might imply single ownership of the whole plot. However, even if held by Danes, parts of the site may have been let out to both English and Danish tenants (Perring 1981, 45). It is possible that ownership was soon transferred to English hands because the English probably always formed the majority in Lincoln, although other evidence such as moneyers' names and street names reveals a population of mixed origins (Hill 1965, 31–5). The structures at Flaxengate conform to what is known of building in early medieval England, and no intrusive elements are detectable, Scandinavian or otherwise. Even if there were two groups of different origins living here, their cultural differences are not discernible archaeologically; in some respects the finds confirm this assessment.

The few vessel sherds of soapstone (*146–9*, see above, p 20) are almost certainly of Norwegian origin. Only five fragments in all were found; two of these are adjoining sherds of the same vessel, of which one was found in the late 9th century levelling pre-dating the construction of the first timber buildings, the other in an early 10th century context. Their occurrence in such early levels suggests that soapstone vessels were possibly brought as treasured possessions from the homeland by the earliest settlers; while this one clearly did not survive long in use, others may have been handed down from generation to generation. The remaining vessel sherds are from later levels and may well be residual. One (*146*) from the western end of the site was in a context which can only be loosely dated to between the late 9th and the late 11th century. The remaining two (*148, 149*) are both from 12th century pits. It is possible but unlikely that soapstone was acquired by means of trade (see below, p 47), and these fragments may therefore indicate the presence of Scandinavian settlers at Flaxengate.

Several objects are of typically Scandinavian Viking-age forms, such as the rectangular bone die (*98;* see above, p 13) and the conical clay spindle-whorl (*184;* p 22). The clamps (*287, 288;* p 30) made of bone are paralleled only on Scandinavian and Viking-age settlements, although this may be the result of our failure in Britain to recognize such tools, or a consequence of their being sometimes made of wood and not surviving elsewhere. Similarly, a few pieces are paralleled only on Anglo-Saxon sites, such as the ivory playing piece (*99;* p 13) and the single-pointed pinbeaters (*209–13*, p 25). The majority of the finds, however, are neither specifically Anglo-Saxon nor Scandinavian for objects similar in form and decoration have been found on both Anglo-Saxon and Scandinavian sites. Among these are pins with expanded, perforated heads, single-sided composite combs, and bone skates.

During the mid to late 11th century the expansion of building along the Grantham Street frontage coincided with the end of a period of intensive industrial activity. This was perhaps due to a change in ownership of the property and therefore in investment (Perring 1981, 45). At around the same time, changes in butchery and slaughtering practices are also evident (O'Connor 1982, 49). Although these factors, together with changes in pottery forms (Adams & Young 1981), may reflect the impact of the arrival of the Normans it had no visible effect on domestic life at Flaxengate as evidenced by the finds discussed here.

Over a third of the material represents personal possessions, ornaments and household utensils, mostly made from readily available and easily worked materials. Nothing survived of the internal furnishings of the houses, but the use of wooden boxes or caskets is implied by a number of ornamented bone mounts (*132–8*). The bone sneck (*139*) seems to have functioned as a swivelling catch, perhaps for securing a shutter.

Most of the domestic utensils, such as spoons and ladles, storage vessels, and tableware, were probably made of wood, and thus have not survived. The two bone spatulae (*144, 145*) were probably kitchen tools, while the few soapstone vessels served as cooking pots, as evidenced by carbon deposits on the external surfaces of two sherds (*147, 149*). Grinding of grain is attested by several well-worn fragments of quern stones (*150–5*). A number of implements may have been used as much for domestic activity as for craft work, such as the knives and bodkins of which only the bone handles survive (*140–3*), and the hones (*221–86*), some of which were perforated for suspension.

Domestic refuse and manufacturing debris alike were scattered around the site, without any apparent systematic disposal. Only a small proportion of the finds discussed here (approximately 15%) came from pits and, although a considerable number of those excavated appeared to be rubbish pits (others with traces of wood or wicker linings were clearly for storage), none held any quantity of manufacturing debris from bone-, antler-, or jet-working. Similarly, no features were found that could be identified as refuse dumps, although much of the waste material occurred in the make-up outside individual structures, or in the levelling dumps associated with the demolition and rebuilding of a sequence of structures. It is possible that temporary dumps existed, but were levelled out with each period of rebuilding, and thus the waste was eventually scattered throughout the excavated area.

Very few (approximately 0·04%) of the finds were trampled into or lay within the floor surfaces of the buildings, perhaps because they had been removed by regular cleaning and the renewal of flooring materials. Finished articles were no doubt carefully stored until removed for use, or for sale or exchange. A considerable amount (approximately 30%) of the material was found in association with a structure or series of structures on the same site, with no apparent discrimination between ordinary household and manufacturing debris. Although this suggests that the structures served both as domestic quarters and workshops, the relationship may be purely fortuitous and the result of successive levelling and reconstruction. The likelihood of both contamination and finds being residual is further increased by such regular shifting of earth and debris. It is thus impossible to determine whether those crafts which are in evidence at Flaxengate (discussed below) were practised only within particular structures, or in them all, during any one period. Similarly, the precise relationship between these and other activities of a domestic or industrial character must remain a matter of conjecture.

Textile working

The spindle-whorls, pinbeaters and other tools found in contexts either within, or associated with, many of the structures suggest that textile working may have been practised in most, if not all households. Whether this simply catered for family needs, or whether a surplus was produced for sale or exchange, is impossible to determine.

Spinning is well attested by over 50 whorls *(156–207)*, many of which are of bone, and were no doubt made as required. The evidence for weaving is slight by comparison, consisting of a single stone loomweight *(208)* and five pinbeaters *(209–13)*. A single linear feature (F17) within structure 20 (Period 6: dated *c* 1040–1060/70) may have been used for the placement of a vertical loom; similar features are thus interpreted at Tilleda, in Germany (Grimm 1968, 97). Such an interpretation for Flaxengate, however, is 'not completely satisfactory in the light of the feature's context' (Perring 1981, 42) because it is inside a structure which, on other evidence, was used for copperworking.

The virtual absence of loomweights may be of considerable significance in relation to the techniques used in weaving. Many contemporary Anglo-Saxon loomweights are made of baked clay (eg at St Neots: Addyman 1973, fig 18, 1, 2); if such weights had been extensively used at Flaxengate, it is probable that some would have survived, even in a fragmentary state. Alternatively, it is possible that for the most part the fibres were spun at Flaxengate and then taken elsewhere for weaving.

The general absence of loomweights in late Anglo-Saxon contexts is possibly due to the use of a two-beam vertical loom. That found in the Oseberg burial (as illustrated in Hoffman 1964, fig 137) stands on a base and clearly differs from the loom depicted in the 11th century manuscript of Hrabanus Maurus (Monte Cassino MS 132; as illustrated in Hoffman 1964, fig 136), where the lower beam is closer to the ground and the weaver apparently sits with his feet in a pit. Hoffman, however (*ibid*, 329–30), suggested that both types of loom may have been used for producing specialized rather than everyday fabrics. The 9th century Utrecht psalter illustrates a loom which is closely related to the late Roman two-beam vertical loom and, although this is not necessarily representative of those used in contemporary western Europe (*ibid*, 327–9 & fig 135), it seems likely that the use of such a loom may have spread further north to England as well as to the Continent, gradually replacing the warp-weighted type for the weaving of ordinary fabrics (*ibid*, 332).

The treadle-operated horizontal loom appears to have come into use in central Europe around the beginning of the 11th century (*ibid*, 258) and its introduction into England might then explain the lack of loomweights in late Anglo-Saxon levels. Its use in England at an earlier date is implied by two fragmentary wooden objects, both suggested to be warping-boards, which were recovered from 9th and 10th century contexts at Gloucester (Hodges in Heighway *et al* 1979, 191 & fig 13b, 5 & 14). The continued use of the warp-weighted loom is suggested, however, by the recovery of a clay loomweight from a 10th century context on the same site (*ibid*, 191 & fig 18, 8). There is insufficient evidence to conclude that either the two-beam vertical or the treadle-operated horizontal loom was used at Flaxengate, although the Scandinavian settlement could certainly have brought with it changes and improvements in weaving techniques.

The finishing of cloth is suggested by several fragmentary glass objects of a type commonly found on late Anglo-Saxon and Scandinavian Viking-age sites.[2] These are generally thought to have been used for removing the wrinkles from linen and are known as 'linen-smoothers', although they may also have been used for pressing the seams of finished garments, much like a primitive iron. Two stone objects *(425, 426)* may have served the same purpose. The majority of the spinning and weaving tools are from 10th and 11th century contexts, possibly suggesting a peak in activity at this time, and a decline thereafter in the 12th century (see Table 2 & n 31, p 41, above).

No textiles survived, but the varying weights of the spindle-whorls (see above, pp 22, 25) suggest that different types of yarn, perhaps wool and flax, were

Table 2 *Textile-working tools*

Type	Date						
	late 9th C	10th C	10/11th C	11th C	12th C	Post-timber & unstrat	Total
spindle-whorl	2	6	13	18	7	6	52
loomweight	–	–	1	–	–	–	1
pinbeater	–	3	1	1	–	–	5
linen-smoother	2	1	1	1	2	–	7

spun at Flaxengate. In turn, this, together with the linen-smoothers and possible polishers, implies the production of different types of cloths, linen as well as woollen. Comparison of yarn-working with weaving and finishing tools (Table 2) suggests that whereas spinning may have taken place in most, if not all households, weaving and finishing may have been more restricted. The relationship between these activities remains uncertain.

In York, spindle-whorls and weaving tools from Anglo-Scandinavian contexts on a number of sites imply a thriving textile industry, although the surviving fragments of woollen and linen cloth, as MacGregor suggests (1978a, 56), were not necessarily made there. Activity on a similar scale in Southampton has been inferred from the number of implements recovered (Addyman & Hill 1969, 72–3), but textile preservation there is poor (although a fragment of fine woollen cloth was found in a Middle Saxon context; see Holdsworth 1976, 45). There is no reason as yet to suppose that textile production in Lincoln differed from that in York or Southampton and other towns, or that the activity at Flaxengate formed other than a small part of a more broadly based cottage industry.

Antler-, bone-, and horn-working

Offcuts, partially worked fragments and discarded raw materials indicate that both bone- and antler-working were practised at Flaxengate; a limited use of horn may also be supposed from the occurrence of three waste cores *(388–90)*. Many of the simple types of bone object, such as toggles, could have been made by anyone as and when needed since they would have been comparatively easy to produce, whereas the more complex combs (of both bone and antler) were probably made by specialist craftsmen.

The range of bone products is demonstrated by the unfinished pieces, such as the pins *(50, 303)*, a spindle-whorl *(161)*, a pinbeater or awl *(304)*, and a flute *(126)*. Some objects lack final trimming and smoothing, such as the tallow-holders *(160–2)* and possibly the skates *(129–31)*, while most of the casket mounts may be rejects *(132, 134–7)*.

The bones of cattle, sheep and pigs were most frequently used; these were readily available, as shown by a study of the unworked remains from the site. Slaughtered carcasses were probably delivered intact for butchery, although it is possible that some animals were killed on site (O'Connor 1982, 46). No specific dumps or pits for butchery (or kitchen) refuse were identified, although small temporary heaps may have existed (see above, p 42). It is thus impossible to determine whether the material was acquired by scavenging, or whether the bone-workers dealt directly with the butchers and so had an organized supply. Equally, there were no dumps or pits of bone-working refuse, but the quantity found was in any case small.

By contrast, numerous pieces of waste antler were found, representing debris from comb making, although there were few half-finished and completed articles. Some of the combs *(1; 3–13)* may have been produced on site, but the only other finished object is the pendant or tool *(334)*. The few unfinished pieces include a gaming counter *(100)*, several handles *(335–7)*, a wedge *(338)*, and what may be a terminal *(340)*, all probably made from the comb-making waste.

Antler was available from two distinct sources, as shown by the discarded burrs *(342–53)*. Of these, seven are cast, while five are still attached to, or have been hacked from the skull. This suggests that shed antlers were collected from nearby areas during the appropriate season, ie March to May for red deer, and October to November for roe deer (although only two fragments of the latter were found). Rather fewer antlers came from carcasses, at least some of which must have been the result of hunting. Examination of the unworked material shows that red deer are represented mostly by antler, but a few post-cranial bones indicate a limited consumption of venison (O'Connor 1982, 40). Again, dumps or pits for refuse were not found, the waste being scattered about the excavated area. A quantity of antler waste was found within or overlying the late 9th and 10th century north–south road surface; this was presumably deposited by successive levelling and reconstruction of the earliest buildings in the adjacent area to the west of the street.

The preponderance of shed antler in contemporary towns such as Dublin (Ó'Ríordáin 1976, 137–8) and York (MacGregor 1978a, 46) has been taken to indicate the existence of a professional, urban industry requiring a year-round supply, with organized intensive collection in the immediate neighbourhood. At Hedeby, however, Ulbricht (1978, 141) suggests that local resources were insufficient to meet the demand for raw materials, necessitating the import of reindeer antler from Norway. The Hedeby comb makers are seen as permanent inhabitants who were forced to supplement their income by combining comb making with some other primary activity.

A recent study of Viking-age comb making (Ambrosiani, 1981), based mainly on evidence from Birka and Ribe, concludes however that combs were made almost exclusively by professional craftsmen, itinerants who travelled from one market to another and only temporary seasonal occupants (not always in the same spot) of a number of settlements in turn. Their raw material could thus be readily obtained at the markets where their products were sold, and such 'foreign' material as the elk antler which occurs at both Hedeby and Ribe could have been brought by the comb makers themselves, rather than by an import trade (*ibid*, 52–3).

It is impossible to draw any conclusions regarding the nature of the comb making in Lincoln on the basis of one site alone. If, however, this was a specialized craft, the few fragments of sawn antler strip *(382–7)* identified as comb-making waste together with the waste burrs, crowns, and tines may indeed imply the presence of professional craftsmen. The split-rib connecting plates *(13–18, 26–8)* and tooth segments *(19–25)* indicate that bone was used to supplement antler. The amount of waste, however, is small and, unless further excavations demonstrate that comb makers were permanently settled elsewhere in the town, the raw material required would not have been sufficient to necessitate an organized year-round supply. At Flaxengate we may have an example of Ambrosiani's itinerant craftsmen; other evidence from the site points to an important role for Lincoln as a local market.

The tools used for antler-, bone-, and horn-working were similar to those for carpentry (Wilson 1968); at Hedeby a range of implements was found and others were inferred from the toolmarks visible on partially worked fragments of antler (Ulbricht 1978, 33–50). Although identification of such tools from Flaxengate must await conservation of the metalwork, two bone

Table 3 *Antler, bone and horn, partially worked and waste pieces*

Material	late 9th C	10th C	10/11th C	11th C	12th C	Post-timber & unstrat	Total
			Date				
antler	14	15	12	8	4	1	54
bone	–	11	14	10	2	1	38
horn	–	–	–	–	3	–	3

objects (*287, 288,* see p 30) may be fragments of clamps.

Toolmarks on the bone and antler fragments indicate that cleavers and saws were used for chopping and cutting, and knives for rough trimming and shaping. Draw-knives, files, and polishers were needed for smoothing and finishing. Handles were probably hollowed out with gouges, and rivet holes made with augers, while use of the lathe is perhaps demonstrated by the ornamentation of the bone 'peg' *292* (as also by a number of the stone spindle-whorls: *210, 213, 214*). Much of the decoration was produced by simple knife-cut incisions, but the ring-and-dot motif in single, double or triple form suggests the use of a specialized tool, or a range of tools. Ring-and-dot is seen on several objects, including the dice (*97, 98*), a handle (*140*), one of the combs (*4*), and most of the bone mounts (*132–7*). In all cases, the rings of each motif are remarkably regular, and the concentric circles of the multiple motifs are evenly separated, although an error has been made on one piece (*296*). Many Anglo-Saxon and Viking-age objects are ornamented with ring-and-dot, the majority displaying this same regularity and neatness of execution. Ulbricht suggests that the design was applied with a tool resembling a pair of compasses, but with fixed, non-adjustable arms; the point producing the central dot would be longer than the one or two points producing the surrounding rings, as the dot was deeper than the circles (Ulbricht 1978, 44). No such tool has yet been found.[3]

The distribution and quantity of the finds suggests that both bone- and antler-working (i.e. comb making) took place on a small scale; this could support Ambrosiani's thesis as regards comb making, while simpler bone articles could have been made by the householder as required. Analysis of the waste material, as far as can be judged, shows that the bone-working continued at a reasonably steady level throughout the 10th to the late 11th centuries. By contrast, a peak in antler-working seemingly occurred during the late 9th and 10th centuries, gradually declining thereafter (see Table 3 and n 31, p 41, above). This may not be peculiar to Flaxengate (or to Lincoln), since a decline in antler-working is noted also in York, but from the late 12th or 13th century, with a probable increase in the trade of the horners as a result (MacGregor 1978a, 46). Although there is insufficient evidence for this at Flaxengate, it may be significant that the only fragments of waste horn occurred in 12th century contexts.

Study of the Hedeby comb-making material demonstrated that there a switch was made from antler to bone for raw material, and Ulbricht (1978, 140–1) suggests that this was a result of innovation in hunting law which restricted hunting to a privileged social class, consequently limiting the supply of antler to the craftsmen. Ambrosiani (1981, 56, 164), however, argues that the supply was probably unaffected since it was mostly derived from collection of naturally shed antler rather than from hunting. With urban growth, the population, and hence the demand for combs, increased, and heretofore itinerant comb makers could now settle profitably in the larger communities. But the total amount of antler available locally did not increase, and the need for a year-round supply of raw material obliged the comb makers to supplement the seasonally produced antler with bone and horn.

The availability of antler as raw material may have decreased in late Anglo-Saxon England, since the forest laws introduced after the Norman Conquest to protect the royal deer were foreshadowed by Cnut in the early 11th century, when trespassers on the royal preserve risked heavy penalties (Whitelock 1968, no 50 cl 80.1). This restriction may have contributed at least in part to the decline of antler-working in favour of both bone and horn. At Flaxengate, however, some bone was nearly always used in combs for toothplates irrespective of date, and for connecting plates from the 10th and 11th centuries onwards. This suggests that local supplies of antler may always have been insufficient, even for an irregular demand.

Looking at the comb-making debris as a whole (both bone and antler), there are far fewer fragments in 11th and 12th century contexts at Flaxengate than in earlier levels. That this reflects a decline in the craft itself is unlikely, and it may reinforce the suggestion that comb makers were only intermittently resident here, at market times. As such, they would no doubt be in competition with other itinerant craftsmen, and thus not necessarily able to occupy the same spot from one visit to the next. It may be no coincidence that the evidence for jet-working (see below) comes mainly from 11th century levels, or that copperworking activity (see above, p 1) apparently increases at this time. Whether comb making and other crafts were initially practised by itinerant professionals and whether comb makers eventually established permanent residence elsewhere in the town are possibilities which will be proved or disproved only by evidence from further excavation.

Jet-working

A group of objects consisting of partially worked pieces and waste flakes (*396–409*) suggests that jet-working was practised at Flaxengate in the early medieval period. These are almost all from 11th century contexts, and the majority are from the eastern end of the site. Much of the waste material, in the form of minute chips and flakes, was found in the accumulation encroaching on to, or in the levelling between, successive road surfaces. There are also two unworked fragments (*395, 410*), three unfinished finger-rings (*77–9*), and two probable pendants (*393, 394*).

It is possible that this jet constitutes part of a small 'hoard', originally of Roman date. Although many jet (and shale) objects were found in the Roman levels at Flaxengate, there was neither evidence of jet-working at that period, nor any proof that such an industry existed elsewhere in Lincoln, as in Roman York (RCHMY 1, 141–4).

A limited use was made of jet in Anglo-Saxon England, eg at Whitby where it occurs naturally (Peers & Radford 1943, figs 19 & 24), but the material only reappears in considerable quantities after the Scandinavian settlement. The Vikings may have regarded it as having magical properties, and it was sufficiently prized to be imported into Norway and used in fashioning a variety of small objects such as finger-rings, beads, bracelets, pendants and playing-pieces. Lignite, a related material, was also used in the manufacture of bracelets and finger-rings, as at the Norse settlement of Jarlshof (Hamilton 1956, fig 56, 5–8) and in Dublin (Wallace 1981, 26). There is evidence for jet-working at York in the form of a bead from Pavement, broken during manufacture (MacGregor 1978a, fig 23, 1); other finds include pendants (Waterman 1959, fig 21, 3; MacGregor 1978a, fig 23, 2, 3), while finger-rings and unworked fragments were found during recent excavations at Coppergate.[4] Evidence for the working of jet and lignite comes mainly from York, Dublin, and Jarlshof, suggesting that the revival of this industry was stimulated by Scandinavian influence and tastes.

The source of the jet used at Flaxengate was almost certainly the Whitby area of the east coast; it may have been brought via York (see below), from whence it may also have been exported to Scandinavia (MacGregor 1978a, 40). The tools employed in manufacturing were probably much the same as those used for bone- and antler-working. The unfinished pieces are only roughly chipped out, and several of the partially worked fragments have 'pecked' edges, as though further shaping was done by punching with a rather blunt tool. The quantity found suggests that this was carried out on a small scale, mainly during the 11th century.

Trade

Lincoln was well situated for trade, since it stood at the junction of two major Roman roads—Ermine Street running from north to south and providing links with both York and London, and the Fosse Way running south-westwards towards Exeter. Good water communications were ensured by the River Witham flowing south-east to the Wash. Access to the Trent at Torksey, and thence via the Humber and the Ouse to the north-east coast and to York, was perhaps provided by the Foss Dyke. This waterway was reopened in 1121, but whether the obstruction was only temporary is unknown (Hill 1965, 173).

The raw materials, such as bone and antler, for the majority of the objects discussed above would have been readily available in the town or within the immediate vicinity, but others are from further afield. In this respect the sources of the stones used illustrate a variety of trading contacts on both a national and international level.

Many of the spindle-whorls are made from soft limestone *(186–207)*, locally available, while one of the querns *(155)* is of grit from the Spilsby area, some 25 miles to the east of Lincoln. The loomweight of felspathic grit *(208)* is probably from a Lincolnshire source, while the pendant of siderite-bearing rock *(83)* may have come from either Lincolnshire or Northamptonshire. The Millstone Grit querns *(153, 154)* were probably brought from the Pennines of Derbyshire or Yorkshire, and jet from the Whitby area of the east coast. Materials were also brought in from the south, as demonstrated by a number of the hones; three *(280–2)* are of Kentish Rag from the Weald (although two of these may in fact be Roman), a single limestone fragment *(284)* is likely to have come from the Purbeck Beds, and those of Coal Measures Sandstone *(270–9)* are possibly from the Bristol or Forest of Dean coalfields.

To some extent this pattern of trade is mirrored by the pottery, although much was imported from East Anglia, eg Thetford ware; a few sherds of St Neots ware were found, and also single sherds of Ipswich ware (probably of the 9th century) and Grimston ware (dating to the 11th century). Stamford ware was brought from south Lincolnshire, while from further west came Torksey and Nottingham wares of the 10th to 12th centuries. The northern link is illustrated by a single sherd of 10th century York ware, several sherds of York splashed wares of the 11th and 12th centuries, and Yorkshire gritty wares of the 11th century, with 12th century glazed pottery from the Humber basin. Two vessel sherds of Winchester ware, and a series of 'early medieval' vessels in fabrics perhaps originating in the southern coastal counties, all probably dating to the 11th century, also hint at contacts with the south.[5]

Identification of the coins[6] suggests similar contacts. A St Edmund memorial penny from an East Anglian mint, *c* 905, was found in an early 10th century pit, while an Edward the Confessor penny, possibly minted at Rochester *c* 1042–4, came from a late 11th century context. Contact with York is again suggested by a penny of Anlaf Quaran Sihtricsson, minted *c* 943, from the 10th/11th century dump at the western end of the site. Links with western Britain are indicated by pennies of Alfred from a West Midlands mint (?Chester: minted *c* 890s; from an early 10th century context) and of Cnut from Hereford (unstratified). The southern connection is suggested by coins of Edward the Confessor from Hertford (minted *c* 1059–62; from a late 11th century hearth) and of William I, minted at Wallingford *c* 1072–4, from a mid 12th century context.

Jet and other goods may have been brought from the north-east via York and from there by road or direct by coastal shipping, landing at a port on the Wash coast. Boston, at the mouth of the Witham, would be a convenient spot, but the early history of this town is unclear; it is traditionally thought to have been founded after the Norman Conquest. By the late 12th century however, it had become one of the most important English medieval ports (Carus-Wilson 1962–3, 182), and its use as an outport for Lincoln may well have begun considerably earlier. Coastal trade may also have been responsible for imports from the south; the Purbeck marble for Lincoln Cathedral was probably transported in this way from Dorset in the 13th century (*ibid*, 188). Trade along the waterways and the coast may also have provided links with the market centres of East Anglia, such as Ipswich and Norwich.

Trade links with the south-west could have followed the prehistoric route of the Jurassic Way through Northamptonshire to the Cotswolds; the existence of a south-west to north-east route in late Anglo-Saxon times is also suggested by finds of Stamford ware pottery in the Oxford region (Mellor 1980, 19). Similarly, contact with the south may have foreshadowed the later medieval route from the central Midlands via Oxford to Southampton, where Midland rock types occur in late Anglo-Saxon levels (Addyman & Hill 1969, 81).

Less evidence of international trade is provided by the finds, although they indicate contact with both Norway and the Rhineland. Trade with the latter is suggested by the three lava querns *(150–2)* from the Mayen-Niedermendig area. Exploitation of the lava outcrops in this region was virtually continuous from prehistoric times, forming the basis of a flourishing Roman trade (Crawford & Röder 1955). Finds of lava querns on Anglo-Saxon sites in England, eg Southampton (Addyman & Hill 1969, 79) and Thetford (Dunning 1956, 232), and in north-west Germany and the Low Countries suggest that this trade continued unbroken. Dorestad and later Hedeby may have served as entrepôts; an unfinished quern found at Hedeby, without the central perforation, suggests that they were shipped as rough-outs to prevent breakage during transit (*ibid*, 232). Expansion of the trade northwards is evidenced by finds of lava querns at Danish Viking-age sites such as Ribe (Graham-Campbell 1980, 17, no 49) and Trelleborg (Nørlund 1948, 125 & Taf XX).

Trade in Norwegian Rag ('schist') hones (and perhaps also of phyllite, see above, p 41 n 30) to the north and east of England is seemingly connected with the Scandinavian settlement and import continued well into medieval times (see above, p 30 & Table 1).

Amber *(80, 82, 392)* and ivory *(99, 391)* were imported, the former probably from the Baltic (although it might have been collected from the North Sea coast), the latter probably from the Arctic. The only other pieces of foreign origin are the soapstone vessel sherds, although these are not necessarily evidence of trade. The existence of strong local pottery traditions, and consequently of an ample supply of ceramic vessels for both cooking and storage diminishes the likelihood of an import trade in soapstone vessels, and the Flaxengate fragments may simply represent personal possessions (see above, p 42), gifts, or curios left behind by some passing traveller. Whether the presence of soapstone is taken as evidence of trade or not, the hones still demonstrate links with Norway, though not necessarily direct contact.

One possibility is that Norwegian trade to England was directed through the Low Countries, and may have been under the control of the Frisians from an early date. In the 8th and 9th centuries Dorestad traded not only with England, but with the eastern coasts of the North Sea and down the Rhine. Although at times overstated, the activities of the Frisian merchants in Carolingian times have been likened to those of the Hanseatic League at a later date (Jellema 1955). A trading colony existed at York in the 8th century (Whitelock 1968, 725), and the possibility of Frisian activity in Lincoln cannot be discounted. (The antler connecting plate *29*, which could have been part of a handled single-sided composite comb, and the three tallow-holders *160–2*, may be signs of Frisian influence here.)

Sherds of imported pottery found at Flaxengate may indicate early trade with the Low Countries and the Rhineland. Badorf ware sherds were found in a level pre-dating the construction of the earliest timber buildings, while early Continental glazed sherds, perhaps of Low Countries origin, have been recognized from early 10th century contexts (Adams 1979b). Of perhaps greater significance are the Chinese Yüeh stoneware sherds of the 8th or 9th century (Adams 1979b) and several fragments of an Islamic vessel of the early 9th century (Adams 1979a), from levels pre-dating the first timber structures. Whether these, like the soapstone vessels, arrived as personal possessions, gifts or curios, or whether a foothold in the international market had already been established in Lincoln prior to the Danish conquest and settlement are, however, beyond the scope of this discussion.

Conclusions

The construction of the earliest timber buildings at Flaxengate may have been a direct result of the Danish conquest of Lincoln in 874, possibly representing part of a planned reorganization of both street systems and land-holdings in this area. A few soapstone vessel sherds in the earliest levels suggest that at least some of the inhabitants were of Scandinavian origin, but the majority of the finds are neither specifically Scandinavian nor Anglo-Saxon, implying that the Danes were soon assimilated into the local population.

The initial occupation at Flaxengate was primarily residential, the finds suggesting normal domestic activities such as spinning, perhaps producing a surplus for sale or exchange. There is comparatively little evidence of weaving, but both woollen and linen cloth may have been made. Bone and antler were worked, the small scale of the refuse generated (together with the lack of specific dumps or pits for waste materials) perhaps indicating that these crafts were pursued on an individual or seasonal basis, thus obviating the necessity for organized waste disposal. Alternatively, rubbish may have been deliberately removed from the site.

In the mid to late 10th century a period of intensive industrial activity began, coinciding with the partial development of the Grantham Street frontage. Perring (1981, 45) suggests that this may reflect a change in ownership of the property and consequently in investment, possibly as a result of Edmund's reconquest of the Danelaw in 942. The structures were probably used both as dwellings and workshops; the finds include personal and domestic objects as well as tools, half-finished products, and waste materials relating to a number of crafts.

Spinning (and weaving?) continued, as did the bone- and antler-working, but the major activities were glass- and metalworking. The production of jet (and amber?) pendants and finger-rings may have been connected with the manufacture of the other jewellery such as the glass rings and beads, and the copper-alloy tags.[7] The possibility of such a link is demonstrated by recent finds from a jeweller's workshop at Fishamble Street, Dublin, where trinkets of lignite, amber, and glass were all produced within successive structures on the same spot (Wallace 1981, 26).

Most of the material discussed here is from late 10th and 11th century contexts, suggesting that these activities reached a peak at that time, and thereafter declined (but see n 31, p 41 above). Although other factors may have been at least partially responsible, as with the comb making (see above, p 45), this may reflect a further change in ownership of the property (and of investment) following the Norman Conquest (Perring 1981, 45).

Excavations elsewhere in Britain show that the domestic crafts and industrial activities found at Flaxengate were common to many contemporary towns, but the coexistence here of several crafts at various times, ie comb making with glass-working and jet-working with copperworking, perhaps indicates that this site lies on the fringe of an industrial or jewellery-making quarter. Whether Flaxengate was part of such a quarter or not, evidence from contemporary towns suggests that such activities are to be expected elsewhere in Lincoln, certainly in the case of domestic production of yarn, and small-scale bone-working. Comb making may have been practised elsewhere, especially from the 11th century onwards, while small-scale metalworking was no doubt taking place at other sites,[8] although whether this resembled that at Flaxengate, or was similarly linked to other crafts, can only be demonstrated by further excavation.

The very existence of a range of crafts at Flaxengate suggests that Lincoln played an important role as a local market centre, probably exchanging manufactured goods for raw materials and agricultural produce from the surrounding countryside, and the sources of the imported stones suggest a variety of trading contacts on both a national and international scale. It is tempting to see the Danish settlement as stimulating the economy with its increased possibilities of tapping into far-flung and well-established Viking-age trade routes. Crafts at Flaxengate however, were on a small scale and mainly domestic in nature until well into the 10th century, when the major phase of industrial activity began, and as regards trade, the imported pottery from the site (see above, p 47) suggests the possibility of prior contact with the Carolingian empire. While international trade and external influences were no doubt of some significance, too great an emphasis should not be placed on these while so little is known at present of Lincoln's relationship with the surrounding area, and its role in the local economy.

Even if the development of Flaxengate was a result of Danish settlement there may have been similar activity at a prior date in other areas, with an earlier focus of both trade and manufacture nearer the waterside. The excavations at Flaxengate have contributed much towards our understanding of Lincoln between the late 9th and the late 12th centuries, but many problems remain unanswered, and only further excavations elsewhere in the town can provide the solutions.

Notes

1 With a margin of error of about 15 years in either direction; see Perring 1981, 36.
2 The linen-smoothers are included with the glass objects from the site; publication forthcoming, AL **14**/2.
3 A three-pronged iron tool found during recent excavations at Spong Hill may have been used for incising ring-and-dot. Unpublished (1012 ELN Urn 3216/1); information from Mrs C Morris.
4 Information from Dominic Tweddle (Assistant Director), York Archaeological Trust.
5 Information regarding the pottery is from Dr Lauren Adams and Mrs Jane Young. These and other wares, both local and imported, are fully discussed in AL **17**/2, publication forthcoming.
6 The coins were identified by Professor M Dolley and Mr Mark Blackburn; fully discussed in AL **6**/2, publication forthcoming.
7 Glass production may be further linked with lead-working at Flaxengate; these, and the copperworking are discussed in the forthcoming publication on industrial activity, AL **14**/2.
8 Copperworking and glass-working crucibles have been found at a number of other sites including Holmes Grainwarehouse and St Paul-in-the-Bail.

Catalogue

The finds are listed by type and subdivided where necessary by material. For ease of reference, the catalogue number of each object (eg *1*) is used in both text and illustrations. The inventory number (eg F76 B20) is that allocated to each find on excavation and will be retained when the material is transferred to the City and County Museum, Lincoln. This is listed after the measurements (in millimetres) which are given thus: H = height, W = width, L = length, Th = thickness, D = diameter. Wt = weight, given in grammes. An asterisk denotes an object from which a thin-section was taken.

The dates given for each context are those of the structural periods to which they are related. Context codes are given in brackets. The chronological sequence (for the establishment of which see Perring 1981, 36) is as follows:

7th–9th century	Pre-timber (a)
late 9th century	Pre-timber (b–d)
c 870/80–900	Timber period 1
c 900–930/40	Timber period 2
c 930/40–970	Timber period 3
c 970–1000/10	Timber period 4
c 1000/10–1040	Timber period 5
c 1040–1060/70	Timber period 6
c 1060/70–1080/90	Timber period 7
c 1080/90–1100	Timber period 8
c 1100–1120	Timber period 9
c 1120–1140	Timber period 10
c 1140–1160	Timber period 11
c 1160–1180	Timber period 12
c 1180–1200	Timber period 13

A few objects were found in late 12th century contexts post-dating the timber structures but pre-dating the construction of the medieval stone buildings, while some occurred residually in later medieval contexts. For the structural sequence to which these are related, see Jones 1980, 9.

Cat No	*Fig*	*Description and context*
		COMBS
		Single-sided composite:
1	3	Terminal; plano-convex antler connecting plates secured by iron rivets (2 remaining), ornamented with paired longitudinal lines. 3 bone tooth segments in place with coarse teeth (4/5 per cm); terminal segment perforated and teeth graduated. Upper edge of connecting plates flush with upper edge of tooth segments; lower edge notched from saw-cutting of teeth. L: 42 mm. H: 31 mm. F76 B20 Late 9th C Levelling, central area (BDM)
2	3	Terminal; bone. Plano-convex connecting plates secured by iron rivets (2 remaining), ornamented with single vertical band of incised zig-zag beyond second rivet. 2 tooth segments remaining but coarse teeth (4 per cm) broken; terminal segment with graduated teeth. Upper edge of connecting plates flush with upper edge of tooth segments. L: 54 mm. H: 28 mm. F76 B29 Late 9th C Levelling over area of Roman building (BJL)
3	3	Terminal; plano-convex antler connecting plates secured by iron rivets (2 remaining); ornamented with end panel of converging oblique lines. 4 vertical lines indicate border of central ornamental panel of lozenges, formed by crossed double oblique lines. End tooth segment of bone projects slightly above connecting plates; coarse graduating teeth (5 per cm) broken at tip. L: 59 mm. H: 28 mm. F76 B38 *c* 930/40–970 Pit F670 (BNG)
4	3	Terminal; end tooth segment of bone with coarse, graduating teeth (5/6 per cm) projects above and beyond plano-convex (?antler) connecting plates. Outer edges of this segment have scalloped profile; ornamented with irregularly spaced line of single ring-and-dot. Terminal suggests inturned animal head; snout undercut to separate from connecting plates, with double horizontal nick representing nostrils, ring-and-dot suggesting eye (?). Connecting plates ornamented with terminal band of incised step-pattern; vertical band of zig-zag beyond first iron rivet (2 remaining). L: 38 mm. H: 37 mm. F75 B41 *c* 970–1060/70 Assoc structures 14/15, 18, & 21 (B87)
5	3	Terminal, obliquely cut; end bone tooth segment with coarse, graduating, beaded teeth (5 per cm) projects above and beyond plano-convex antler connecting plates. Secured by iron rivet; ornamented with terminal band of paired vertical lines. L: 41 mm. H: 30 mm. F74 B14 *c* 1140–1160 Pit F734 (ABP)
6	3	Fragment. Plano-convex antler connecting plates ornamented with longitudinal panel of double interlocked step-pattern, unevenly executed. Single bone tooth segment remaining, secured by two iron rivets. Coarse teeth (6 per cm) beaded. Lower edges of connecting plates notched by saw. L: 66 mm. H: 34 mm. F75 B109 *c* 900–1060/70 Levelling dump, west of structures 6, 9, 13, 17, & 20 (J10)
7	3	Fragment. Plano-convex antler connecting plates with ?central ornamental panel. 2 horizontal zones of double zig-zag, divided by horizontal double line, with borders of panel marked by three pairs of vertical lines. Lower edge notched from saw-cutting of coarse teeth (5 per cm). Smooth and polished; secured by iron rivets. Numerous (?bone) teeth, rivets, fragments of plain connecting plate and tooth segments; too badly damaged for further reconstruction. F73 B25 *c* 1080/90–1100 Levelling over structure 23 (AGG)
8	3	Connecting plate fragment, antler; plano-convex. Panel of carelessly executed vertical lines at one end, the other fractured across a rivet hole. Lower edge notched from saw-cutting of coarse teeth (4 per cm). Surface rough. L: 38 mm. H: 15 mm. F76 B45 Late 9th C Levelling over area of Roman building (BRT)
9		Connecting plate fragment, antler; plano-convex. Unevenly shaped, surface rough. One end fractured across band of vertical incised lines. One iron rivet remaining. Lower edge notched from saw-cutting of coarse teeth (5 per cm). L: 53 mm. H: 15 mm. F75 B101 *c* 900–1000/1010 External dump to west of structures 6, 9, & 13 (H53)
10	3	Connecting plate fragment, antler; plano-convex. Both ends fractured across rivet hole, one iron rivet remaining. Surface rough; ornamented with ?central panel of paired oblique lines, bordered by three double verticals. Lower edge notched from saw-cutting of coarse teeth (4 per cm). L: 81 mm. H: 17 mm. F74 B13 *c* 1040–1060/70 Levelling over structure 18 (AWR)

Cat No	*Fig*	*Description and context*
11	3	Connecting plate fragment, antler; plano-convex. Surface polished, ornamented with paired and triple oblique lines. Lower edge notched from saw-cutting of coarse teeth (5 per cm). L: 22 mm. H: 15 mm. F73 B18 *c* 1080/90–1100 Levelling over structure 23 (IG)
12		Connecting plate terminal, antler; plano-convex. End obliquely sawn; fractured across rivet hole. L: 15 mm. H: 12 mm. F76 B68 *c* 900–930/40 Levelling over structures 3 & 5 (BHR)
13		Connecting plate terminal, bone; split cattle rib. Rivet hole at end; corners broken. Surface smooth and polished. L: 68 mm. H: 16 mm. F75 B73 *c* 900–970 Road surface F748 (E85)
14		Connecting plate fragment, bone; split ?sheep rib. Fractured across rivet holes at both ends. Slight iron staining visible round one perforation. Surface smooth and polished. L: 53 mm. H: 13 mm. F75 B94 *c* 900–1060/70 Levelling dump west of structures 6, 9, 13, 17, & 20 (H30)
15		Connecting plate fragment, bone; split rib. Unfinished—edges uneven, surface rough. Both ends fractured across perforation. L: 53 mm. H: 12 mm. F75 B142 *c* 930/40–1060/70 Road surface F748 (B102)
16	4	Connecting plates, bone; split (?cattle) rib. Terminal of pair of thin plates, secured by iron rivet. Fractured across second perforation. Surface smooth and polished. L: 55 mm. H: 13 mm. F75 B119 *c* 1000/10–1060/70 Road surface F748 (E79)
17		Connecting plate fragment, bone; split rib. Unevenly shaped, with rough surface. Iron rivet remaining. L: 53 mm. H: 12 mm. F75 B42 *c* 1060/70–1080/90 Levelling over structure 20 (BAF)
18		Connecting plate terminal, bone; split rib. Of uneven shape, with rivet hole at end, and fractured across second perforation. L: 76 mm. H: 14 mm. F73 B28 *c* 1140–1200 Levelling external to structures 40 & 44 (ADR)
19	4	Tooth segment, bone, with 8 coarse (4 per cm) graduated teeth, beaded from wear. Fractured across rivet holes at both ends; traces of iron staining visible. L: 20 mm. H: 30 mm. F76 B9 *c* 900–930/40 Levelling: central area (BDG)
20		Tooth segment, bone; fractured. 2 beaded, coarse teeth (5 per cm) remaining. L: 9 mm. H: 31 mm. F75 B104 *c* 900–930/40 Levelling west of structure 6 (J32)
21		Tooth segment, bone. 2 of 7 coarse teeth (4 per cm) remaining. L: 16 mm. H: 33 mm. F76 B27 *c* 930/40–970 Pit F669 (BHY)
22		Tooth segment, bone, with rivet hole at each end. 10 coarse teeth (4/5 per cm) of uneven width, beaded. L: 21 mm. H: 37 mm. F75 B82 *c* 930/40–1000/10 Assoc structures 10 and 14/15 (F94)
23	4	Tooth segment, bone; fractured across rivet hole. Upper portion of segment ornamented with oblique lines. 2 beaded, coarse teeth (4 per cm) remaining. L: 9 mm. H: 40 mm. F75 B63 *c* 930/40–1040 Assoc structures 9, 13, & 17 (E71)
24		Tooth segment, bone, with rivet hole at one end. 8 beaded, coarse teeth (5 per cm). L: 18 mm. H: 32 mm. F76 B5 *c* 1040–1060/70 Pit F675 (BDD)
25		Tooth segment, bone; fractured, but iron rivet remaining. 5 coarse teeth (5 per cm) of uneven width. L: 13 mm. H: 33 mm. F73 B24 *c* 1140–1160 Levelling north of structure 42/43 (ACE)

Comb cases

Cat No	*Fig*	*Description and context*
26		Connecting plate fragment, bone; split cattle rib. End obliquely cut and perforated for rivet. Of uneven width, but with smooth, polished surface. Slight green discolouration due to corrosion products of copper fragments in vicinity. L: 87 mm. H: 15 mm. F75 B64 *c* 970–1060/70 Assoc structures 13, 17, & 20 (E28)
27	4	Connecting plate, bone; split cattle rib. Iron rivet at each end, one corner fractured. Surface smooth, with slight polish. L: 137 mm. H: 15 mm. F73 B38 *c* 1060/70–1080/90 Posthole (F453) associated with hearth (F20) external to structure 25 (AMC)
28	4	Terminal of tapering bone strip (split cattle rib); plano-convex. Small iron rivet at end; ornamented with groups of triple transverse lines; pair of shallow grooves running parallel to each side barely visible. L: 56 mm. H: 19 mm. F74 B1 *c* 1140–1160 Pit F732 (AKF)

Double-sided composite comb

Cat No	*Fig*	*Description and context*
29	4	Connecting plate terminal, antler; plano-convex. 2 adjoining fragments, with 3 rivet holes. Both edges notched from saw-cutting of coarse teeth (6 per cm, 2 per cm). Surface smooth and polished. L: 109 mm. H: 15 mm. F75 B95 *c* 930/40–970 Assoc structures 10, 11, & 12 (G98, G103)

PINS: BONE

Ball-headed

Cat No	*Fig*	*Description and context*
30		Fragment; top of head faceted to slight cone. Circular-sectioned shank. Polished. L: 23 mm. F76 B44 9th C Levelling: central area (BNH)
31		Fragment; large head flattened on one side. Circular-sectioned shank. Surface rough but with slight polish. L: 28 mm. F76 B40 9th C Levelling: central area (BNZ)
32	6	Fragment; traces of faceting on small head and swollen circular-sectioned shank. Slight polish. L: 63 mm. F76 B31 Late 9th C Robber trench (F45) of Roman building (BLO)
33		Fragment; head and swollen circular-sectioned shank faceted. Slight polish. L: 64 mm. F76 B15 Late 9th C Levelling over Roman building (BKK)

Cat No	*Fig*	*Description and context*
34		Large mis-shapen head; thick, circular-sectioned shank tapers to blunt point. Slight polish. L: 69 mm. F76 B64 *c* 870/80–900 Structure 5, destruction (BZF)
35	6	Large mis-shapen head; thick, circular-sectioned shank, with central swelling and blunt point. Smooth and polished. L: 67 mm. F76 B65 *c* 870/80–900 Structure 5, destruction (BZF)
36		Fragment; slight faceting on head; circular-sectioned shank bent and flattened on one side. Smooth and polished. L: 83 mm. F76 B7 *c* 900–930/40 Levelling over Roman building (BCU)
37		Fragment; slight faceting on head, slight hipping of upper circular-sectioned shank. Smooth and polished. L: 45 mm. F76 B13 *c* 900–930/40 Levelling over structures 3 & 5 (BEX)
38		Fragment; slight faceting on head and circular-sectioned shank. Faint polish. L: 44 mm. F75 B55 *c* 1000/10–1040 Assoc structure 17 (F32)
39		Slight faceting on small head and circular-sectioned shank. Broken and reused; fracture ?trimmed, shows signs of wear. Very smooth, highly polished. L: 62 mm. F74 B24 *c* 900–1060/70 Pit F693 (AVV)
40		Fragment; large mis-shapen head, circular-sectioned shank. Slight polish. L: 23 mm. F74 B9 *c* 1060/70–1080/90 Levelling over structure 20 (AOV)
		Nail-headed
41	6	Fragment; one side of head broken. Slight faceting on head and circular-sectioned shank. L: 45 mm. F75 B52 *c* 870/80–1060/70 Levelling dump assoc with pitting at western end (H6)
42		Fragment; small stump projects from centre of head. Traces of faceting on circular-sectioned shank but smooth and polished. L: 57 mm. F74 B21 *c* 900–1060/70 Robber trench (F384) of Roman building (ASO)
		Expanded perforated head
43		Traces of working on curved and ovoid-sectioned shank, but smooth and polished. Top of head flattened to almost triangular shape. L: 107 mm. F74 B20 *c* 870/80–900 Robber trench/pit F55 (AYJ)
44		Fragment; head trimmed almost square, ovoid-sectioned shank. Surface rough. L: 15 mm. F75 B107 *c* 900–970 Assoc structures 7 & 10 (H81)
45	6	Head rounded; traces of tooling on fractured and ovoid-sectioned shank but smooth and highly polished. L: 98 mm. F76 B16 *c* 930/40–970 Levelling over structure 7 & road surface F748 (BGA)
46		Fragment; head almost triangular, ovoid-sectioned shank. Surface rough. L: 23 mm. F76 B17 *c* 930/40–970 Levelling over structure 7 & road surface F748 (BGA)
47		Fragment, rounded head; traces of faceting on ovoid-sectioned shank. L: 56 mm. F74 B158 *c* 1000/10–1040 Structure 18, floor (AZK)
48		Fragment; traces of tooling on ovoid-sectioned shank but smooth with slight polish. L: 78 mm. F75 B134 *c* 1000/10–1080/90 Assoc structures 17, 20, & 26 (E13)
49	6	Top flattened to form triangular head; traces of faceting on curved, ovoid-sectioned shank. Smooth and highly polished. L: 70 mm. F74 B22 *c* 1140–1160 Pit F729 (AEJ)
50	6	Unfinished: top of head untrimmed. Lower half of ovoid-sectioned shank cut away in preparation for shaping of point. L: 59 mm. F76 B80 *c* 900–930/40 Levelling over structures 3 & 5 (CAT)
		Perforated decorative head
51	6	Four notches around perforated head, presenting scalloped appearance. Ovoid-sectioned shank evenly tapered, smooth and highly polished. L: 80 mm. F75 B40 *c* 870/80–1060/70 Levelling dump assoc with pitting, western end (E6)
		Fragments
52		Slender, circular-sectioned, with traces of tooling; tapers to blunt point. L: 41 mm. F76 B26 9th C Destruction of Roman building (BKJ)
53		Circular-sectioned, with traces of faceting; slight hip above blunt, worn point. L: 56 mm. F76 B46 9th C Levelling: central area (BNE)
54		Slender & circular-sectioned, with slight faceting; tapers to sharp point. Smooth and polished. L: 59 mm. F76 B14 Late 9th C Levelling over Roman building (BKK)
55		?Unfinished: sharply faceted and circular-sectioned with slight hip; tapers to sharp point. L: 52 mm. F76 B19 Late 9th C Levelling over Roman building (BKK)
56		Circular-sectioned with slight faceting, unevenly shaped. Tapers to blunt point. L: 74 mm. F76 B32 Late 9th C Levelling: central area (BDS)
57		Circular-sectioned, slender, tapering to sharp point. L: 35 mm. F76 B39 Late 9th C Levelling: central area (BDS)
58		Circular-sectioned, slender, tapering to sharp point. L: 26 mm. F76 B42 Late 9th C Levelling: central area (BRL)
59		Thick, of circular section, with slight hip. L: 52 mm. F76 B92 Late 9th C Levelling: central area (BNX)
60		Circular-sectioned with slight hip. L: 66 mm. F76 B78 Late 9th C Levelling: eastern end (CAI)
61		Circular-sectioned with slight hip; tapers to worn, blunt point. Smooth and polished. L: 60 mm. F75 B93 *c* 900–930/40 Levelling over Roman building (BCL)

Cat No	*Fig*	*Description and context*
62		Ovoid-sectioned with rough surface; tapering. L: 31 mm. F76 B18 *c* 930/40–970 Levelling over structure 7 & road surface F748 (BGA)
63		Tapering, ovoid-sectioned, faceted; slight polish. L: 47 mm. F75 B87 *c* 900–1040 Assoc structures 6, 9, 13, & 17 (G51)
64		Ovoid-sectioned with traces of tooling; smooth, with slight polish. Tapers to sharp point. L: 50 mm. F75 B68 *c* 930/40–1040 Assoc structures 10, 14/15, & 18 (E81)
65		Ovoid-sectioned with traces of faceting but smooth, with slight polish. L: 54 mm. F75 B66 *c* 970–1040 Assoc structures 14/15 & 18 (H18)
66		Circular-sectioned, smooth, polished. L: 24 mm. F75 B133 *c* 870/80–1060/70 Levelling dump assoc with pitting: west end (E47)
67		Circular-sectioned, with slight faceting; slender, tapering to sharp point. L: 71 mm. F76 B23 *c* 900–1060/70 Pit F691 (BIE)
68		Of faceted circular section with slight hip; tapers to sharp point. L: 70 mm. F74 B27 *c* 900–1060/70 Robber trench F384 (ASO)
69		Circular-sectioned, with slight hip; tapers to blunt, worn point. L: 56 mm. F75 B65 *c* 1000/10–1080/90 Assoc structures 17, 20, & 26 (E13)
70		Ovoid-sectioned shank, bent but evenly tapered; smooth and polished. L: 55 mm. F75 B135 *c* 1000/10–1080/90 Assoc structures 17, 20 & 26 (E13)
71		Of circular section, with rough surface. L: 28 mm. F75 B137 *c* 1000/10–1080/90 Assoc structures 17, 20 & 26 (E13)
72		Circular-sectioned, with slight hip; smooth and polished. L: 32 mm. F74 B12 *c* 1060/70–1080/90 Structure 24, floor (AVG)
73		Circular-sectioned, faceted; tapers to sharp point. L: 30 mm. F73 B29 *c* 1100–1120 Levelling over structure 27/28 and area of road (F749) (AEE)
74		Circular-sectioned, tapering; surface damaged but with slight polish. L: 47 mm. F74 B5 Unstratified

FINGER-RINGS

Jet

Cat No	*Fig*	*Description and context*
75	7	Fragment; plain, D-sectioned band. Smooth and polished. Int D: *c* 17 mm. F75 M98 *c* 970–1040 Assoc structures 14/15 & 18 (B95)
76		Fragment; plain, D-sectioned band. Smooth and polished. Int D: *c* 20 mm. F73 M121 Unstratified
77	7	Unfinished: fragment. Crudely shaped, of uneven section. Int D: *c* 16 mm. F74 M59 *c* 1040–1060/70 Levelling over road surface F748 (AWS)
78		Unfinished: fragment of plain, D-sectioned band. Internal surface rough; traces of faceting and filing on exterior. Int D: *c* 20 mm. F74 M27 *c* 1060/70–1080/90 Levelling over road surface F749 (AQQ)
79	7	Unfinished: fragment of thick, plain D-sectioned band. Internal surface rough; traces of faceting on exterior. Int D: *c* 18 mm. F73 M84 *c* 1120–1140 Levelling over structure 35 (ZL)

Amber

Cat No	*Fig*	*Description and context*
80	7	Fragment; plain, D-sectioned band with median ridge on internal surface. Int D: *c* 20 mm. F75 M146 *c* 900–1000/10 Assoc structures 7, 10, & 14/15 (G94)

PENDANTS

Bone

Cat No	*Fig*	*Description and context*
81	8	Fragment: axe-shaped. Fractured across socket (suspension loop). L: 45 mm. F76 B88 *c* 900–930/40 Levelling over Roman building (BFC)

Amber

Cat No	*Fig*	*Description and context*
82	8	Fragment: small chunk from upper end of ?pendant, fractured across perforation. L: 13 mm. F74 M55 *c* 1000/10–1040 Pit F671 (AXF)

Stone

Cat No	*Fig*	*Description and context*
83	8	* Unfinished; fragment. Siderite-bearing rock. Square-sectioned, crudely shaped; perforation drilled through tapering head. L: 47 mm. W: 10 mm. Th: 10 mm. F75 M152 *c* 900–930/40 Levelling west of structure 6 (J28)
84	8	*Fragment; ?Coal Measures Sandstone. Square-sectioned, tapering; upper end fractured across drilled perforation. Slight faceting on sides; smooth and polished. L: 57 mm. W: 11 mm. Th: 11 mm. F73 M77 Late 12th–mid 13th C Levelling dump over latest timber buildings (WL)
85	8	Limestone; triangular with drilled perforation through rounded apex. Smooth and polished. L: 34 mm. W: 20 mm. Th: 7 mm. F72 M5 Late 12th–mid 13th C Levelling dump over latest timber buildings (AS)

TOGGLES: BONE

Cat No	*Fig*	*Description and context*
86		Pig metacarpal, unfused, with central anterior-posterior perforation. Smooth, with slight polish on anterior and posterior surfaces. L: 55 mm. F75 B96 *c* 900–970 Assoc structures 7 and 10 (G93)
87	9	Pig metacarpal, unfused, with off-centre anterior-posterior perforation. Ends and part of shaft trimmed; slight polish on anterior and posterior surfaces. L: 47 mm. F75 B78 *c* 930/40–970 Assoc structure 9 and earlier levelling (G50)

Cat No	*Fig*	*Description and context*
88	9	Fragment: pig metacarpal, unfused; fractured across second of two anterior-posterior perforations. L: 29 mm. F75 B100 *c* 900–1000/1010 Assoc structures 7, 10, & 14/15 (G94)
89	9	Pig metatarsal, unfused, with central anterior-posterior perforation of irregular shape. Lip of perforation roughly chipped away on both surfaces. L: 65 mm. F75 B126 *c* 970–1040 Assoc structures 14/15 & 18 (F36)
90		Pig metatarsal, unfused, with anterior-posterior perforation. Slight polish on anterior and posterior surfaces. L: 61 mm. F74 B26 *c* 1000/1010–1040 Structure 18: destruction (AZE)
91		Pig metacarpal, unfused, with medio-lateral perforation. Small pit 1·5 mm below perforation on one surface. Slight polish. L: 61 mm. F75 B50 *c* 870/80–1060/70 Levelling dump assoc with pitting, west end (F6)
92		Pig metacarpal, unfused, with anterior-posterior perforation of irregular shape. Anterior and posterior surfaces smooth, with slight polish. L: 62 mm. F76 B74 *c* 900–1060/70 Pit F700 (BLG)
93		Pig metacarpal, unfused, with central anterior-posterior perforation of irregular shape. Slight polish on anterior and posterior surfaces. L: 60 mm. F75 B89 *c* 970–1080/90 Assoc structures 13, 17, 20, & 26 (G33)
94		Pig metacarpal, unfused, with central medio-lateral perforation of irregular shape. Small pit 3 mm below perforation on one surface. Smooth, with slight polish. L: 54 mm. F73 B42 *c* 1060/70–1080/90 Structure 24: ?beam-slot F465 (AMV)
95		Fragment: pig metatarsal with anterior-posterior perforation of irregular shape. Surface rough. L: 63 mm. F74 B153 *c* 1060/70–1100 Pit F710 (AWL)
96		Pig metatarsal with central anterior-posterior perforation, a little irregular in shape. Anterior and posterior surfaces smooth, with slight polish, and bevelled lip to perforation. L: 56 mm. F73 B33 *c* 1080/90–1100 Structure 30: floor (ACV)

DICE: BONE

Cat No	*Fig*	*Description and context*
97	10	Cube; ring-and-dot markings only partially visible. 10 × 9 × 9 mm. F73 B31 *c* 1120–1140 Levelling over structure 33 (AED)
98	10	Fragment; ?rectangular. Ring-and-dot markings; smooth and polished. 18 × 15 × ?15 mm. F73 B43 *c* 1100–1120 Levelling over structure 27/28 and area of road F749 (AEW)

GAMING PIECES

Ivory

Cat No	*Fig*	*Description and context*
99	11	Plano-convex; 2 concentric zones of ring-and -dot on upper face. D (max): 20 mm. Th: 6 mm. F73 B46 *c* 1140–1200 Levelling to north of structure 42/43 (AMD)

Antler (red deer)

Cat No	*Fig*	*Description and context*
100	11	Unfinished; roughly shaped disc with central perforation. Saw-marks on sides and one surface. D (max): 53 mm. Th: 7 mm. F74 B36 *c* 900–1060/70 Pit F689 (AYB)

Ceramic disc

Cat No	*Fig*	*Description and context*
101	12	Body sherd, Roman grey ware, roughly chipped. D: 28 mm. Th: 8 mm. F76 P24 9th C Destruction of Roman building (BCX)
102		Fragment; body sherd, Roman grey ware; edges ground smooth. D: 32 mm. Th: 8 mm. F76 P37 Late 9th C Levelling over Roman building (BKK)
103		Body sherd, Roman amphora (?S. Spanish); edges ground smooth. D: 64 mm. Th: 16 mm. F76 P17 Late 9th C Levelling over Roman building (BJL)
104	12	Fragment; base sherd, Roman grey ware; edges ground smooth. D: 61 mm. Th: 12 mm. F76 P29 Late 9th C Robber trench F45 of Roman building (BPZ)
105		Roman tile, roughly chipped. D: 46 mm. Th: 15 mm. F76 P30 Late 9th C Levelling: central area (BDQ)
106		Body sherd, Roman grey ware; roughly chipped. D: 48 mm. Th: 14 mm. F76 P47 Late 9th C Levelling: eastern end (BXN)
107		Fragment; body sherd, Roman grey ware; edges ground smooth. D: ?50 mm. Th: 8 mm. F76 P74 Late 9th C Levelling: eastern end (BXN)
108		Body sherd, Roman black-burnished ware; roughly chipped. D: 50 mm. Th: 6 mm. F76 P48 Late 9th C Levelling: eastern end (CAI)
109	12	Roman tile, roughly chipped. D: 57 mm. Th: 19 mm. F76 P66 Late 9th C Levelling: eastern end (CAI)
110		Roman tile, roughly chipped. D: 54 mm. Th: 20 mm. F76 P51 *c* 870/80–900 Road surface F747 (BOU)
111		Fragment; body sherd, Roman grey ware; roughly chipped. D: ?34 mm. Th: 8 mm. F75 P500 *c* 1000/10–1040 Assoc structure 17 (E10)
112		Body sherd, Roman grey ware; roughly chipped. D: 36 mm. Th: 10 mm. F74 P470 *c* 900–1060/70 Robber trench F384 (ASO)
113		Body sherd, Roman mortarium (ironstone gritting: ?Lower Nene Valley *c* 3rd-4th C); roughly chipped. D: 40 mm. Th: 13 mm. F74 P323 *c* 900–1060/70 Pit F693 (AVV)
114		Base sherd, Roman grey ware; roughly chipped. D: 64 mm. Th: 10 mm. F75 P471 *c* 1000/10–1080/90 Assoc structures 17, 20, & 26 (E13)

Cat No	*Fig*	*Description and context*
115		Fragment; body sherd, Saxon sandy ware; roughly chipped. D: ?60 mm. Th: 7 mm. F74 P283 *c* 1060/70–1080/90 Levelling over structure 20 (AOV)
116	12	Base sherd; hand-made, medium-fine Saxon shelly ware, roughly chipped. D: 40 mm. Th: 9 mm. F73 P7 *c* 1120–1140 Structure 37, floor (MU)
117		Fragment; body sherd, Roman grey ware; edges ground smooth. D: ?30 mm. Th: 11 mm. F73 P11 *c* 1140–1200 Levelling dump north of structure 42/43 (AGN)
		Limestone disc
118		Edges partially ground smooth; surface cracking from heat. D: 48 mm. Th: 12 mm. F76 St30 Late 9th C Levelling: central area (BNB)
		Micaceous sandstone disc
119		Roughly chipped. D: 53 mm. Th: 13 mm. F76 St31 7th–9th C Robber trench/gully assoc with destruction of Roman building (BPW)
120	12	Of irregular shape but edges ground smooth. D: 34 mm. Th: 14 mm. F76 St10 7th–9th C Pit F745 assoc with destruction of Roman building (BCV)
121	12	Edges ground smooth. D: 73 mm. Th: 21 mm. F76 St 7 9th C Levelling over Roman building (BFI)
122	12	Roughly chipped. D: 45 mm. Th: 17 mm. F76 St52 Late 9th C Levelling: eastern end (CAH)
123		Edges partially ground smooth. D: 62 mm. Th: 19 mm. F76 St37 *c* 870/80–900 Structure 2, posthole F163 (BOE)
124		Fragment; edges ground smooth. D: ?50 mm. Th: 13 mm. F75 M123 *c* 1000/10–1080/90 Assoc structures 17, 20, & 26 (F33)
125		Of irregular shape but edges ground smooth. D: 41 mm. Th: 15 mm. F74 M29 *c* 1060/70–1080/90 Levelling north of structure 21 (AQQ)
		MUSICAL INSTRUMENTS: BONE
126	13	Flute; (?unfinished) fragment (swan ulna). Fractured across blow-hole and below first finger-hole. Both perforations made through anterior surface; toolmarks on bevelled lip of blow-hole and around roughly chipped finger-hole. Slight polish. L: 175 mm. D: 12 mm. F75 B76 *c* 930/40–970 Assoc structure 9 and earlier activity (F70)
127	14	Flute, fragment. Small sliver from shaft of goose bone, fractured across each of 2 finger-holes. Smooth, with slight polish. L: 27 mm. D: ?8 mm. F75 B156 *c* 1140–1160 Pit F733 (ATK)
128	14	Flute/pipe mouthpiece, fragment. Shaft of sheep tibia, crudely ornamented with random incised dots and oblique lines. Single perforation (blow-hole) with bevelled lip abuts double-collared terminal. Upper end longitudinally split; lower end fractured. Smooth and polished. L: 63 mm. D: 15 mm. F75 B44 *c* 870/80–1060/70 Levelling dump assoc with pitting at western end (E6)
		SKATES: BONE (cattle metacarpal)
129	15	Anterior surface roughly cut; distal end (unfused) broken. Slight oblique trimming at proximal end. L: 151 mm. F76 B87 *c* 900–930/40 Levelling: central area (BDG)
130	15	Slight trimming and smoothing of anterior surface; distal condyles obliquely trimmed to form upswept toe. Proximal end trimmed to sub-rectangular shape, with small shallow perforation in articular facet. L: 180 mm. F75 B123 *c* 900–970 Assoc structures 8 & 11 (G106)
131	15	Anterior surface roughly worked; distal condyles obliquely trimmed to form upswept toe. Proximal end broken. L: 178 mm. F75 B122 *c* 930/40–970 Assoc structures 10, 11, & 12 (F98)
		MOUNTS: BONE
132	16	Fragment; flat strip (animal scapula), ornamented with double ring-and-dot. 2 rivet holes interrupt ornament; both ends fractured. L: 23 mm. W: 14 mm. Th: 1·5 mm. F75 B56 *c* 870/80–1060/70 Levelling dump assoc with pitting, western end (H6)
133	16	Flat strip (cattle/pig rib), one end obliquely cut; ornamented with double ring-and-dot. Fractured across rivet hole at each end, and both corners of longest (polished) edge broken off. L: 84 mm. W: 16 mm. Th: 2 mm. F74 B6 *c* 1080/90–1100 Levelling over structure 26 (ATV)
134	16	Fragment: (cattle/pig rib) plano-convex strip with crudely applied ring-and-dot ornament. Central dots perforate bone; one rivet hole remaining. L: 48 mm. W: 15 mm. Th: 2 mm. F74 B7 *c* 1080/90–1100 Structure 27/28: postholes F564 & 565 (ANN)
135	16	Fragment; terminal of flat strip (animal rib), ornamented with triple ring-and-dot. L: 17 mm. W: 8 mm. Th: 1·5 mm. F73 B20 *c* 1160–1180 Levelling north of structure 46 (ZT)
136	16	Fragment; terminal of flat strip (sheep/pig rib) ornamented with triple ring-and-dot. L: 40 mm. W: 13 mm. Th: 1·5 mm. F73 B32 *c* 1140–1200 Pit F735 (IH)
137	16	Fragment; flat strip fractured across triple ring-and-dot motif. L: 25 mm. W: 7 mm. Th: 2 mm. F73 B11 Late 12th C Levelling dump over latest timber buildings (ND)
138	16	?Mount. Fragment of short, thick strip with obliquely cut ends. Fractured along second of 2 deep longitudinal grooves. L: 29 mm. W: 7 mm. Th: 4 mm. F76 B58 *c* 870/80–900 Pit F658 (BNK)

Cat No	*Fig*	*Description and context*
		SNECK: BONE
139	17	Thick, plano-convex bone strip with rounded terminals and off-centre perforation. Zoomorphic ornament incised on upper surface; circular wear-marks around perforation on underside. Fractured across perforation; one fragment stained green. Smooth and polished. L: 118 mm. W: 18 mm. F75 B46 (i) *c* 970–1000/10 Assoc structure 13 (E29) (ii) *c* 970–1060/70 Assoc structures 16, 19, & 22 (B99)
		HANDLES: BONE
140	18	?Unfinished. Hollow, tapering, of rectangular section. Both ends trimmed, but broken. One surface ornamented with zone of ring-and-dot at terminal L: 95 mm. F76 B93 Late 9th C Levelling: central area (BDM)
141	18	Broken; hollow, oval-sectioned fragment of sheep metatarsal with double-collared moulding at each end. 2 zones of deeply incised ornament separated by zig-zag between parallel transverse lines. Split, with fragment broken away from one side, but smooth and polished. L: 58 mm. F75 B103 *c* 900–1000/10 Assoc structures 6, 10, & 14/15 (J54)
142	18	Broken; hollow fragment of cattle metatarsal. Two-thirds of length ornamented with alternate grooves and mouldings; remaining third with panel of alternating incised obliques, surmounted by triple collar. This terminal blackened by heat; fragment of shaft broken away. Smooth and polished. L: 75 mm. F73 B34 *c* 1100–1120 Levelling over structure 30 (ACU)
143	18	Fragment; hollow, tapering rectangular section. Ornamented with series of roughly incised shallow transverse grooves. L: 55 mm. F76 B25 Unstratified
		SPATULAE: BONE
144	19	Fragment, spatulate terminal broken; handle terminal sawn across. L: 118 mm. F75 B59 *c* 970–1040 Assoc structures 14/15 & 18 (H15)
145	19	Natural ridges at spatulate terminal trimmed and smoothed. Shaft trimmed; handle terminal sawn across and smoothed. Slight polish. L: 141 mm. F73 B50 *c* 1160–1180 Levelling north of structure 46 (XF)
		VESSEL SHERDS: SOAPSTONE
146		?Rim sherd; small, abraded. Th: 15 mm. F75 M158 *c* 870/80–1060/70 Levelling dump assoc with pitting at western end (E6)
147		Adjoining body sherds with triple-grooved ornamental band. Carbon deposit on external surface. Th: 8 mm. F75 M159 (i) Late 9th C Levelling: eastern end (BXN) (ii) *c* 900–930/40 Levelling: west of structure 6 (J69)
148		Body sherd. Th: 7 mm. F73 M191 *c* 1120–1140 Pit F717 (AFD)
149		Body sherd. Carbon deposit on external surface. Th: 12–14 mm. F74 M156 *c* 1140–1160 Pit F732 (AKF)

Cat No	*Fig*	*Description and context*
		ROTARY QUERNS
		Mayen Lava
150	20	Fragment; upper stone. Angled handle socket through upper surface and side. Series of radial grooves on grinding surface and edge. D: *c* 460 mm. Th: 67 mm. F76 St28 *c* 900–930/40 Levelling over Roman building (BCU)
151	20	Fragment; upper stone with collared central perforation, of D: 80 mm. Th: 39 mm. F76 St3 *c* 930/40–970 Road surface F748 (BEA)
152		Fragment; series of radial grooves on worn grinding surface and outer edge. D: *c* 400 mm. Th: 45 mm. F75 St14 Late 9th C–*c* 1060/70 Levelling dump assoc with pitting; western end (F5)
		Millstone Grit
153		Fragment; upper stone. Series of radial grooves on worn grinding surface. D: *c* 440 mm. Th: 79 mm. F74 St 5 *c* 1000/1010–1040 Structure 18: floor (AZK)
154		Fragment; upper stone. Series of shallow pecked concentric grooves on worn grinding surface. D: *c* 380 mm. Th: 63 mm. F74 St3 *c* 1060/70–1080/90 Levelling over structure 20 (AON)
		?Spilsby Grit
155		Fragment; upper stone. Series of shallow radial grooves on worn grinding surface. Th: 55 mm. F74 St11 *c* 1040–1060/70 Road surface F749 (AZL)
		SPINDLE-WHORLS
		Bone
		Perforated cattle femur heads, fused or fusing *(U)* = unfused
156		(U) D: 37 mm. H: 17 mm. Wt: 9·4 g. F76 B84 Late 9th C Levelling, east end (BHV)
157		D: 39 mm. H: 16 mm. Wt: 7·9 g. F75 B84 *c* 930/40–970 Road surface F748 (F97)
158		D: 42 mm. H: 21 mm. Wt: 12·2 g. F75 B116 *c* 930/40–1000/1010 Assoc structures 10 & 14/15 (J76)
159		D: 44 mm. H: 27 mm. Wt: 23 g. F75 B67 *c* 930/40–1040 Assoc structures 9, 13, & 17 (E70)
160	21	Square perforation on upper surface. D: 42 mm. H: 26 mm. Wt: 22·4 g. F74 B23 *c* 1000/1010–1040 Levelling over structure 13 (AUU)
161	21	Unfinished; with hole bored from underside, small pit on upper surface. D: 47 mm. H: 28 mm. Wt: 27·4 g. F75 B132 *c* 870/80–1060/70 Levelling dump assoc with pitting: western end (E8)
162		D: 38 mm. H: 21 mm. Wt: 13 g. F74 B4 *c* 900–1060/70 Pits F696, F697, F698 (ASE)

Cat No	*Fig*	*Description and context*
163		(U) Lip of perforation bevelled flat on upper surface. D: 41 mm. H: 19 mm. Wt: 14·2 g. F75 B72 *c* 1000/1010–1060/70 Assoc structures 18 & 21 (E36)
164		(U) D: 40 mm. H: 19 mm. Wt: 11·6 g. F76 B30 *c* 1040–1060/70 Pit F675 (BDA)
165		Square perforation on both surfaces. D: 36 mm. H: 19 mm. Wt: 9·5 g. F74 B11 *c* 1060/70–1080/90 Levelling dump assoc with pitting: western end (AJP)
166		Sub-triangular perforation on upper surface. D: 44 mm. H: 28 mm. Wt: 16·1 g. F74 B31 *c* 1060/70–1080/90 Levelling, west end, in preparation for structure 24 (AVT)
167		Fragment. (Wt: 9·5 g.) F74 B25 *c* 1060/70–1080/90 Levelling over structure 20 (AOV)
168		Slight bevelling of lip of perforation on upper surface. D: 43 mm. H: 21 mm. Wt: 14·2 g. F74 B37 *c* 1060/70–1080/90 Levelling over structure 20 (ARJ)
169		Broken: surface chipped and cracked. D: 44 mm. H: 21 mm. (Wt: 12·5 g.) F74 B30 *c* 1060/70–1080/90 Rubble consolidation F652 for structure 26 (ARS)
170		D: 39 mm. H: 23 mm. Wt: 15·9 g. F74 B18 *c* 1080/90–1100 Levelling over structure 24 (ASX)
171		Fragment. (Wt: 2·7 g.) F73 B27 *c* 1080/90–1160 Levelling dump north of structures 26 to 42/43 (YZ)
172		D: 42 mm. H: 20 mm. Wt: 14·4 g. F73 B26 *c* 1160–80 Levelling north of structure 46 (XU)
173		D: 41 mm. H: 27 mm. Wt: 18 g. F75 B113 Unstratified
174		D: 42 mm. H: 19 mm. Wt: 15·3 g. F75 B114 Unstratified
175		D: 40 mm. H: 20 mm. Wt: 13·8 g. F76 B2 Unstratified
		Ceramic: perforated disc
176		Fragment; body sherd of Roman grey ware with edges ground smooth. D: 46 mm. H: 8 mm. (Wt: 11·4 g.) F75 P243 *c* 900–930/40 Levelling west of structure 6 (J51)
177		Body sherd of Roman fine ware with uneven edges ground smooth. D: 40 mm. H: 8 mm. Wt: 14 g. F76 P9 *c* 900–930/40 Levelling over structure 2 (BEU)
178		Fragment; sherd of Roman tile with edges ground smooth. D: 42 mm. H: 13 mm. (Wt: 12·2 g.) F76 P23 *c* 900–930/40 Levelling over structure 2 (BEU)
179		Fragment; base sherd of fine (local) Saxon shelly ware; edges untrimmed. D: 51 mm. H: 10 mm (max). (Wt: 19 g.) F74 P34 *c* 900–1060/70 Pit F693 (AVV)
180		Fragment: base sherd of Saxon shelly ware. D: *c* 50 mm. H: 7 mm. (Wt: 6·2 g.) F75 P507 *c* 900–1060/70 Levelling dump assoc with pitting: west end (F49)
181	21	Body sherd of fine (local) Saxon shelly ware, crudely trimmed. D: 44 mm. H: 7 mm. Wt: 13·1 g. F74 P322 *c* 1080/90–1100 Structure 27/28: ?floor (AKY)
182	21	Base sherd of (local) Saxon sandy ware, Type I; edges ground smooth. D: 40 mm. H: 10 mm. Wt: 19·7 g. F75 P510 Unstratified
		Fired clay
183		Fragment; perforated disc of coarse red clay. D: *c* 43 mm. H: 15 mm. (Wt: 15·8 g.) F75 P319 *c* 870/80–1060/70 Levelling dump assoc with pitting: west end (E8)
184	21	Fragment; conical; fine red clay. D: 32 mm. H: 22 mm. (Wt. 10·3 g.) F74 P321 *c* 1000/10–1040 Structure 18, floor (AZK)
		Chalk
185	21	Fragment; cylindrical disc. D: 32 mm. H: 18 mm. (Wt: 12·9 g.) F76 St42 870/80–900 Structure 5: destruction (BZF)
		Limestone
		Cylindrical
186	21	Tall, slightly tapering. D: 34 mm. H: 26 mm. Wt: 42·1 g. F75 M100 *c* 930/40–1040 Assoc structures 9, 13, & 17 (E71)
		Disc
187	21	Fragment; crudely incised irregular ornament around faceted sides. D: 31 mm. H: 16 mm. (Wt. 14·5 g.) F74 M30 *c* 1060/70–1080/90 Levelling over structure 20 (AOO)
		Sub-conical
188	21	Crudely incised ornament: 8-pointed star on upper surface and base. Sides ornamented with upper zone of alternating horizontals, verticals and obliques, lower zone of zig-zag. D: 34 mm. H: 20 mm. Wt: 31·2 g. F76 St20 *c* 930/40–970 Levelling over structure 7 (BML)
		Truncated conical
189		Fragment. D: *c* 30 mm. H: 15 mm. (Wt: 6·3 g.) F75 M84 *c* 1000/10–1040 Assoc structure 18 (G16)
190	22	?Broken: base rough. D: 28 mm. H: 7 mm. Wt: 6·4 g. F75 M87 *c* 930/40–1060/70 Assoc structures 11, 12, 16, 19, & 22 (B104)
191		Fragment. D: *c* 30 mm. H: 8 mm. (Wt: 3·3 g.) F75 M97 *c* 970–1060/70 Assoc structures 16, 19, & 22 (B99)

Cat No	*Fig*	*Description and context*
192	22	?Broken: base rough. Crudely incised random ornament around sides. D: 32 mm. H: 16 mm. Wt: 14·6 g. F75 St17 *c* 1000/10–1080/90 Assoc structures 17, 20, & 26 (E13)
		Hemispherical
193		Fragment. D: *c* 34 mm. H: 19 mm. (Wt: 11·7 g.) F75 M138 *c* 930/40–1060/70 Assoc structures 9, 13, 17 & 20 (G53)
194	22	Fragment. Sides and base ornamented with alternate plain and decorative panels, latter consisting of opposed obliques. Similar arrangement on base, but ornamental panels of ladder pattern. D: *c* 30 mm. H: 23 mm. (Wt: 10·8 g.) F75 M73 *c* 970–1060/70 Assoc structures 14/15, 18, & 21 (B87)
195	22	Alternating plain and incised ladder-pattern panels around sides: radial lines incised on base. D: 31 mm. H: 19 mm. Wt: 20·7 g. F73 M154 *c* 1040–1060/70 Structure 21: floor (AEP)
196	22	Alternating plain and incised ladder-pattern panels around sides. Slight traces of burning. D: 28 mm. H: 18 mm. Wt: 17·2 g. F74 M36 *c* 1060/70–1100 Pit F709 (AWZ)
197		Fragment. D: *c* 40 mm. H: 18 mm. (Wt: 10·4 g.) F74 M1 *c* 1080/90–1100 Levelling over structure 26 (AI0)
		Globular
198	22	Crudely incised chain-loop ornament around sides. D: 31 mm. H: 20 mm. Wt: 19·1 g. F74 M35 *c* 1000/10–1040 Structure 18: destruction (AZE)
199	22	Surface painted black, with red band between double incised zig-zag line around sides. D: 31 mm. H: 19 mm. Wt: 20·2 g. F75 M95 *c* 970–1060/70 Assoc structures 13, 17, & 20 (F30)
200	22	Crudely incised crosses around sides; faint traces of red paint. D: 32 mm. H: 22 mm. Wt: 24·4 g. F74 M16 *c* 1140–1160 Pit F733 (ATK)
		Bi-conical
201		Traces of red paint. D: 33 mm. H: 21 mm. Wt: 25·9 g. F74 St23 *c* 1060/70–1100 Pit F709 (AWZ)
202		Fragment. Shallow, irregular grooves around widest part. D: 30 mm. H: 21 mm. (Wt: 8·9 g.) F73 M101 *c* 1160–1180 Levelling north of structure 46 (XF)
203	22	Shallow turned grooves. D: 34 mm. H: 20 mm. Wt: 26·8 g. F74 M26 *c* 1160–1180 Pit F737 (ALQ)
204		Surface irregularities. D: 33 mm. H: 21 mm. Wt: 26·4 g. F74 M2 *c* 1140–1200 Pit F724 (APX)

Cat No	*Fig*	*Description and context*
205	22	Surface ornamented with shallow radial grooves connecting perforations. Traces of burning. D: 34 mm. H: 22 mm. Wt: 26·2 g. F73 M71 *c* 1180–1200 Backfill hearth F32; post-dates destruction structure 46 (FQ)
206		Fragment. Shallow turned grooves faintly visible. D: 34 mm. H: 21 mm. Wt: 11·9 g. F73 M80 Late 12th C Levelling north of structure 51 (XB)
		Annular
207	22	Ornamented with shallow turned grooves. D: 27 mm. H: 9 mm. Wt: 9 g. F73 M116 Late 12th C Levelling over road F750 (ABM)
		LOOMWEIGHT
208	23	Fragment; coarse felspathic grit. Intermediate form, of irregular cross-section (produced by wear?) D: *c* 80 mm. H: 50 mm. F75 M99 *c* 1000/10–1060/70 Assoc structures 17 & 20 (F53)
		PINBEATERS
		Single-pointed, bone
209	24	Of oval section with point worn at angle to shaft. Faces flattened, upper end worn to tapered, almost spatulate shape. Very smooth, highly polished. L: 105 mm. F75 B75 *c* 930/40–1000/10 Assoc structures 9 & 13 (F72)
210	24	Of oval section, fractured in mid-shaft; upper end broken and trimmed smooth. Faces flattened, shaft fairly smooth and polished. L: 138 mm. F75 B88 *c* 970–1000/10 Assoc structure 13 (H12)
211	24	Fragment; of oval section tapering to blunt and broken point. One face flattened; shaft extremely smooth, highly polished. L: 82 mm. F75 B150 *c* late 9th C–*c* 1060/70 Levelling dump assoc with pitting, west end (F5)
212	24	Fragment; of oval section. Damaged upper end with concave facet on both faces. Smooth and polished. L: 58 mm. F73 B49 *c* 1080/90–1100 Levelling over structure 23 (IG)
		?Weaving tool/pinbeater: single-pointed, bone
213	24	Of rectangular section with rounded edges; blunt point worn at angle to shaft. Faces flattened at upper end; shaft extremely smooth, highly polished. L: 103 mm. F75 B105 *c* 930/40–970 Assoc structures 10 & 14/15 (J56)
		NEEDLES: BONE
214	25	Fragment; small circular eye in tapering, pointed head. Circular-sectioned shank flattened around eye; point broken off. Smooth and polished. L: 80 mm. F76 B83 *c* 900–930/40 Levelling over structure 3 (CCB)
215	25	Fragment; single circular eye in flattened head. Oval-sectioned shank smooth and polished. L: 37 mm. F75 B61 *c* 970–1060/70 Assoc structures 13, 17 & 20 (F29)

Cat No	*Fig*	*Description and context*
216	25	(Pig fibula) Rounded head with large, circular eye. Trimming of oval-sectioned shank visible above blunt point; unfinished? L: 125 mm. F73 B22 *c* 1140–1160 Levelling north of structure 42/43 (ACE)

BODKIN: BONE

Cat No	*Fig*	*Description and context*
217	25	Cattle ulna trimmed to blunt point. Small circular eye. Shank rough; internal tissue of bone partially exposed. L: 163 mm. F72 B2 *c* 1120–1140 Structure 40: floor (BO)

TALLOW-HOLDERS: BONE

Cat No	*Fig*	*Description and context*
218	26	Cattle metatarsal with longitudinal perforation through proximal end to natural cavity. Shaft obliquely sawn and crudely trimmed. Slight polish. L: 67 mm. F76 B89 *c* 900–930/40 Levelling over structure 2 (BEU)
219		Unfinished. Cattle metatarsal with longitudinal perforation through proximal end to natural cavity. Shaft obliquely chopped. L: 55 mm. F76 B94 *c* 930/40–970 Road surface F748 (BEA)
220		Cattle metatarsal with longitudinal perforation through proximal end to natural cavity. Shaft obliquely chopped and crudely trimmed. Base of holder trimmed and smoothed. Slight polish. L: 58 mm. F75 B60 *c* 970–1060/70 Assoc structures 13, 17, & 20 (F30)

HONES

Norwegian Rag

Cat No	*Fig*	*Description and context*
221	27	*Fragment; both ends broken. Rectangular-sectioned, both broad faces well worn. Small pit drilled at top and bottom of one broad face. L: 112 mm. W: 33 mm. Th: 9 mm. F76 St34 Late 9th C Levelling over area of Roman building (BRT)
222		*Fragment, both ends broken. Rectangular-sectioned, both broad faces well worn. L: 27 mm. W: 21 mm. Th: 15 mm. F76 St21 *c* 900–930/40 Levelling over structures 3 & 5 (BEX)
223		*Sliver of triangular section. L: 71 mm. W: 23 mm. Th: 10 mm. F75 M103 *c* 930/40–970 Assoc structure 9 and earlier dumping (E48)
224		Sliver of triangular section. L: 26 mm. W: 11 mm. Th: 6 mm. F75 M128 *c* 930/40–970 Assoc structure 9 and earlier dumping (G48)
225	27	Fragment; one end and one side fractured. Rectangular-sectioned; all faces well worn. L: 68 mm. W: 18 mm. Th: 8 mm. F75 M137 *c* 930/40–1000/10 Assoc structures 10 & 14/15 (F94)
226		*Fragment, both ends broken. Rectangular-sectioned, slight wear on all faces. L: 57 mm. W: 25 mm. Th: 14 mm. F75 M131 *c* 900–1040 Assoc structures 7, 10, 14/15 & 18 (F81)
227		*Sliver of triangular section. L: 55 mm. W: 16 mm. Th: 5 mm. F75 M107 *c* 870/80–1060/70 Levelling dump assoc with pitting, west end (D46)
228	27	*Rectangular-sectioned; broad faces and rounded ends extremely worn. L: 84 mm. W: 22 mm. Th: 12 mm. F75 M69 *c* 900–1060/70 Levelling dump assoc with pitting, west end (AVI)
229	27	*Rectangular-sectioned; broad faces and rounded ends extremely worn. L: 80 mm. W: 22 mm. Th: 11 mm. F74 M25 *c* 1040–1060/70 Levelling over structure 18 (AWR)
230	27	*Fragment, tapering; both ends broken. Rectangular-sectioned, slight wear on broad faces. Small pit drilled on one broad face near end. L: 61 mm. W: 20 mm. Th: 8 mm. F74 M60 *c* 1040–1060/70 Levelling over structure 18 (AWR)
231		* ?schist. Sliver of triangular section. L: 40 mm. W: 22 mm. Th: 16 mm. F74 M66 *c* 1040–1060/70 Levelling over structure 18 (AWR)
232	27	*Fragment, both ends broken. Rectangular-sectioned, one broad face worn. L: 41 mm. W: 39 mm. Th: 18 mm. F74 M46 *c* 1040–1060/70 Levelling to west of structure 21 (ALK)
233	27	*Fragment, rectangular-sectioned. Horizontally grooved upper end broken, central area of both broad faces well worn. L: 87 mm. W: 13 mm. Th: 10 mm. F75 M139 *c* 1000/10–1080/90 Assoc structures 17, 20, & 26 (E13)
234		*Large sliver of triangular section. L: 101 mm. W: 34 mm. Th: 14 mm. F75 M72 *c* 1000/10–1080/90 Assoc structures 17, 20, & 26 (E13)
235	27	*Fragment, rectangular-sectioned; one end broken. Well worn on both broad faces and remaining rounded end. L: 89 mm. W: 30 mm. Th: 9 mm. F74 M14 *c* 1060/70–1080/90 Levelling over structure 21 (AWG)
236	29	*Fragment, oval-sectioned. Upper end perforated, lower end broken. Slight wear on broad faces. L: 29 mm. W: 13 mm. Th: 6 mm. F74 M62 *c* 1060/70–1100 Pit F709 (AWZ)
237		*Sliver of rectangular section. L: 76 mm. W: 15 mm. Th: 6 mm. F74 M58 *c* 1060/70–1100 Pit F709 (AWZ)
238		*Fragment, rectangular-sectioned; one end broken. Slight wear on broad faces and remaining rounded end. L: 63 mm. W: 24 mm. Th: 18 mm. F74 M10 *c* 1080/90–1100 Levelling over structure 26 (ATV)
239		* ?Norwegian Rag—atypical. Sliver of triangular section. L: 99 mm. W: 30 mm. Th: 13 mm. F73 M106 *c* 1080/90–1100 Levelling over structure 23 (AGG)
240		*Fragment, rectangular-sectioned; both ends broken. L: 51 mm. W: 28 mm. Th: 10 mm. F73 M194 *c* 1120–1140 Levelling over structure 35 (ZN)
241	27	*Fragment, both ends broken. All faces well worn, producing lozenge-shaped section. L: 68 mm. W: 21 mm. Th: 17 mm. F73 M156 *c* 1120–1140 Levelling over structure 35 (ZL)

Cat No	Fig	Description and context
242	27	Fragment, rectangular-sectioned; both ends broken. Extremely worn on broad faces. L: 70 mm. W: 30 mm. Th: 21 mm. F73 M115 *c* 1080/90–1160 Levelling dump north of structures 26 to 46 (YZ)
243		*Fragment, rectangular-sectioned; both ends broken. Slight wear on broad faces. L: 25 mm. W: 20 mm. Th: 9 mm. F73 M195 *c* 1080/90–1160 Levelling dump north of structures 26 to 46 (YZ)
244	27	*Fragment, one end broken. Rectangular-sectioned, with shallow groove on one broad face. All faces well worn. L: 70 mm. W: 20 mm. Th: 12 mm. F74 M63 *c* 1140–1160 Pit F729 (AEJ)
245	27	*Fragment, both ends broken. Rectangular-sectioned, with horizontal groove around upper end. All faces well worn. L: 94 mm. W: 21 mm. Th: 16 mm. F74 M13 *c* 1140–1160 Pit F731 (AKE)
246		*Fragment, longitudinally split, both ends broken. L: 124 mm. W: 29 mm. Th: 27 mm. F73 M119 *c* 1140–1160 Pit F731 (ABN)
247		*Fragment, rectangular-sectioned; both ends broken. One broad face worn. L: 30 mm. W: 18 mm. Th: 14 mm. F73 M110 *c* 1140–1160 Road surface F750 (ABT)
248		*Fragment, sub-rectangular section. Both ends broken. L: 140 mm. W: 21 mm. Th: 20 mm. F73 M120 *c* 1140–1200 Levelling dump north of structure 36 (AGM)
249		Fragment, both ends broken. All faces worn to produce lozenge-shaped section. L: 150 mm. W: 42 mm. Th: 23 mm. F73 M64 Late 12th C Levelling dump over latest timber structures (ND)
250		Fragment, rectangular-sectioned; both ends broken. L: 32 mm. W: 26 mm. Th: 12 mm. F72 M6 Late 12th–mid 13th C Levelling dump over latest timber structures (AS)
251		*Fragment, rectangular-sectioned; both ends broken. Broad faces worn. L: 104 mm. W: 26 mm. Th: 14 mm. F75 M91 Unstratified
		Phyllite (BP = 'Blue phyllite')
252		BP. Sliver of irregular semi-circular section. L: 34 mm. W: 11 mm. Th: 4 mm. F76 St 6 *c* 900–930/40 Levelling over structure 2 (BEU)
253	28	*BP. Almost complete hone with diagonally opposite corners broken; fractured across perforation at upper end. Rectangular-sectioned, broad faces well worn. L: 58 mm. W: 23 mm. Th: 14 mm. F76 St26 *c* 930/40–970 Road surface F748 (BOH)
254	28	*Fragment, fractured below perforated upper end. Worn to irregular hexagonal section. L: 31 mm. W: 24 mm. Th: 10 mm. F76 St25 *c* 930/40–970 Levelling over structure 8 (BOL)
255		*BP. Fragment, rectangular-sectioned. One end broken, remaining end worn. L: 24 mm. W: 12 mm. Th: 7 mm. F75 M119 *c* 930/40–970 Assoc structure 11 (E104)
256		BP. Sliver, longitudinally fractured across unfinished perforation. L: 30 mm. W: 3 mm. Th: 2 mm. F75 M150 *c* 900–1000/10 Assoc structures 7, 10 & 14/15 (G94)
257		*Fragment, longitudinally split, both ends broken. Slight wear on narrow face. L: 76 mm. W: 11 mm. Th: 8 mm. F75 M153 *c* 930/40–1000/10 Assoc structures 10 & 14/15 (J76)
258		*BP. Fragment, both ends broken. Rectangular-sectioned with small perforation. L: 30 mm. W: 11 mm. Th: 3 mm. F75 M93 *c* 870/80–1060/70 Levelling dump assoc with pitting, western end (G6)
259	28	*Almost complete; rectangular-sectioned. Upper end fractured across central perforation; second hole drilled below and to one side, with small horizontal nicks across adjacent edges of hone. Broad faces and lower end worn. L: 63 mm. W: 20 mm. Th: 8 mm. F76 St8 *c* 900–1060/70 Pit F700 (BKN)
260		*BP. Fragment of triangular section; both ends broken; longitudinally split. L: 58 mm. W: 18 mm. Th: 8 mm. F75 M126 *c* 900–1060/70 Levelling dump, assoc with pitting, western end (F49)
261		*BP. Sliver of triangular section. Small pit (unfinished perforation) drilled at one end. L: 57 mm. W: 10 mm. Th: 6 mm. F75 M136 *c* 970–1060/70 Assoc structures 14/15, 18 & 21 (F55)
262		* ?BP. Fragment; one end broken, remaining end worn. Rectangular-sectioned, slight wear on broad faces. L: 61 mm. W: 22 mm. Th: 10 mm. F75 M127 *c* 970–1060/70 Assoc structures 13, 17, & 20 (E28)
263	28	*BP. Fragment, both ends broken. Of tapering, rectangular section; both broad faces well worn. Trace of horizontal notches on one broad face. L: 150 mm. W: 27 mm. Th: 13 mm. F75 M83 *c* 970–1060/70 Assoc structures 16, 19, & 22 (B99)
264	29	*BP. Rectangular-sectioned, with small drilled perforation through upper end. Lower end rounded; slight wear on broad faces. L: 46 mm. W: 10 mm. Th: 4 mm. F75 M120 *c* 1000/10–1080/90 Assoc structures 17, 20, & 26 (E13)
265	28	*BP. Fragment, notched upper end longitudinally split, lower end broken. Broad faces worn. L: 83 mm. W: 10 mm. Th: 9 mm. F75 M106 *c* 1000/10–1080/90 Assoc structures 17, 20, & 26 (E13)
266		*BP. Fragment, rectangular-sectioned; longitudinally split. Fractured across perforation. L: 19 mm. W: 14 mm. Th: 3 mm. F74 M31 *c* 1060/70–1080/90 Levelling over structure 20 (AON)
267		*BP. Fragment, both ends broken; sub-rectangular section. Broad faces well worn, upper end perforated. L: 66 mm. W: 17 mm. Th: 7 mm. F74 M41 *c* 1060/70–1080/90 Levelling, western end (AJP)

Cat No	Fig	Description and context
268		*BP. Triangular-sectioned fragment. L: 79 mm. W: 11 mm. Th: 10 mm. F74 M12 *c 1060*/70–1080/90 Levelling north of structure 21, over road surface F749 (AQQ)
269	28	*Fragment, rectangular-sectioned. Upper end perforated, lower end broken. Broad faces well worn to produce lozenge-shaped section. L: 59 mm. W: 13 mm. Th: 10 mm. F74 M11 *c* 1140–1160 Pit F733 (ATK)

Coal Measures Sandstone

Cat No	Fig	Description and context
270	30	*Fragment, rectangular-sectioned block, both ends broken. Shallow longitudinal groove on one broad face. This and one narrow face worn. L: 85 mm. W: 60 mm. Th: 25 mm. F76 St47 Late 9th C Levelling, eastern end (CAH)
271		*Fragment, one end broken. Rectangular-sectioned, tapering from wear on all faces. Longitudinal groove on one broad face. L: 52 mm. W: 22 mm. Th: 12 mm. F76 St24 *c* 870/80–900 Pit F659 (BNI)
272	30	*Fragment, both ends broken. Rectangular-sectioned, tapering from wear on all faces. L: 53 mm. W: 34 mm. Th: 21 mm. F76 St4 *c* 900–930/40 Levelling over area of Roman building (BFB)
273		*Fragment, of sub-rectangular section; both ends broken. One edge chipped, all faces well worn. L: 36 mm. W: 26 mm. Th: 17 mm. F76 St5 *c* 930/40–970 Road surface F748 (BEA)
274		*Fragment, rectangular-sectioned; both ends broken. All faces worn. L: 80 mm. W: 41 mm. Th: 21 mm. F75 M90 *c* 970–1040 Assoc structures 13 & 17 (D30)
275	30	*Fragment; tapering, lozenge-shaped block of irregular hexagonal section with diagonally opposite corners broken. L: 109 mm. W: 53 mm. Th: 16 mm. F74 M51 *c* 900–1060/70 Pit F693 (AVV)
276		*Fragment, block of sub-rectangular section; both ends broken. One broad, one narrow face worn. L: 139 mm. W: 58 mm. Th: 26 mm. F73 M176 *c* 1120–1140 Levelling over structure 35 (ABU)
277		*Fragment, rectangular-sectioned block, both ends broken. One broad face extremely worn. L: 79 mm. W: 83 mm. Th: 29 mm. F73 M109 *c* 1140–1160 Pit F729 (AEJ)
278	30	*Fragment, rectangular-sectioned; both ends broken. Two shallow grooves on one broad face; well worn. L: 97 mm. W: 37 mm. Th: 15 mm. F73 M88 *c* 1160–1180 Levelling north of structure 46 (XG)
279	29	*Fragment, rectangular section. Upper end broken, lower end tapering, rounded. Both broad faces well worn. L: 37 mm. W: 13 mm. Th: 4 mm. F73 M127 *c* 1160–1180 Levelling north of structure 46 (XU)

Kentish Rag

Cat No	Fig	Description and context
280		*Fragment, rectangular-sectioned; both ends broken. Slightly tapered from wear on all faces. L: 35 mm. W: 19 mm. Th: 16 mm. F76 St13 Late 9th C Levelling, central area (BDS)
281	30	*(coarse-grained variant) Fragment, rectangular-sectioned; both ends broken. Two shallow longitudinal grooves on one broad face; all faces worn. L: 148 mm. W: 33 mm. Th: 21 mm. F76 St58 Late 9th C Levelling, eastern end (BHV)
282	30	*Fragment, ovoid section; both ends broken. Tapering slightly from wear, L: 44 mm. W: 23 mm. Th: 19 mm. F76 St9 *c* 1060/70–1080/90 Structure 23, floor (BFG)

Other

Cat No	Fig	Description and context
283		*Quartz-bearing limestone. Rectangular-sectioned, both ends broken. Slight wear on broad faces. L: 27 mm. W: 18 mm. Th: 9 mm. F76 St64 *c* 870/80–900 Pit F656 (BFK)
284		*Limestone (?Purbeck Beds). Fragment, rectangular-sectioned block; both ends broken. All faces worn. L: 165 mm. W: 53 mm. Th: 50 mm. F76 St14 *c* 1000/10–1040 Levelling over structure 14/15 (BGZ)
285	29	Contact rock. Fragment, rectangular-sectioned. Upper end broken, lower end rounded. Slight wear on broad faces. L: 37 mm. W: 10 mm. Th: 6 mm. F73 M91 *c* 1160–1180 Levelling north of structure 46 (XG)
286		* Micaceous siltstone. Fragment, rectangular-sectioned; both ends broken. All faces worn. L: 51 mm. W: 31 mm. Th: 13 mm. F73 M70 Late 12th C Levelling over latest timber structures (ND)

BONE CLAMPS

Cat No	Fig	Description and context
287	31	Fragment; plano-convex strip with rounded terminal. Fractured across rivet hole. L: 72 mm. W: 22 mm. Th: 12 mm. F75 B51 *c* 1000/10–1040 Assoc structure 17 (D32)
288	31	Fragment; plano-convex strip, longitudinally fractured. L: 74 mm. F75 B92 *c* 900–1000/10 External dump to west of structures 6, 9, & 13 (H11)

SOCKETED BONE POINTS

Cat No	Fig	Description and context
289	32	Cattle right metatarsal cut and trimmed to point. Hole bored in proximal articular surface connects with medullary cavity. Point smooth and polished. L: 153 mm. F76 B90 *c* 870/80–900 Pit F658 (BNK)
290		Cattle right metatarsal cut and trimmed to point. Hole bored in proximal articular surface connects with medullary cavity. Point smooth, faintly polished; extreme tip broken. L: 123 mm. F76 B91 *c* 900–1060/70 Pit F700 (BLG)
291		Cattle right tibia cut and trimmed to point. Hole bored in distal articular surface connects with medullary cavity. Point smooth, faintly polished. L: 83 mm. F74 B154 *c* 1080/90–1100 Levelling over structure 26 (ATV)

Cat No	*Fig*	*Description and context*
		MISCELLANEOUS OBJECTS
		Bone
292	33	Peg-like object. One-third of shaft of square, tapering section; remaining two-thirds of circular section, ornamented with series of transverse grooves and mouldings. Small pit in corresponding end: lathe-turned? 2 longitudinal grooves on adjacent sides at right angles to one another. L: 49 mm. D: 11 mm. F73 B30 *c* 1060/70–1080/90 Rubble consolidation F654 for construction of structure 23 (AJR)
293	33	?Unfinished wedge or peg. Upper half of shaft of tapering rectangular section; lower half circular. Traces of filing. L: 58 mm. Th: 13 mm. D: 9 mm. F73 B16 *c* 1160–1180 Levelling north of structure 46 (ZS)
294	33	Ring; section of cattle metatarsal, both ends sawn. Turned exterior. D: (ext) 24 mm. Th: 8 mm. F75 B77 *c* 970–1040 Assoc structures 13 & 17 (G29)
295	33	Fragment; thin ring. Cut from scapula. D: (ext) *c* 18 mm. Th: 1 mm. F73 B40 *c* 1060/70–1080/90 Structure 25, floor (APB)
296	33	Fragment, rectangular-sectioned strip; split cattle rib. Both ends fractured across incised ring-and-dot; one motif bungled. Surface and sides smooth and polished. L: 22 mm. W: 15 mm. Th: 2 mm. F73 B37 *c* 1040–1060/70 Levelling over structure 18 (AEY)
297	33	Terminal of tapering, plano-convex strip with incised ornament on all surfaces. Burnt. L: 23 mm. W: 12 mm. Th: 6 mm. F74 B38 *c* 1040–1060/70 External surface, west of structure 21 (AOX)
298	33	Terminal; strip of tapering oval section. Fractured across perforation. L: 18 mm. W: 15 mm. Th: 5 mm. F73 B47 *c* 1060/70–1080/90 Structure 25, floor (AMP)
299	33	Fragment, longitudinally fractured and ends broken. One surface abraded and highly polished. L: 40 mm. F74 B161 *c* 1140–1160 Pit F732 (ATN)
300	33	Terminal of thin, perforated, oval-sectioned strip. Curved and fractured. L: 26 mm. W: 5 mm. Th: 2 mm. F76 B50 Late 9th C Levelling over area of Roman building (BJL)
301	34	Fragment of cylinder. ?Sheep femur shaft, both ends sawn across and smoothed; longitudinally fractured. Group of incised transverse lines at each end. L: 38 mm. D: (ext) *c* 15 mm. F74 B15 *c* 1060/70–1100 Pit F709 (AWZ)
302	34	Fragment cattle metacarpal, longitudinally split; incised ring-and-dot at one end. L: 46 mm. F75 B108 *c* 900–930/40 External levelling, west of structure 6 (J50)
303	34	Fragment ?cattle metatarsal, longitudinally split; irregular incised cross-hatching on surface. L: 37 mm. F74 B16 *c* 1060/70–1080/90 Levelling over structure 20 (AOY)
304	35	Fragment, crudely knife-trimmed to point. L: 37 mm. F74 B159 *c* 900–930/40 Levelling over area of Roman building (APN)
305		Fragment, crudely knife-trimmed to point. L: 34 mm. F74 B160 *c* 900–930/40 Levelling over area of Roman building (APN)
306	35	Fragment, pig fibula; lower shaft crudely trimmed. L: 86 mm. F75 B130 *c* 930/40–970 Road surface F748 (G97)
307	35	Unfinished pinbeater/awl? Length of bone, shaft roughly cut to point. Upper end cut across, one broad surface cut and filed. L: 130 mm. W: 11 mm. Th: 8 mm. F74 B29 *c* 1060/70–1100 Pit F710 (AWV)
308	35	Fragment, cattle rib with edges trimmed. Cut to sharp point at one end. L: 139 mm. Th: 5 mm. F75 B102 *c* 900–930/40 External levelling west of structure 6 (J31)
309	36	Fragment split rib, one end cut to rounded shape. Fractured near rivet hole. L: 42 mm. W: 15 mm. Th: 3 mm. F75 B147 *c* 900–1040 Assoc structures 6, 9, 13, & 17 (G51)
310	36	Fragment, rectangular plate; 2 adjacent edges sawn, one face filed smooth. L: 26 mm. W: 14 mm. Th. 3 mm. F75 B140 *c* 970–1040 Assoc structures 13 & 17 (G11)
311	36	Fragment plano-convex strip of split ?pig rib. L: 43 mm. W: 16 mm. Th: 3 mm. F75 B149 *c* 1000/10–1040 Assoc structure 18 (G54)
312	36	Fragment tapering plano-convex strip; split ?pig rib. L: 45 mm. W: 11 mm. Th: 3 mm. F75 B90 *c* 1000/10–1040 Assoc structure 17 (H28)
313	36	Fragment rectangular-sectioned strip, split rib. L: 30 mm. W: 14 mm. Th: 2 mm. F75 B79 *c* 970–1060/70 Assoc structures 13, 17, & 20 (E28)
314	36	End fragment rectangular-sectioned strip, split cattle rib. Surface and edges polished; end partly sawn then snapped. L: 21 mm. W: 14 mm. Th: 3 mm. F74 B3 *c* 1120–1140 Levelling over structure 33 (ABE)
315	36	Fragment partially worked plano-convex strip. Edges trimmed, surfaces partially filed smooth. L: 48 mm. W: 17 mm. Th: 7 mm. F73 B48 Late 12th C Levelling over latest timber buildings (NZ)
316		Fragment sheep metatarsal; hole bored through proximal articular surface to medullary cavity. Longitudinally fractured. L: 54 mm. F75 B131 *c* 900–1040 Assoc structures 6, 9, 13, & 17 (G51)
317	37	Fragment sheep right tibia; hole bored through proximal articular surface to medullary cavity. L: 78 mm. F75 B145 *c* 970–1040 Assoc structures 14/15 & 18 (G57)

Cat No	*Fig*	*Description and context*
318	37	Cattle right metatarsal; hole bored through proximal articular surface to natural cavity. Obliquely cut to detach from shaft. L: 118 mm. F75 B120 *c* 870/80–1060/70 Levelling dump assoc with pitting, west end (C7)
319	37	Cattle right metatarsal; hole bored through proximal articular surface to natural cavity. Shaft crudely trimmed. L: 107 mm. F75 B121 *c* 930/40–1060/70 Assoc structures 11, 12, 16, 19, & 22 (B105)
320	37	Sheep right metatarsal; hole bored through proximal articular surface to natural cavity. Shaft fractured, untrimmed. L: 78 mm. F75 B151 *c* 930/40–1060/70 Road surfaces F748, F749 (G75)
321	37	Sheep left tibia; transverse perforation through to natural cavity. Shaft fractured, untrimmed. L: 151 mm. F75 B143 *c* 900–970 Assoc structures 7, 8, 10, 11, & 12 (G100)
322	37	Fragment sheep right mandible; blood-vessel hole enlarged by drilling. L: 56 mm. F75 B124 *c* 930/40–1000/10 Assoc structures 10, 11, 12, 14/15 & 16 (E101)
323	37	Fragment sheep right scapula; transverse perforation. L: 87 mm. F75 B125 *c* 970–1040 Assoc structures 14/15 & 18 (F35)
324	37	Cattle right metatarsal, distal end, sawn from shaft. L: 61 mm. F74 B10 *c* 1040–1060/70 Levelling over structure 18 (AWR)
325	37	Pig metatarsal, distal end, cut from shaft. L: 31 mm. F73 B53 *c* 1080/90–1100 Levelling over structure 23 (AGG)
326	37	Fragment cattle thoracic vertebra chopped lengthwise; cut surface smoothed. Burnt. L: 28 mm. F75 B83 *c* 900–970 Assoc structures 7 & 10 (F96)
327	37	Fragment, rectangular-sectioned; shaft trimmed, one end obliquely cut to rough point. L: 36 mm. W: 8 mm. Th: 6 mm. F75 B144 *c* 930/40–970 Assoc structure 9 and earlier dumping (G49)
328	37	Surface fragment rib, longitudinally split; oblique groove. L: 21 mm. F75 B58 *c* 870/80–1060/70 Levelling dump assoc with pitting, west end (H6)
329		Surface fragment long bone, longitudinally split; both ends and one edge sawn. Rough and weathered. L: 52 mm. F75 B129 *c* 870/80–1060/70 Levelling dump assoc with pitting, west end (G7)
330	37	Fragment sheep vertebra, ends deliberately flattened. L: 18 mm. F75 B139 *c* 970–1060/70 Assoc structures 14/15, 18 & 21 (F55)
331	37	Fragment, trimmed to strip of irregular oval section. One end sawn, traces of smoothing. L: 24 mm. F75 B146 *c* 970–1060/70 Assoc structures 14/15, 18 & 21 (F75)
332	37	Fragment, sheep right femur shaft with 2 transverse and 1 longitudinal (?saw-) cuts on posterior surface. L: 59 mm. F73 B52 *c* 1060/70–1080/90 Levelling over road surface F749 (AHR)
333	37	Surface fragment rib, longitudinally split, with oblique groove. L: 32 mm. F74 B17 *c* 1080/90–1100 Levelling over structure 26 (ATV)

Antler

Cat No	*Fig*	*Description and context*
334	38	(Red deer?) Curved and tapering object of irregular pentagonal section with transverse perforation through broad sub-circular collar of upper terminal. Projecting double-collared pentagonal moulding above rather blunt point. L: 97 mm. F75 B69 *c* 930/40–1040 Assoc structures 10, 14/15, & 18 (E86)
335	39	Tapering fragment red deer tine, both ends sawn across. Partially hollowed out from each end, but unfinished. L: 47 mm. F76 B28 *c* 870/80–900 Pit F663 (BJZ)
336	39	Fragment roe deer tine with base sawn across and surface trimmed. Upper end broken, partially hollowed out. L: 87 mm. F75 B81 *c* 970–1060/70 Assoc structures 14/15, 18, & 21 (F75)
337	39	Fragment red deer tine, partially hollowed out; longitudinally fractured. L: 50 mm. F75 B136 *c* 1000/10–1080/90 Assoc structures 17, 20, & 26 (E13)
338	39	Red deer tine, sawn across base; point crudely worked (and gnawed). L: 80 mm. F75 B86 *c* 930/40–970 Assoc structures 11 & 12 (F106)
339	39	Lunate fragment of red deer antler, cut from base of tine. L: 30 mm. F75 B45 *c* 1000/10–1040 Assoc structure 18 (F17)
340	39	Red deer tine, with traces of faceting on point, producing beak-shaped terminal. L: 106 mm. F74 B157 *c* 900–1060/70 Robber trench F384 (ASO)
341	39	Brow tine, sawn from beam. Surface knife-trimmed. L: 85 mm. F74 B163 *c* 1060/70–1080/90 Consolidation F652 for structure 26 (ARS)

Burrs

(Red deer)

Cat No	*Fig*	*Description and context*
342	40	Cast; 1st to 3rd tines partially sawn then snapped. Beam sawn between these tines and longitudinally split. F76 B54 *c* 870/80–900 Road surface F746 (BSY)
343		Cast; 1st tine partially sawn then snapped; 2nd chopped/snapped. 3rd tine and crown sawn. F76 B55 *c* 870/80–900 Road surface F746 (BSY)
344		Attached to skull. 1st tine and beam sawn. F76 B71 *c* 870/80–900 Road surface F747 (BOU)
345		Cast; beam and 1st tine obliquely sawn just above burr. F76 B6 *c* 930/40–970 Road surface F748 (BEA)
346	40	Attached to right frontal skull. Beam sawn and snapped just above burr. F75 B128 *c* 930/40–1060/70 Assoc structures 11, 12, 16, 19, & 22 (B105)

Cat No	*Fig*	*Description and context*
347		Cast; beam and 1st tine obliquely sawn just above burr. F75 B85 *c* 930/40–1060/70 Assoc road surfaces F748, F749 (F90)
348		Cast; 1st tine partially chopped/sawn then snapped. Beam obliquely sawn and snapped. F75 B115 *c* 1040–1060/70 Levelling west of structure 21 (ALK)
349		Hacked from skull below burr. 1st tine and beam obliquely sawn then snapped. F74 B35 *c* 1040–1060/70 Road surface F749 (AZL)
350	40	Attached to frontal skull. Beam sawn and snapped immediately above burr; remaining fragment split down to frontal bone. F73 B44 *c* 1060/70–1080/90 Rubble consolidation F654 for structure 23 (AJR)
351	41	Cast; beam and 1st tine obliquely sawn just above burr. F74 B32 *c* 1060/70–1080/90 Pit F707 (AUL)
352		Cast; beam and 1st tine obliquely sawn and snapped just above burr. F73 B51 *c* 1160–1180 Levelling north of structure 46 (ZG)
353		Chopped from skull. Beam and 1st tine obliquely sawn just above burr. F76 B35 *c* 1140–1200 Pit F726 (BLM)
		Tines (Red deer)
354	40	Crown with tines attached, sawn from beam. F76 B33 *c* 870/80–900 Structure 3: internal levelling (BOD)
355		Brow/1st tine, sawn and snapped from beam. F76 B61 *c* 870/80–900 Road surface F747 (BOU)
356		Tine partially sawn then snapped from beam. F76 B67 *c* 870/80–900 Road surface F747 (BOU)
357		Brow tine, sawn from beam; shaft broken. F74 B162 *c* 900–1060/70 Pit F693 (AVV)
358		3rd tine, damaged and rodent-gnawed; sawn from beam. F76 B49 *c* 900–1060/70 Pit F700 (BLG)
359		Crown; 3rd tine broken, 4th tine sawn. F76 B79 Unstratified
		Beam fragments (red deer)
360	41	Fragment from near base of ?1st tine; 1 transverse and 2 oblique saw-cuts. Partial faceting on lower surfaces. F76 B52 *c* 870/80–900 Road surface F746 (BSY)
361		From between 1st and 2nd tines? Base sawn, top snapped. F76 B53 *c* 870/80–900 Road surface F746 (BSY)
362	41	From base of crown; beam and 3 tines sawn. F75 B110 *c* 870/80–930/40 Assoc with road surfaces F746–7 (H85)
363		From base of crown. Beam and 2 tines sawn, remaining tine ?gnawed. F76 B4 *c* 900–930/40 Levelling encroaching onto road (BEB)
364		From base of (2nd/3rd?) tine; tine sawn, beam split longitudinally at junction with tine. F76 B21 *c* 930/40–970 Road surface F748 (BEA)
365		From base of crown; beam and 3 tines sawn. F76 B3 *c* 930/40–970 Road surface F748 (BEM)
366		From base of crown; beam and 2 tines sawn. F75 B111 *c* 900–1000/10 Assoc structures 7, 10, & 14/15 (G94)
367		From base of 3rd tine; beam and tine sawn. F75 B48 *c* 970–1060/70 Assoc structures 16, 19, & 22 (B98)
		Tine points (red deer; * = roe deer)
368		Extreme tip, shaft sawn. F76 B66 *c* 870/80–900 Levelling over structure 4 (CAD)
369		Shaft sawn. F76 B59 *c* 900–930/40 Levelling over area of Roman building (BIH)
370		Shaft sawn. F76 B10 *c* 900–930/40 Levelling, central area (BDG)
371		Shaft sawn, tip snapped. Small transverse saw-cut on one surface. F76 B69 *c* 900–930/40 Levelling over structures 3 & 5 (BHR)
372		Shaft sawn, tip snapped. F76 B34 *c* 930/40–970 Levelling over structure 8 (BOL)
373	41	Shaft sawn. F76 B36 *c* 930/40–970 Road surface F748 (BOH)
374		Shaft sawn. F75 B80 *c* 930/40–1000/10 Assoc structures 10, 11, 12, 14/15, & 16 (E101)
375		Shaft snapped, tip sawn. F75 B141 *c* 930/40–1040 Structures 10, 14/15, & 18 (E93)
376		Shaft sawn. F74 B8 *c* 900–1060/70 Robber trench F384 (ASO)
377		Shaft sawn, tip snapped. F76 B24 *c* 900–1060/70 Robber trench F384 (ASO)
378	41	Shaft partially sawn then snapped. Transverse saw-cuts and faceting on lower shaft. F75 B49 *c* 930/40–1060/70 Assoc structures 11, 12, 16, 19, & 22 (B104)
379	41	?*Shaft sawn from opposite sides and snapped. F76 B12 *c* 1040–1060/70 Pit F674 (BDB)
380		Shaft sawn. F73 B35 *c* 1120–1140 Levelling over structure 34 (ACY)

Cat No	*Fig*	*Description and context*
381		Shaft sawn. F73 B15 *c* 1160–1180 Levelling north of structure 46 (ZJ)
		Surface fragments, beam (red deer)
382	41	One end sawn. L: 52 mm. W: 21 mm. Th: 10 mm. F76 B63 *c* 870/80–900 Structure 5, floor (BZP)
383		One end sawn. L: 57 mm. W: 45 mm. Th: 18 mm. F76 B76 *c* 870/80–900 Structure 5: destruction (BZF)
384		One end sawn, transverse saw-cuts on external surface. L: 63 mm. W: 39 mm. Th: 27 mm. F76 B86 *c* 870/80–900 Structure 5: destruction (BZF)
385	41	Both ends sawn. L: 46 mm. W: 28 mm. Th: 11 mm. F76 B72 *c* 870/80–900 Road surface F747 (BOU)
386		One end sawn. L: 70 mm. W: 25 mm. Th: 15 mm. F76 B77 *c* 900–930/40 Levelling over structures 3 & 5 (BHR)
387	41	Both ends sawn. L: 30 mm. W: 26 mm. Th: 8 mm. F75 B148 *c* 900–1000/10 Assoc structures 7, 10, & 14/15 (G94)
		Horn
388		Cattle left horn core obliquely sawn just above base. F74 B28 *c* 1140–1160 Pit F729 (AEJ)
389	42	Cattle left horn core sawn across at base and tip. F74 B164 *c* 1140–1200 Levelling dump north of structure 42/43 (AGM)
390		Sheep horn core sawn off at base. F73 B54 *c* 1140–1200 Pit F724: ?lining (AJL)
		Ivory
391	43	Terminal fragment of rectangular-sectioned strip; both broad faces ornamented with 4 shallow longitudinal grooves, abutting single transverse line approx 5 mm from terminal. Small pits placed in intervening spaces. L: 33 mm. W: 15 mm. Th: 2 mm. F72 B3 *c* 1080/90–1100 Structure 29, floor (DV)
		Amber
392		Small unworked pebble-shaped fragment with surface weathering. F75 M140 *c* 900–1040 Assoc structures 7, 10, 14/15, & 18 (F81)
		Jet
393	44	Sub-rectangular fragment with rounded corners; rectangular-sectioned. L: 31 mm. W: 14 mm. Th: 4 mm. F74 M3 *c* 1080/90–1100 Levelling over structure 26 (ATV)
394	44	Sub-rectangular fragment with one long edge bevelled; rectangular-sectioned. L: 26 mm. W: 14 mm. Th: 3 mm. F73 M102 *c* 1080/90–1160 Levelling dump north of structures 26 to 46 (YZ)
395		Pebble-shaped fragment, unworked. F75 M67 *c* 870/80–1060/70 Levelling dump associated with pitting, western end (C6)
396	44	Sub-rectangular fragment of irregular section. L: 32 mm. W: 17 mm. Th: 11 mm. F74 M24 *c* 1040–1060/70 Levelling over road surface F748 (AWS)
397		Waste flake. F74 M33 *c* 1040–1060/70 Levelling over road surface F748 (AWS)
398		Waste flake. F74 M34 *c* 1040–1060/70 Levelling over road surface F748 (AWS)
399	44	Waste flake, wedge-shaped section. F74 M20 *c* 1060/70–1080/90 Levelling over road surface F749 (AQQ)
400		Waste flake, wedge-shaped section. F74 M28 *c* 1060/70–1080/90 Levelling over road surface F749 (AQQ)
401		53 small waste flakes, chips. F74 M6 *c* 1060/70–1080/90 Levelling over road surface F749 (ATS)
402		8 small chips. F74 M7 *c* 1060/70–1080/90 Levelling over road surface F749 (ATS)
403	44	Small flake of irregular shape, fractured across ?perforation. F74 M162 *c* 1060/70–1080/90 Levelling over road surface F749 (ATS)
404		Semicircular flake of wedge-shaped section; outer edge 'pecked'. D: 29 mm. F74 M163 *c* 1060/70–1080/90 Levelling over road surface F749 (ATS)
405	44	Semicircular flake of wedge-shaped section; outer edge 'pecked'. D: 28 mm. F74 M164 *c* 1060/70–1080/90 Levelling over road surface F749 (ATS)
406		Minute sliver of wedge-shaped section, fractured across perforation. L: 12 mm. W: 3 mm. Th: 2 mm. F74 M165 *c* 1060/70–1080/90 Levelling over road surface F749 (ATS)
407	44	Thin flake with rounded outer edge, fractured across ?perforation. D: *c* 40 mm. F74 M166 *c* 1060/70–1080/90 Levelling over road surface F749 (ATS)
408		Sub-circular fragment. D: *c* 30 mm. F74 M167 *c* 1060/70–1080/90 Levelling over road surface F749 (ATS)
409	44	Semicircular fragment, outer edge faceted and worked. D: *c* 40 mm. F74 M168 *c* 1060/70–1080/90 Levelling over road surface F749 (ATS)
410		Unworked pebble-shaped fragment. F74 M19 *c* 1080/90–1100 Levelling over structure 26 (ATV)

Cat No	*Fig*	*Description and context*
		Chalk
411	45	Sub-rectangular block; transverse cut-marks and wear on one face. L: 74 mm. W: 54 mm. Th: 43 mm. F75 M129 *c* 970–1000/10 Assoc structure 16 (B96)
412	45	Block; tapering faceted ovoid section. L: 79 mm. W: 75 mm. Th: 53 mm. F73 M189 *c* 1060/70–1080/90 Levelling over west end for structure 25 (AAA)
413		Small block; tapering faceted ovoid section. L: 46 mm. D: 28 mm. F73 M159 *c* 1060/70–1080/90 Structure 25: floor (AMP)
414		Small block; tapering faceted ovoid section. L: 23 mm. D: 18 mm. F73 M207 *c* 1060/70–1080/90 Structure 25: floor (AMP)
415	45	Small block; tapering sub-rectangular section. L: 60 mm. W: 23 mm. Th: 21 mm. F72 M11 *c* 1120–1140 Structure 40; floor (BO)
416		Small block; square-sectioned, tapering to rectangular. L: 24 mm. W: 17 mm. Th: 17 mm. F27 M200 *c* 1120–1140 Structure 40: floor (BO)
417		Small block; tapering faceted ovoid section. L: 38 mm. D: 28 mm. F72 M201 *c* 1120–1140 Structure 40: floor (BO)
418	45	Small block; faceted circular section; one end obliquely fractured. L: 41 mm. D: 20 mm. F72 M202 *c* 1120–1140 Structure 40: floor (BO)
419	45	Small block; tapering faceted ovoid section. L: 37 mm. D: 28 mm. F72 M10 Late 12th C Levelling over latest timber buildings (BE)
420		Small block; tapering irregular polygonal section. L: 29 mm. W: 21 mm. F72 M203 Late 12th C Levelling over latest timber buildings (BE)
421		Small block; tapering faceted ovoid section. L: 31 mm. W: 25 mm. F72 M204 Late 12th C Levelling over latest timber buildings (BE)
422		Small block; ovoid section, one end obliquely worn. L: 31 mm. W: 22 mm. F72 M205 Late 12th C Levelling over latest timber buildings (BE)
423	45	Small block; tapering irregular polygonal section. L: 42 mm. W: 22 mm. F72 M206 Late 12th C Levelling over latest timber buildings (BE)
424		Small block; tapering rectangular section, one end obliquely worn. L: 29 mm. W: 15 mm. Th: 13 mm. F73 M93 Late 13th/early 14th C Assoc with reconstruction of stone building Ai/ii (YF)
		Stone
425	46	Fragment, smoother/polisher? Rectangular-sectioned, one end worn and tapering. L: 88 mm. W: 32 mm. Th: 28 mm. F76 St33 *c* 870/80–900 Levelling, western end (BOF)
426	46	Fragment, smoother/polisher? Rectangular-sectioned, with rounded edges. L: 58 mm. W: 36 mm. Th: 15 mm. F75 M161 *c* 900–930/40 Levelling over area of Roman building (BCL)
		Ceramic
427	47	Body sherd of late Saxon shelly ware, partially trimmed to disc. L: 51 mm. Th: 6 mm. F74 P509 *c* 870/80–900 Robber trench/pit F55 (AYJ)
428	47	Base sherd of late Saxon shelly ware, partially trimmed to disc; broken. D: *c* 30 mm. Th: 6 mm. F75 P508 *c* 900–930/40 Levelling west of structure 6 (J32)
429	47	Base sherd of Roman grey ware with part of vessel wall attached, fractured across central perforation. D: *c* 70 mm. Th: 6–9 mm. F74 P499 *c* 900–1060/70 Robber trench F384 (ASO)
430	47	Body sherd of Roman grey ware trimmed to irregular polygonal shape; abraded. L: 64 mm. W: 36 mm. Th: 9 mm. F73 P74 *c* 1140–1160 Pit F731 (AKB)

Summary

Excavations by the Lincoln Archaeological Trust revealed a sequence of timber buildings dating from the late 9th to the late 12th century at Flaxengate. The associated finds of antler, bone, stone, horn, ivory, amber, and jet provide useful information about the inhabitants and, by extension, the development of crafts and trade in Lincoln, although they represent only a small proportion of the material recovered from the site. A few objects such as the soapstone vessel sherds suggest the presence there of Scandinavian settlers, but the majority of the finds are of types which occur commonly on both late Anglo-Saxon and Scandinavian Viking-age sites.

The range of crafts evidenced at Flaxengate is typical of many contemporary towns. Tools, partially worked objects, and waste materials indicate that textile manufacture and bone-working were practised although perhaps on a small-scale, individual basis, while comb making may have been practised by itinerant craftsmen. The manufacture of finger-rings and pendants of jet (and amber?) may have been closely linked with the production of rings and trinkets of glass and copper alloy, and Flaxengate may be part of an industrial and craft-working quarter.

The sources of the stone artefacts (supported by the provenances of the pottery and the coins) suggest that Lincoln played an important economic role as a market centre. They demonstrate contacts with the immediate area of the Danelaw (and East Anglia), with Yorkshire, and also with the south and west, while imported materials from Scandinavia and the Rhineland indicate trade on an international level.

Résumé

Les fouilles à Flaxengate, organisées par le Lincoln Archaeological Trust, ont révélé une séquence de bâtiments en bois qui datent de la fin du 9ème siècle à la fin du 12ème siècle. Les trouvailles associées d'andouillers et d'objets en os, pierre, corne, ivoire, ambre, et jais, bien qu'elles ne représentent qu'une petite partie du matériel découvert sur le site, permettent d'obtenir des renseignements utiles sur les habitants et, par extension, sur le développement de l'artisanat et du commerce à Lincoln. Quelques objets, tels que les tessons de vases en stéatite, suggèrent la présence de colons scandinaves, mais la plupart des trouvailles sont d'un type qui apparait communément à la fois sur des sites d'époque anglo-saxonne tardive et viking scandinave.

En matière d'artisanat, la diversité dont témoigne Flaxengate est typique de nombreuses villes contemporaines. Outils, objets en partie travaillés, et déchets indiquent que l'on pratiquait l'industrie textile et le travail de l'os, peut-être sur une échelle modeste et individuelle, tandis que l'industrie du peigne aurait pu être pratiquée par des artisans itinérants. La fabrication de bagues et pendentifs en jais (et ambre?) aurait pu être étroitement liée à la production d'anneaux et breloques en verre et alliage de cuivre, et Flaxengate faisait peut-être partie d'un quartier industriel et artisanal.

La provenance d'objets en pierre (ainsi que celle de poteries et pièces de monnaie) suggère que Lincoln jouait un rôle économique important en tant que centre d'échanges. Elle démontre l'existence de contacts avec les régions proches du Danelaw (et d'East Anglia) avec le Yorkshire, et aussi avec le sud et l'ouest, cependant que l'importation de marchandises de Scandinavie et de Rhénanie indique des relations commerciales à un niveau international.

Zusammenfassung

Ausgrabungen durch den Lincoln Archaeological Trust in der Flaxengate haben eine Holzbautenfolge erbracht, die vom späten 9. Jahrhundert bis in das ausgehende 12. Jahrhundert reicht. Die zugehörigen Funde aus Geweih, Knochen, Stein, Horn, Elfenbein, Bernstein und Pechkohle geben brauchbare Auskunft über die Einwohner, und im weiteren Sinne, über die Entwicklung von Handwerk und Handel. Sie stellen jedoch nur einen geringen Teil des Materials dar, das von dieser Ausgrabungsstelle geborgen wurde. Einige wenige Gegenstände, wie etwa Gefäßscherben in Seifenstein weisen auf die Anwesenheit skandinavischer Siedler hin. Die Mehrzahl der Funde gehört jedoch in die Kategorien, die so wohl auf spätangelsächsischen als auch auf skandinavischen Fundstellen der Wikingerzeit auftreten.

Die in der Flaxengate vertretenen Handwerke sind typisch für viele Städte der Zeit. Werkzeug, teilweise gefertigte Gegenstände und Abfall weisen daraufhin, daß Textil- und Knochenverarbeitung betrieben wurde, allergings in sehr geringem Maße und in individuellen Werkstätten. Die Herstellung von Kämmen war wahrscheinlich in den Händen fahrender Handwerker. Die Fertigung von Ringen und Anhängern aus Pechkohle (und Bernstein) ist wahrscheinlich eng mit der Herstellung von Ringen und Schmuckstücken aus Glass und Kupferlegierungen verbunden gewesen; und die Flaxengate scheint Teil eines industriellen und handwerklichen Viertels gewesen zu sein.

Die Herkunft der Gegenstände aus Stein (ebenso die Provinenz der Keramik und der Münzen) deuten daraufhin, daß Lincoln eine wirtschaftlich wichtige Rolle als Marktzentrum besaß. Sie weisen hin auf Kontakte mit der angrenzenden Region des Danelags (und Ostanglia) mit Yorkshire und weiter nach Süden und Westen. Fernhandel ist bezeugt durch importierte Waren aus Skandinavien und dem Rheinland.

Acknowledgments

The Lincoln Archaeological Trust is indebted to the Lincoln City Council and their officers and staff for providing access to the site and for their cooperation throughout the excavations, and to the Department of the Environment who financed most of the work, with additional grants from the Lincoln City Council and the Lincolnshire County Council. The finds and records are to be deposited in the collections of Lincolnshire Museums.

It is impossible to mention by name all those who assisted in the processing of the finds and in the preparation of this report, but the work of Mrs J Green was especially valuable. Information on the stratigraphy was provided by Mr Dom Perring and on the pottery by Dr L Adams and Mrs J Young; Mr T O'Connor identified the animal bones. I am particularly grateful to Mr D T Moore for his work on the hones and Mrs Carole Morris for many helpful suggestions. Many other individuals provided information and specialist advice; they are credited, where appropriate, in the text. Mr M J Jones directed the post-excavation research while Dr D M Wilson gave much advice and encouragement.

A generous grant from the Society of Antiquaries enabled me to visit a number of Scandinavian museums to examine comparative material. Thanks are due to the staffs of those museums, in particular to Mrs E Roesdahl of Århus University and Dr I Ulbricht of the Schleswig-Holstein Landesmuseum. Mr B O'Ríordáin of the National Museum of Ireland generously provided access to the material from recent excavations in Dublin, and he and his staff were most helpful. The visit was made possible by a grant from the J W Wright Trust.

I am grateful to Mr J Graham-Campbell for his careful reading of the report in typescript, and for suggesting many improvements to the text. Miss C Thorne and Mr R Sutton drew the finds. Mrs J Peacock provided Figs 1 and 2 and Mr H N Hawley took the photograph in Fig 5. The summary was translated by Mireille Galinou into French and by Katrin Aberg into German. Mrs. A Morton typed the report and Mrs E Nurser edited the text for publication with patience and good humour.

Bibliography

Adams, L, 1979a Early Islamic pottery from Flaxengate, Lincoln, *Medieval Archaeol*, **23**, 218–19

————, 1979b Imported pottery of the 9th–11th centuries from Flaxengate, Lincoln, *Lincoln Archaeological Trust seventh annual report*, 30–4

Adams, L, & Young, J, 1981 Eleventh-century domestic scene at Flaxengate, *FLARE Annual Newsletter*, May

Addyman, P V, 1964 A Dark Age settlement at Maxey, Northants, *Medieval Archaeol*, **8**, 20–73

————, 1973 Late Saxon settlements in the St Neots area III: the village or township at St Neots, *Proc Cambridge Antiq Soc*, **64**, 45–99

Addyman, P V, & Hill, D H, 1969 Saxon Southampton: a review of the evidence; Part II: Industry, trade and everyday life, *Proc Hampshire Field Club Archaeol Soc*, **26**, 61–96

Addyman, P V, & Priestley, J 1977 Baile Hill, York: a report on the Institute's excavations, *Archaeol J*, **134**, 115–56

Alcock, L, 1963 *Dinas Powys: An Iron Age, Dark Age and early medieval settlement in Glamorgan*

————, 1972 *'By South Cadbury is that Camelot...' The excavation of Cadbury Castle 1966–1972*

Allen, J R, 1904 A carved bone of the Viking Age, *The Reliquary and Illustrated Archaeologist*, **10**, 270–5

Ambrosiani, K, 1981 *Viking age combs, comb making, and comb makers in the light of finds from Birka and Ribe*, Stockholm Studies in Archaeology, **2**

Andersen, H H, Crabb P J, & Madsen, H J, 1971 *Århus Søndervold: en byarkaeologisk undersøgelse*

Arbman, H, 1943 *Birka 1, Die Gräber*

Arne, T J, 1934 *Das Bootgräberfeld von Tuna in Alsike*

Baldwin Brown, G, 1915 *The arts in Early England, Vol 3: Saxon art and industry*

Biddle, M, 1962–3 The deserted medieval village of Seacourt, Berkshire, *Oxoniensia*, **26–7**, 70–201

Blindheim, C, 1969 Kaupangundersøkelsen avsluttet, *Viking*, **33**, 5–40

Blomqvist, R, 1942 Kammar från Lunds Medeltid, *Kulturen*, 133–62

Brade, C, 1978 Knöcherne Kernspaltflöten aus Haithabu, in *Berichte über die Ausgrabungen in Haithabu 12: Das archäologische Fundmaterial III der Ausgrabung Haithabu* (ed K Schietzel)

Brodribb, A C C, Hands, A R, & Walker, D R, 1971 *Excavations at Shakenoak Farm near Wilcote, Oxfordshire I: Sites A and D*, 2nd edn

————, 1972 *Excavations at Shakenoak Farm, near Wilcote, Oxfordshire III: Site F*

Bruce-Mitford, R L S, 1975 *The Sutton Hoo ship-burial, Vol 1: Excavations, background, the ship, dating and inventory*

Bulleid, A, & Gray, H St George, 1917 *Glastonbury Lake Village*, Vol 2

Bushe-Fox, J P, 1949 *Fourth report on the excavations of the Roman fort at Richborough, Kent*, Rep Res Cttee of Soc Antiq London, **16**

Carus-Wilson, E, 1962–3 (1964) The medieval trade of the ports of the Wash, *Medieval Archaeol*, **6–7**, 182–201

CGM, 1908 *Catalogue of the collection of London antiquities in the Guildhall Museum*

Clarke, H, & Carter, A 1977 *Excavations in King's Lynn 1963–1970*, Soc for Medieval Archaeol monog ser, **7**

Collis, J, & Kjølbye-Biddle, B, 1979 Early medieval bone spoons from Winchester, *Antiq J*, **59**, 2, 375–91

Colyer, C, & Jones, M J (eds), 1979 Excavations at Lincoln, Second interim report: excavations in the lower walled town 1972–8, *Antiq J*, **59**, 1, 50–91

Coppack, G, 1973 The excavation of a Roman and medieval site at Flaxengate, Lincoln, *Lincolnshire Hist Archaeol*, **8**, 73–114

Crane, F, 1972 *Extant medieval musical instruments (a provisional catalogue by types)*

Crawford, O G S, & Röder, J, 1955 The quern-quarries of Mayen in the Eifel, *Antiquity*, **29**, 68–76

Cunliffe, B W, 1964 *Winchester excavations, 1949–1960, Vol 1*

————, 1968 *Fifth report on the excavations of the Roman fort at Richborough, Kent*, Rep Res Cttee of Soc Antiq London, **23**

————, 1971 *Excavations at Fishbourne 1961–1969, Vol 2: The finds*, Rep Res Cttee of Soc Antiq London, **27**

————, 1975 *Excavations at Portchester Castle, Vol 1: Roman*, Rep Res Cttee of Soc Antiq London, **32**

————, 1976 *Excavations at Portchester Castle, Vol. 2: Saxon*, Rep Res Cttee of Soc Antiq London, **33**

Curle, A O, 1938–9 A Viking settlement at Freswick, Caithness, *Proc Soc Antiq Scot*, **73**, 71–109

Dunning, G C, 1956 Trade relations between England and the Continent in the late Anglo-Saxon period, in *Dark Age Britain: Studies presented to E T Leeds* (ed D B Harden), 218–33

Dunning, G C, Hurst, J G, Myres, J N L, & Tischler, F, 1959 Anglo-saxon pottery: a symposium, *Medieval Archaeol*, **3**, 1–78

Ellis, S E, 1969 The petrography and provenance of Anglo-Saxon and medieval English honestones, with notes on some other hones, *Bull Brit Mus (Natur Hist), Mineralogy*, **2**, no 3, 135–87

Evison, V I, 1975 Pagan Saxon whetstones, *Antiq J*, **55**, 1, 70–85

Fanning, T, 1969 The bronze ringed pins in the Limerick City Museum, *N Munster Antiq J*, **12**, 6–11

Galloway, P, 1976 Note on descriptions of bone and antler combs, *Medieval Archaeol*, **20**, 154–7

Gilmour, B, 1979 The Anglo-Saxon church at St Paul-in-the-Bail, Lincoln, *Medieval Archaeol*, **23**, 214–17

Graham-Campbell, J, 1980 *Viking artefacts: a select catalogue*

Grieg, S, 1933 *Middelalderske Byfund fra Bergen og Oslo*

Grimm, P, 1968 The royal palace at Tilleda, *Medieval Archaeol*, **12**, 83–100

Hamilton, J R C, 1956 *Excavations at Jarlshof, Shetland*

Heighway, C M, Garrod, A P, & Vince, A G, 1979 Excavations at 1 Westgate Street, Gloucester, 1975, *Medieval Archaeol*, **23**, 159–213

Hill, J W F, 1965 *Medieval Lincoln*

Hills, C, 1977 *The Anglo-Saxon cemetery at Spong Hill, North Elmham; Part 1: Catalogue of cremations, nos 20–64 and 1000–1690*, East Anglian Archaeology Res Rep **6**

————, 1981 Barred zoomorphic combs of the migration period, in *Angles, Saxons, and Jutes, Essays presented to J N L Myres* (ed V I Evison), 96–125

Hoffman, M, 1964 *The warp-weighted loom,* Studia Norvegica, **14**
Holdsworth, P, 1976 Saxon Southampton; a new review, *Medieval Archaeol,* **20,** 26–61
Howarth, E, 1899 *Catalogue of the Bateman collection of antiquities in the Sheffield Public Museum*
Jankuhn, H, 1943 *Die Ausgrabungen in Haithabu 1937–1939*
Jellema, D, 1955 Frisian trade in the Dark Ages, *Speculum,* **30,** 15–36
Jones, R H, 1980 *Medieval houses at Flaxengate, Lincoln, The archaeology of Lincoln,* **11/1**
Kenyon, K M, 1948 *Excavations at the Jewry Wall site, Leicester,* Rep Res Cttee of Soc Antiq London, **15**
Knocker, G M, & Hughes, R G, 1950 Anglo-Saxon Thetford, Part 2. *Archaeological Newsletter,* **3,** no 3, 41–6
Lawson, A J, 1975 Shale and jet objects from Silchester, *Archaeologia,* **105,** 241–76
Lawson, R G, 1980 Stringed musical instruments in excavations, United Kingdom Institute of Conservation Occasional Papers, **1,** 12–13
LMMC, 1940 *London Museum medieval catalogue*
Long, C D, 1975 Excavations in the medieval city of Trondheim, Norway, *Medieval Archaeol,* **19,** 1–32
MacGregor, A, 1972–4 The Broch of Burrian, North Ronaldsay, Orkney, *Proc Soc Antiq Scot,* **105,** 63–118
———, 1975 Problems in the interpretation of microscopic wear patterns: the evidence from bone skates, *J Archaeol Sci,* **2,** 385–90
———, 1976a Bone skates: a review of the evidence, *Archaeol J,* **133,** 57–74
———, 1976b *Finds from a Roman sewer system and an adjacent building in Church Street, The archaeology of York,* **17/1**
———, 1978a Industry and commerce in Anglo-Scandinavian York, in *Viking Age York and the North* (ed R A Hall), CBA Res Rep **27,** 37–57
———, 1978b *Roman finds from Skeldergate and Bishophill, The archaeology of York,* **17/2**
———, 1979 Taking the lid off the past, in *Interim,* Bull York Archaeol Trust, **6** no 3, 6–8
Mårtensson, A W (ed), 1976 *Uppgrävt forflütet för Pkbanken i Lund: en investering i arkeologi,* Archaeologica Lundensia, **7**
Megaw, J V S, 1960 Penny whistles and prehistory, Antiquity, **34,** 6–13
———, 1961 An end-blown flute or flageolet from White Castle, *Medieval Archaeol,* **5,** 176–80
Mellor, M, 1980 Late Saxon pottery from Oxfordshire: evidence and speculation, *Medieval Ceramics,* **4,** 17–27
Moore, D T, 1978 The petrography and archaeology of English honestones, *J Archaeol Sci,* **5,** 61–73
Müller-Wille, M, 1973 Eisengeräte aus Haithabu (Ausgrabung 1963–1964), in *Berichte über die Ausgrabungen in Haithabu, 6: Das archäologische Fundmaterial 2* (ed K Schietzel), 23–37
Murray, H J R, 1952 *A history of board-games other than chess*
Myres, J N L, & Green, B, 1973 *The Anglo-Saxon cemeteries of Caistor-by-Norwich and Markshall, Norfolk,* Rep Res Cttee Soc Antiq London, **30**
Nerman, B, 1958 *Grobin-Seeburg: Ausgrabungen und Funde*
Nørlund, P, 1948 *Trelleborg*
O'Connor, T P, 1982 *Animal bones from Flaxengate, Lincoln, The archaeology of Lincoln,* **18/1**
Ó'Ríordáin, A B, 1976 The High Street excavations, *Proc Seventh Viking Congress* (eds B Almqvist & D Greene), 135–40
Peers, C, & Radford, C A R, 1943 The Saxon monastery of Whitby, *Archaeologia,* **89,** 27–88
Perring, D, 1981 *Early medieval occupation at Flaxengate, Lincoln, The archaeology of Lincoln,* **9/1**
Petersen, J, 1951 *Vikingetidens Redskaper*
Platt, C, & Coleman-Smith, R, 1975 *Excavations in medieval Southampton, Vol 2: The finds*
Radcliffe, F, 1962–3 Excavations at Logic Lane, Oxford (the prehistoric and early medieval finds), *Oxoniensia,* **26–7,** 38–69
RCHMY 1, 1962 *An inventory of the historical monuments in the city of York 1: Eburacum, Roman York,* 1962, Royal Commission on Historical Monuments, England
Richardson, K M, 1959 Excavations in Hungate, York, *Archaeol J,* **116,** 51–114
Roes, A, 1963 *Bone and antler objects from the Frisian terp-mounds*
Rygh, O, 1885 *Norske Oldsager*
Schietzel, K, 1970 Hölzerne Kleinfunde aus Haithabu (Ausgrabung 1963–1964), in *Berichte über die Ausgrabungen in Haithabu, 4: Das archäologische Fundmaterial I (1963–1964)* (ed K Schietzel), 77–91
Schwarz-Mackensen, G, 1976 Die Knochennadeln von Haithabu, in *Berichte über die Ausgrabungen in Haithabu 9* (ed K Schietzel)
Shetelig, H (ed), 1940 *Viking antiquities in Great Britain and Ireland*
Tempel, W D, 1970 Die Kämme aus Haithabu (Ausgrabung 1963–1964), in *Berichte über die Ausgrabungen in Haithabu, 4: Das archäologische Fundmaterial I (1963–1964)* (ed K Schietzel), 34–45
Ulbricht, I, 1978 Die Geweihverarbeitung in Haithabu, *Die Ausgrabungen in Haithabu, 7*
VMD, 1980 *Viking and medieval Dublin: National Museum excavations, 1962–73. Catalogue of exhibition,* 3rd edn
Wallace, P F, 1981 Wood Quay, Dublin, *Pop Archaeol,* March 1981, 24–7
Waterman, D M, 1959 Late Saxon, Viking, and early medieval finds from York, *Archaeologia,* **97,** 59–105
Wheeler, R E M, 1927 *London and the Vikings,* London Mus Catalogues, **1**
———, 1943 *Maiden Castle, Dorset*
Wheeler, R E M, & Wheeler, T V, 1932 *Report on the prehistoric, Roman, and post-Roman site in Lydney Park, Gloucestershire,* Rep Res Cttee Soc Antiq London, **9**
Whitelock, D, 1961 *The Anglo-Saxon Chronicle*
——— (ed), 1968 *English historical documents I: c 500–1042,* 3rd edn
Williams, F, 1979 Excavations on Marefair, Northampton, 1977, *Northamptonshire Archaeol,* **14,** 38–79
Williams, J H, 1979 *St Peter's Street Northampton, excavations 1973–1976,* Northampton Development Corporation
Wilson, D M, 1964 Anglo-Saxon ornamental metalwork 700-1100 (in the British Museum)
———, 1968 Anglo-Saxon carpenters' tools, in *Studien zur europäischen Vor- und Frühgeschichte* (eds M Claus *et al*), 143–50
Wilson, D M, & Hurst, D G, 1964 Medieval Britain in 1962 and 1963, *Medieval Archaeol,* **8,** 231–99
——— & ———, 1966 Medieval Britain in 1965, *Medieval Archaeol,* **10,** 177–219